Daisy Bates

By the same author

Daisy Bates

"THE GREAT WHITE QUEEN OF THE NEVER NEVER"

ELIZABETH SALTER

ANGUS AND ROBERTSON

First published in Great Britain in 1972 by

ANGUS AND ROBERTSON (PUBLISHERS) PTY LTD
221 George Street, Sydney
2 Fisher Street, London
107 Elizabeth Street, Melbourne
167 Queen Street, Brisbane
89 Anson Road, Singapore

National Library of Australia
card number and ISBN 0 207 12271 7

Registered in Australia for transmission by post as a book
PRINTED IN AUSTRALIA BY HALSTEAD PRESS, SYDNEY

DEDICATION

To Pauline and Bill O'Halloran Giles
and to J.M.B.

ACKNOWLEDGMENTS

If I were to list the many hundreds of Australians who helped me in my researches for this book; those who sent me letters, anecdotes, personal memories, advice; those whom I interviewed and those who arranged interviews for me, my list would run to many pages. Because of them this book has an extra dimension. I most gratefully acknowledge the fact; and my thanks are due to each and every contributor, and especially to: Margaret Bullock, my tireless secretary; Kerry James, who advised on anthropological matters; Sir Harold White, former Librarian of the National Library in Canberra and his assistants Mrs Fanning and Mrs Carroll, whose help was invaluable; Messrs Richard Wright and Charles Mountford; Professors Elkin, Berndt, Fitz-Herbert and T. G. H. Strehlow, and Sir John Cleland for advice on Aboriginal and other affairs; writers Mary Durack and E. L. Grant Watson for permission to quote from their books; Mr Max Fatchen and Mr and Mrs Barry Lintner for my visit to Yalata, and their Aboriginal friends on the reserve to whom I spoke; my friends Jean Jukes, Isobel Durack and Lady Price who gave me their time; H. L. Richardson, Gordon Heaslip, Charles Carney and J. Steel, who voluntarily took on research jobs for me; the Mickan family, Ivy Watkins, artist Desmond Norman, writer Jo Samuel, photographers Douglas Glass and Hal Missingham; Dr R. Y. Mathew and J. F. Pollitt; Daisy Bates's personal friends, among them Mrs Ernestine Hill, Lady Casey, the late Lady Hayward, Mrs Jolly, Mrs Thomson, Miss Kathleen Kyffin Thomas; my sisters Vivien and Barbara, Miss Phyllis Whyte, Madeleine Morel and Claudine Perretti; Mr L. Moore for advice; my reader, George Browne C.B.E.; and Mrs Jean Bates for her co-operation.

I am indebted to the State Libraries of Victoria (La Trobe collection), South and Western Australia, the Mitchell Library,

N.S.W.; to the Library of the University of Adelaide; to the National Library of Canberra and to the British Museum; to the Fryer Librarian of the University of Queensland; and to newspapers throughout Australia which kindly published my requests for information.

Last and most importantly, I should like to thank the Australian Commonwealth Literary Fund for the generous grants that made my researches possible, with special thanks to the then secretary, Mr W. R. Cumming and, above all to the chairman at the time, Sir Grenfell Price, for whose encouragement and support I am deeply grateful.

E.S.

CONTENTS

ILLUSTRATIONS

INTRODUCTION

The settlement of Australia is a tale of two colours. Historically, the white invasion is a mere ripple on the surface of a bottomless well. Soundings have been taken that carbon-date the black Australians back to twenty-five or even thirty thousand years. But these are according to white technology that measures black history in its own terms. The Aboriginal is wiser. He allows his ancestry to melt into the "dreaming" as the desert horizon melts into mirage.

His word was legend, his pattern the law. Neither sustained him against the coming of the Europeans who wrote the story of conquest in letters bold enough to obliterate the tracings of a less articulate heritage.

So that, among the shouts of settlement—deservedly self-congratulatory—of the white pioneers, the protesting mutters of a black minority were almost unheard and seldom understood.

Since no official effort was made to communicate with the plundered in their own language, they were forced to attempt to learn the language of the plunderers. Their attempts were ridiculed, as was the tattered clothing they wore in imitation. Patronized at best and despised at worst, their numbers diminishing, not so much because of the white man's weapons as because of his diseases, they grasped at the straws of survival offered by their conquerors. They allowed themselves to be herded into reserves. Tribal groups crowded onto the stations that employed their young men. Miserable little bands of derelicts drifted round the edges of the white communities.

Only in the outback did they retain the individuality that was their right of birth. Here they survived where the white man could not. But the hunter's life is a hard one. Whispers of soft living reached him over the miles of burnt earth, luring him towards the indulgent captivity that was the white man's compromise.

Not least among the reasons that threatened the Australian Aboriginal with extinction was his own willingness to adjust. There were whites who championed his cause but very few who returned the compliment of adjustment. There were fewer still who chose the black in preference to the white way of life.

Among these few, and alone among the women of her day, was Daisy Bates.

A more unlikely example of symbiosis would be difficult to imagine. She was county Irish and a Victorian into the bargain. But she was a hardy transplant, sustained by class attitudes that were woven into the fabric of her personality. Her adoption of the black community was at first an intellectual rather than an emotional choice. Not for a moment did she disown her roots. In search of a hobby she found an obsession. But the way of life suited her. The Aborigines became her friends. The historian of their mores, she ended her life in search not of data but of people.

The change took place over fifty years and dated from her arrival in Perth in 1899. By the end of the first decade of the new century she was established as the West Australian authority on the Aborigines. Her acceptance as the first woman member of an Australian scientific expedition in 1910 was greeted with applause rather than surprise. Though the post was unpaid, her appointment in the year 1912 as the first female Protector of Aborigines was unique, as was her title of Justice of the Peace for two States. Her newspaper articles earned her fame as an intrepid traveller of the hazardous inland. She was a member of British as well as Australian anthropological societies.

Not until she settled in Ooldea, to live on the edge of the Nullarbor Plain for the sixteen years between 1919 and 1935 did the sacrificial image take precedence over the scientific investigator. The fantastic little figure, glimpsed by curious passengers on the East-West express in her long skirts, high collars, veiled hats and white gloves, cast a shadow that extended far beyond the red sands of her camping ground. The legend of Daisy Bates was born.

Like all shadows, the projected image was less than the reality. Gone was the ethnologist. Gone was the vivacious lady of education, who could talk with wit on subjects ranging from politics to Charles Dickens. In her place came the martyr, the self-ordained Florence Nightingale of the black people, who endured heat, starvation, even attacks of blindness in the care of her Aboriginal friends.

She paid the price of her fame. Those who suspected that there was more to the story condemned her as a fraud. Certainly in her own attempts to fit reality to popular concept much was lost. The fascination of her personality depended on spontaneity and spontaneity is not the stuff out of which public figures are made. But a shadow is cast by substance. Both aspects of the image were true though neither was the whole truth. Only in the last decade of her long life did she fit fantasy to fact. When her manuscripts were safely lodged on the shelves of Australia's National Library, her work honoured by the King, she left the white world to put up her tent among her black friends. When she died in 1951 her legend was the only legacy she had to leave. The image of the elegant little society lady who endured conditions of living that would defeat the sturdiest of pioneers was firmly fixed in the Australian imagination.

To experience the full impact of the unlikelihood of her story it would be necessary to do as I did; to leave the cities four hundred miles behind, to cross the saltbush sea of the Nullarbor Plain in a landrover; to pass the sullen little row of fettlers' cottages beside the Trans-Australian Railway line; to bounce over the yielding tracks of the ubiquitous sandhills and to come to rest on the rise that was her camp.

I was driven by the superintendent of Yalata, one of the Aboriginal reserves. A man of impatient beneficence, Barry Lintner preferred realism to theory. He showed no compunction in shooting the soft-eyed kangaroos for the benefit of our Aboriginal guides. Close to the urgent problems of assimilation, he dismissed the impractical, be it academic or political. Though he did not know it, he very often echoed Daisy's words.

We lunched on the camp-site, overgrown now but marked by the outline of what was once her windbreak. The two Aborigines picked up an iron peg and a corroded pannikin that had belonged to her.

They remembered her well. On the journey, and before then, in the reserve at Yalata, they discussed her. Surrounded by bush swathed with the smoke of the eternal fires and dotted with wurlies that showed signs of progress in their canvas roofing, the old men sat in a circle round me. The sun beat down on us. In the clear light their clothes were ragged and stiff with dust. The brown eyes sparkled with intelligence. They talked together in the rippling murmurs Daisy had liked so much.

She was Kabbarli, the grandmother who had given them food. She had banished the bad things. (These were left vague.) One had run away from the sight of her when he was a boy. An old man agreed that she had been the keeper of their totem boards but doubted if she had witnessed an initiation ceremony. The younger men remembered that she had been a good hunter. She had gone with them to look for the eggs of mallee hens, for rabbits, even for kangaroos. They laughed as they reminisced. The expression on their faces was indulgent. One had the uneasy suspicion that to them the white civilization was a joke, to which Daisy had been an exception as she had earned their respect.

We drove back across the ninety miles between Ooldea and Yalata. While Barry stopped to put up his short-wave aerial to check in with the Reserve, I wandered a little deeper into emptiness. It was twilight and the endless Plain reflected the violet desert light. A haze over the mulga reminded me of her description of "reptilian heads that loom up and appear to be gliding through the mists". I was standing on one of the oldest land surfaces in the world and the atmosphere was that of prehistory. It was easy at this moment to understand why the pleasures of cities could appear to her as "the pains and penalties of civilization".

I looked down at the pannikin in my hand, rusted but intact after thirty years of exposure, and saw it as a symbol of the obstinate valiance that had dared the lonely immensity with nothing more than a child's belief in God to set against it.

But then was she not Kallower, wife of Leberr of the Dreamtime?—the magician who could choose each night one out of her "floral memories" to lead her back out of emptiness towards the gaiety of girlhood?—who could wake each morning to the echo of the pipes to which she had danced the Irish reel until two in the morning?

E.S.

DAISY BATES'S AUSTRALI

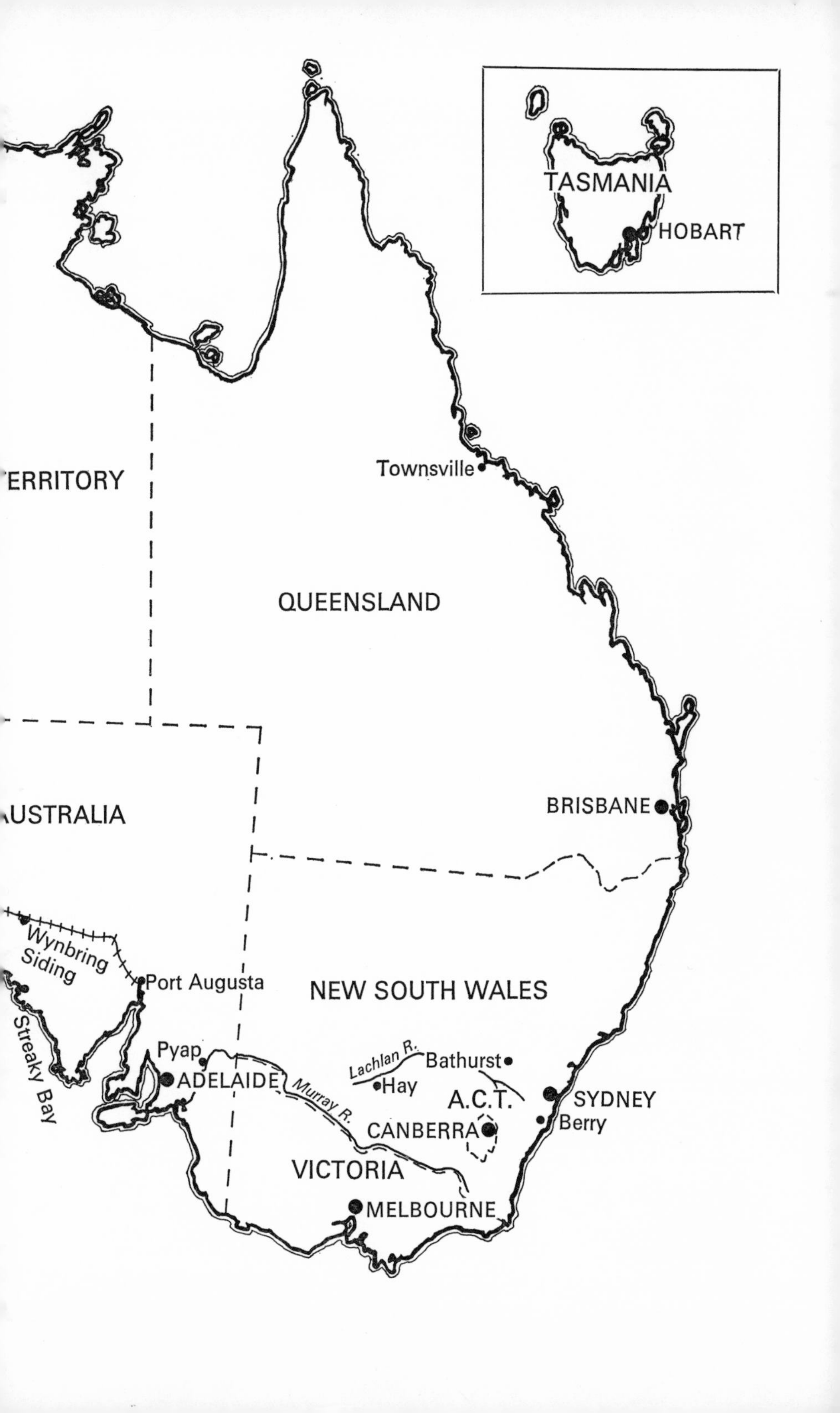
TASMANIA
HOBART
ERRITORY
Townsville
QUEENSLAND
BRISBANE
USTRALIA
Wynbring Siding
Port Augusta
NEW SOUTH WALES
Streaky Bay
Pyap
ADELAIDE
Murray R.
Lachlan R.
Bathurst
Hay
A.C.T.
SYDNEY
Berry
CANBERRA
VICTORIA
MELBOURNE

CHAPTER ONE

Surely the world we live in is but the world that lives in us?—From the Notebooks of Daisy Bates.

In County Tipperary

She was born in Ashberry House, a rambling old building on the wide wet slope of Caraig Hill in County Tipperary, Ireland. Christened Daisy May in the Church of Ireland, she was a daughter of privilege, with a family tree dating back to William O'Dwyer, created Baron of Kilnamanagh by Edward III.

A digression somewhere along the line meant that hers was a Protestant household, militant at that, but the O'Dwyer chin and the O'Dwyer temperament proclaimed her kinship with a clan that combined loyalty to tradition with intolerance of injustice. Their historian informs us that the O'Dwyer chiefs, though not aggressive, were not conspicuous for their obedience. Their resistance to Cromwell's armies scattered them to the four corners of Europe. They turned to soldiering and became officers in the Irish regiments of Spain and France. Those who remained managed as best they could to wrest a living from an overcrowded soil. It was Patrick O'Dwyer's stand against the landlords in the battle of Ballycohey that provided Gladstone with the ammunition he needed to force through his revised land law Act of 1870.

By then, according to the chronology of her marriage certificate, Daisy was seven years old. Her birthdate was given as

16th October 1863. She was the fourth child of Marguerette Hunt and "the loveliest father in Christendom", James Edward O'Dwyer, whose occupation is described with Jane Austen simplicity as "Gentleman".

Her immediate forbears were occupied with the law, and her grandfather, the magistrate, presided over her childhood memories. A hardened drinker, he alternated between sessions in court and at the Kildare Street club in Dublin. His interests were horse-racing and politics in the best Irish tradition. Generally regarded as "a good sport", he gambled on the one and pontificated on the other. That his granddaughter was influenced by his opinions is shown by the number of times she quoted him, especially on the controversial topic of the Church of Rome.

"The Protestants have more honour than the Catholics as a body" was a dictum repeated more often than it deserved.

A taste for French brandy resulted in his being carried "kicking and cursing" to bed at night. But this, according to Daisy, placed more of a strain on the family coffers than on the loyalty of the family retainers, whose respect for the magistrate suffered not one jot from so human a weakness. More snobbish than their master, the O'Dwyer servants divided the "gentry" into those who were born into it and those who bought their way. The O'Dwyers were "born" and so above reproach.

Her mother she remembered only through the portrait that her father had painted. A fragile beauty, her features lit by the false radiance of tuberculosis, she bequeathed to Daisy her blue eyes and a susceptibility to the disease that killed her very soon after the birth of her youngest daughter. The baby, together with Daisy's sisters Marian and Kathleen, aged twelve and six respectively, and her two-year-old brother James, were taken under the matriarchal wing of Grandmother Hunt. This lady showed her disapproval of the hard-drinking O'Dwyers by affixing her name to theirs. The four children, from then on, became known as the "O'Dwyer Hunts".

They were, Daisy said, "a dreadfully happy-go-lucky, careless, misruley lot". They argued incessantly, learnt to ride and to dance the Irish reel to the accompaniment of O'Brien, the fiddler of royal descent. Daisy and her brother Jim explored the misty hills of Caraig and Slieve Na Mon, looking for "goblins and ghosties", armed with the "doggerel curses" learnt from their nurse. Sometimes the magistrate took them to Dublin and they escaped to gorge at the local cake-shop. Presented with an account for 12s.—a great deal of money in those days—their grandfather reproved the attendant for allowing them to run up a bill for pastries.

"Shure, your honour, it wasn't a bill at all they ran up," the woman replied; "they ate them at wanst."

On another occasion they escaped to watch a battle being fought between an old woman and her daughter-in-law. The children settled on a wall and laid bets as to which one would win while the two women rolled down the slope beneath them, clawing at each other's hair and eyes in a fury of female hate. A flick of their grandfather's whip brought them to heel but not to repentance, especially as that respectable gentleman had been enjoying the fight himself.

To balance this masculine indulgence was the family matriarch, Grandmother Hunt. In Daisy's memory she remained as a symbol of minor royalty, a Queen Victoria in her minute realm, the family property at Ballycrine, a townland tucked into the hem of Roscrea and owned in part by Michael Hunt.

Hers was a poverty-stricken domain. Grandmother Hunt spent a great deal of her time behind a spinning-wheel at which she wove cloths, coloured for her grandchildren, plain for the servants. A lady bountiful, she "fed and clothed and doctored" those unfortunates described by Daisy as "hovel Irish, benighted in indolence and superstition with little to separate them from the Australian Aborigine".

Grim tales reached her of a hated landlord's agent buried up to his neck at the mercy of a herd of pigs turned loose to root about him. For the Irish peasants of the 1860s life was a battle for survival, unremitting in its ferocity. Like most children, Daisy absorbed more of the realities than she indicated. The unsanitary wurlies of ailing Aborigines were unable to daunt an Irishwoman born at this moment in time. Not that her memoirs hint at personal deprivation. They are a mere pen sketch, drawn with Victorian reticence over an epoch of starvation and despair that was already producing the greatest exodus of Irish history.

Adults hovered in the background, but, in the main, she and her brother Jim were given the freedom to create their own world. Together they roamed "gaily and irresponsibly" over Knockshegowna. Separated from her not long afterwards, Jim remained as the Peter Pan of her memories, for ever the "nice boy with the curly hair" who taught her, as brothers do, to become a tomboy in order to gain his respect.

The only authority to whom they were required to answer

was that phenomenon of the English middle classes, the family nanny.

Of all the Victorian anomalies, it is hard to find one more remarkable than this habit of entrusting children, body and soul, to the care of an often illiterate nurse, given free rein to teach all that must later be unlearnt. Daisy was luckier than most. Her "Allie" could neither read nor write, but she was soft-hearted and indulgent. With such pliable material, the young Daisy learnt very early to expect from life what she wanted "on demand". There is only one recorded occasion in which Allie exerted her will over her charge. Daisy broke her leg, and Allie, in superstitious terror, took her to the priest instead of to the doctor, "frightening the devil" out of her to say nothing to the matriarch. Fortunately she appears to have come to no harm. The break caused the displacement of a vein that troubled her if she had to stand for long periods, but never prevented her from walking a "cheery nine miles" if she felt like it.

A difficult, spirited little girl, her loves and antipathies were equally passionate. Being the only mother she knew, her nurse had great influence; and with Allie she learnt an early respect for the magic that was the Irish peasant heritage. She went with her to a wake and watched the rite of the placing of a plate of salt on the corpse to ward off the evil spirits. She listened to the keening that was to come back to her, years later, when she heard the "long wild wail" of an Aboriginal lubra. To ensure the obedience she so seldom received, Allie told her of the case of a child placed on a shovel over a fire "to burn the devil out of it". The future Kallower, magician of the black Australians, whose *nowinning* sparked its own light in the blackness of the bush, understood the power of superstition even as her growing intellect rejected it.

The adults of the family soon taught her to laugh at peasant charms and curses, but this did not prevent her from peopling her mist-drenched valleys and peaty brown streams with elves and fairies. Daisy believed in them more fervently than most children if only because her nurse believed in them as well. When she was left alone after the break-up of the family, they became her chosen companions. That she never quite gave them up is shown by an unfinished poem, begun almost seventy years later with the lines:

Oh Ashberry House on the back of the hill where I was born and bred,

And in childhood traced the thirty odd springs that made the wide river bed,
Those little banks by the rainbow springs, the homes of our elfin world,
Where under a leaf or top of a flower the wee baby elves lay uncurled . . .

The attempt ends with the admission that:

I have never grown out of my longing for you and my playmates of long ago. . . .

It is easy to understand why Daisy, a writer of some talent, abandoned the poem, but it is revealing in that it provides the link between her two worlds. That childhood is the most formative period of our lives we know. Daisy's fantasy world was her open sesame into the Aboriginal mind. The Broome legend of the *ngargalulla* spirit babies woke a response that dated back to the elves and fairies curled on the tops of wildflowers. She possessed total recall, and the magic casements were never quite closed on her faery lands forlorn. Reality, by contrast, could be as sordid as it liked. It could never come more than second best.

The death of the matriarch divided the family. Marian, by now a grown-up young lady, and Kathleen, still at school, were taken into the home of a relative. Jim was sent off to yet another O'Dwyer family and Daisy, the youngest, remained with her father.

What happened to Allie is not related; but that Daisy's father was at a loss to know what to do with his daughter was evident. She records a visit across the Irish channel, to the widow of the Dean of Ripon. Again there is a strong suggestion of Jane Austen in her description of the widow's house "in the vicinity of Conway Castle", but the visit is on record mainly because, from the widow of Ripon, Daisy received the Bible that was to remain with her for life. On her return to Dublin she was sent for a while to school, but the enforced discipline, imposed so soon after the break-up of the family, turned her into something of a problem child. Her teachers reported that Daisy "would not learn". James O'Dwyer suggested that they confine themselves to teaching her to speak the right way, this being the only education necessary to a young girl who could already ride to hounds and dance the reel. He was more concerned about what she read, and extracted a promise from her that she was later to regard as a governing factor in her literary taste. If she read the books of his favourite authors she could then choose what she liked. He listed Dickens, Scott, Thackeray and Lytton. Of these, Dickens was first favourite, and Daisy began, under her father's tuition, to absorb the works of an author who came second in her esteem only to the word of God.

"I walked with Nell," she wrote, "and cried with pity and sorrow for her poor wounded feet. And I learned thro' Dickens all things good."

By now the tomboy child was blossoming into the beauty she became. It is a remarkable fact that once she reached her full height of five feet four inches, Daisy's appearance altered scarcely at all throughout her long life. The reasons for this manifested themselves at once. Always on the move, she kept the lithe grace of body of which she was so proud. She seldom walked if she could run, and she loved dancing. She enjoyed sport, and played tennis and hockey at her various schools. Her mother's transparent skin gave delicacy to the decisive lines of her face, so that the colouring rather than the shape of her features was the dominant factor. Her complexion was the traditional Irish peaches and cream. Her eyes were vividly blue, her hair she described as chestnut. In the fashion of the day she cultivated a bang of curls over the impressive brow. Her nose, small and gently aquiline, took on, with time, the taut curve of a bird's beak. The O'Dwyer chin appeared to grow outward with the years and the hint of the voluptuous in the fullness of mouth disappeared into a line of resolution. But, in this transition period between child and girlhood, outlines were round and softly tinted, and the Irish brogue moderated with its charm the carrying voice, already too insistent, given to laughter, to contention and to challenge. The "magnetic personality" so often commented upon in later life must, at this stage, have been rather trying. It is not difficult to imagine the relief with which her father handed her over to the Outram family to be educated with their five children.

The offer came about through the friendship of her grandmother and Lady Outram, widow of the famous Sir James, who had won glory as Lieutenant-General in the Indian army. Lady Outram was a daughter of the family Anderson, whose seat was Emill Castle in County Tipperary. After her husband's death she was no doubt glad to find refuge in the tranquillity that was still possible amid the "ruins and rain" of Ireland. Inevitably her grandchildren met and played with the younger O'Dwyer Hunts. Equally inevitably the matriarch confided her doubts about the suitability of her son-in-law as a guiding influence over his motherless offspring. Sir Francis Outram had known and liked the fragile Marguerette. The "Dowager Lady Outram" as Daisy insisted upon referring to her, would not have found it difficult to persuade her son to accept Daisy as the sixth member of his family of five sons.

No doubt Lady Outram was sorry for the child, deprived so drastically of her brother and sisters, but there was another reason for her charity.

Daisy, who cared "not one shake of a lame mouse's tail" for the opinions of her age group, tended to haunt the company of older people. Good manners were her birthright, and her elders found in this volatile and cheerful child an inquiring mind that provoked their interest without threatening their condescension. Daisy, lacking her own mother, looked for an answer to a need that neither Allie nor her father was capable of supplying. Her grandmother's friends responded. Lady Outram was one of a group of women who had interested themselves in her, among them Elizabeth Knox, to whom Daisy attributed the love of poetry that was to enrich the self-imposed solitude of later years.

In terms of the age she could not have done better in the choice of foster family. A history of service to Queen and Empire had been recognized by the State burial of Sir James Outram in Westminster Abbey. Financially as well as socially, the Outrams were in the privileged stratum of a hierarchic society. The price of glory had been paid, however, and Sir Francis Outram, though not yet forty years old, was confined to a wheelchair through a back injury received in carrying dispatches in the Indian mutiny. A young man so stricken would be compelled to glorify or to reject the cause for which he had fought. Sir Francis Outram's ideal of Empire became Daisy's for life. Exposed at this formative stage to a tradition rendered valid by sacrifice and given substance by personal encounters with royalty, the young Daisy vowed a devotion from which she never wavered.

In her mind she carried the image of Queen Victoria, glimpsed walking in the grounds of Balmoral in her long skirts and beribboned picture hat, to the dreariest wastes of the Australian inland. Driving her camel buggy laden with groceries and tobacco for her sick Aborigines, she comforted herself with the thought of the Queen delivering hampers to her tenants in the royal pony trap. Long after such a concept had become an anachronism, she fought for her ideal of a King's man to rule over her black kingdom.

If she were made to feel an alien in an already overpopulated nest, she does not record the fact. She received, she said, "a funny travelling kind of education". Lessons were given the children by a governess, her "dear Fräulein Reischauer", who "thumped her for her grammar", but whose excellent tuition is manifest. Daisy's handwriting became a model of its kind, rounded and firm, totally legible even on the scraps of newspaper wrappings to which she was later reduced. Her spelling was impeccable. She developed a taste for Latin verse, became fluent in French, read the German philosophers and quoted from Nietzsche and Schopenhauer. A passionate interest in all things scientific was an early and generally considered unsuitable taste. Her reading on the subject must have been wide as there is no other evidence of training to equip her for her future role of anthropologist.

Her education appears to have been completed in a finishing school in Belgium, but of this she speaks not at all. Her gift for total recall went hand in hand with a selectiveness that conveniently forgot all she wished not to remember. Her tour with the Outram family is recorded as a series of vignettes in kaleidoscope.

"Learning a language here and a scrap of needlework there", the children danced as blithely across Europe as if accompanied by the royal fiddler O'Brien. Snowed in on a Swiss frontier they consoled themselves with a meal of boiled rice provided by Fräulein Reischauer. Sitting disconsolate on the pavements of "the gay and dainty Paris of the seventies", the young Daisy wept for a burst "ballon". At Ostend she escaped from the little party to release the caged birds waiting to be sold. She tweaked the pigtail of "that undeniably dull little eaglet, Marie Coecceldi, niece of Napoleon III", and fled from the hooded monks in the streets of that "smelly city, clammy and damp and cold, that was Rome".

From time to time James O'Dwyer descended upon them, carried off his daughter for a meal in Montreux, or some other fashionable resort, and consulted with the good Fräulein on Daisy's deficiencies as a scholar. For all her brilliance, these were real enough. An inborn restlessness combined with the uprootings of her childhood had made concentration difficult. To learn a language was easy because of the stimulus of new places and new people; to sit down long enough to work out the prosaic problems of pounds, shillings and pence was a chore to be avoided at all costs by this mercurial young creature who regarded it as a sin to cage a bird and whose refuge, like theirs, was in flight.

None the less, by the time she returned to Dublin she had absorbed the rules of conduct and the social attitudes of her class.

She was erect of back, fastidious of toilet. She could ride anything, although, she admitted, she "had no hands". Her politics, like her voice, had acquired an English accent. Since there remained a year or two of adolescence before she could be recognized as a debutante, she spent some time with the members of her father's Kildare Street club, imbibing more of the prejudices of these Protestant anglophiles.

In their eyes her country would remain a battlefield between faiths until equipped with a "free, compulsory and secular education". Parnell was a hero because he refused to allow himself to be "swayed by Rome". His downfall was predicted, and Daisy listened to bets being laid as to how the uncrowned king of Ireland would be disqualified in the eyes of his countrymen.

"Ireland has got out of its own hands," she was told. "The better men see it . . . and so leave their country for their own good."

Like all Victorian young ladies she was protected from the young men of her own age, and her companions remained these friends of her father's. Chief among them was Bishop G. H. Stanton. Greatly taken by the vivacious young daughter of James O'Dwyer, the bishop rode with her by day and included her in the long discussions that occupied the evenings of the club members. A favourite subject was Dickens, and a suitable ending for *Edwin Drood* became a challenge as absorbing as the chess that provided an alternative to discussion. The bishop's suggestion that he teach Daisy the game was dismissed by her father, who pronounced her incapable of the necessary concentration. Stanton accordingly confined his encouragement to literature. The publication of two of her poems gave Daisy hope of a literary career, but again her father discouraged the idea.

"Work at it and you may turn out to be a fair versifier," was his verdict.

Faint praise had its effect and Daisy abandoned poetry as she had abandoned chess.

By which it will be seen that her father may well have spoiled but certainly did not spare her. If he had lived she might have learnt to accept the mental discipline he so plainly tried to teach her. But, she wrote, she had just begun to appreciate his "wise counsel" when he died. He remained in her memory as the beloved companion of her adolescence. His opinions became hers, even though, by accepting them, she had to acknowledge her female inferiority. This never appeared to disturb her. She was as indulgent as he had been towards her "scatterbrain" inconsistency. For a woman, he told her, character was more important than brain.

Under his tuition she learnt to keep her private life and her private emotions to herself; to face the world with pride, dignity and, above all, humour. They laughed together at the cartoons in *Punch*, his favourite magazine. Later, when she had officially "come out" they laughed at the acrostics sent her by aspiring suitors, one of which she memorized.

Dost oh dost thou remember the night we first met,
Ah dear the remembrance to me,
I to my death will ne'er forget,
Sweet lady that dance with thee,
Yes that dance made so pleasant by thee!

The sender was gleefully christened "Dost oh dost", and relegated to the ranks of a family joke.

But a nation's tragedy could not be excluded even from the candle-lit ballrooms of Dublin's hunting set. Poverty stalked the streets, penetrating the brave façade of Russell Square, in which were situated the more elegant of the town houses belonging to county families. There was a whispered rumour of two old ladies locked in a mansion filled with valuables they were too proud to sell, who stole out in the cover of darkness to raid the garbage tins for food. Month by month the United Irish brotherhood of New York swelled its numbers with newly arrived immigrants. Those unable to join them braved the three-month voyage to Australia; some to pioneer, like the Durack brothers, the waterless outback.

The death of James O'Dwyer left Daisy with an inheritance somewhat diminished by his conviviality, and with a restless desire to link her life with the friends who wrote so cheerfully from the other side of the world. Among them was Bishop Stanton, now Bishop of North Queensland. He wrote offering hospitality, and Daisy pressed for permission to accept his invitation.

She was told that it was out of the question. It was one thing for Irish manhood to venture so far, it was quite another for a gently brought up young lady.

Alone and lonely, Daisy fretted in Dublin. Then fate played into her hands. A spot on her lungs was diagnosed by the family doctor as a warning of tuberculosis. If she were not to be stricken like her mother she must find a warmer climate.

"So," she wrote, "was Australia brought on my life's map."

Daisy booked her passage and spent the months of waiting in acquiring introductions and a wardrobe luxurious enough to establish her claim to gentility in the Government circles of this new land.

She left on the *Almora*. The year was 1884 and her destination the little community of Townsville, two hundred-odd miles above the tropic of Capricorn on the Queensland coast.

CHAPTER TWO

For me there is always the rainbow beyond the hill.
—Daisy Bates.

A Milkmaid in Queensland

Australia in the 1880s was a challenge to the imagination exploited to the full by the speculators.

For Daisy's compatriots, there was the lure of land. Dr Lang's seven voyages of assault on the English Government had produced results. The immigrant to the new colony of Queensland was offered a bonus of property at least the value of his passage out. The potential squatter was then told of vast areas inland that needed only to be stocked for a tender to be submitted to the Government. Once established, he would be lord of his domain, empowered as magistrate as well as master.

The pot of gold gleamed brightly indeed from the end of the rainbow on the other side of the world. By 1884 the Irish immigrants added up to very nearly a quarter of the entire population of Australia. Amongst them were the many family friends to whom Daisy had been given introductions. Important among these was Philip Gipps, cousin of her friend Hester Cayley and descendant of the former Governor.

In her memoirs the voyage on the *Almora*, like the spot on her lungs, is allowed to vanish without trace. Only a vague mention

The Kildare Street Club, Dublin (*Photo*: National Library of Ireland)

Daisy Bates on her arrival in Australia, 1884 (*Photo*: West Australian Newspapers Ltd)

The *Macquarie* (*Photo*: *Radio Times* Hulton Picture Library)

of parties on board in which the young people "kept themselves to themself", is left as a record of what must surely have been a momentous event in her life.

In those days before radar and stabilizers long voyages were never without incident. The element of danger was there, especially in 1884, when the after-effects of the Krakatoa eruption were still being felt. "Turner-like sunsets" flamed the sky each night. The resultant tidal waves that ravaged the coast of the Malay Archipelago had left a legacy of tragedy to the inhabitants and of nervousness to the captains of passenger ships.

If there were alarms on the *Almora*, Daisy did not bother to record them. No doubt she flung herself into shipboard life as she entered into all things new, with curiosity and a total absence of fear.

Blessed with "Auntie Flo's digestion", she rode the bucking decks without discomfort. She could even enjoy the ship's fare, though not all of it, for the menus were enormous and her capacity always small. In spite of the lack of refrigeration, food was fresher on those early steamers than on the luxury liners of today, for the somewhat macabre reason that each ship carried its own little farm that was consumed on the journey. Passengers were offered a choice of roast or boiled mutton, pork, bacon, or gammon, followed by varieties of fowl and duck and rounded off with English pudding. These sustaining little snacks, set out twice a day, were washed down with beer or wine, included in the price of the ticket. Rifles were provided so that the gentlemen might take a sporting pot at the seabirds overhead. Card games were available in the saloon. Otherwise the passengers must entertain themselves. The young Daisy, whose equanimity was never threatened by *mal de mer*, was no doubt greatly in demand.

Contact was easy for her always. Her gaiety and vigour struck sparks among those who surrounded her. None of the depressing emotions such as homesickness appeared to have assailed her. Not until later years did unhappiness bring with it a nostalgia for "the old country". Her arrival in tropical Townsville was an adventure robbed of all strangeness by the presence of Bishop Stanton. She was officially designated as his ward. At his house she found familiar faces and familiar accents.

"Australia," Daisy wrote, "was just like home."

In fact it could not have been less like. Apart from the heat, which must have melted the starched Victorian collar that encircled her neck and brought with it a retinue of flies and mosquitoes, there were such exotic fauna as snakes, kangaroos and crocodiles, exotic flora of many different kinds. Above all there was the vitality of the little colony. After the weary struggle for survival with which she was surrounded in Ireland, it must have engulfed her like a wave.

Queensland was thrusting ahead. The "blackbirders" had stocked the plantations with more than two thousand South Sea islanders. Traders such as the infamous Ross Lewin, who could sell his human cargo for as much as £7 per head, had seen to it that his "blackbirds" were worth the price. Those that were not had been thrown to the sharks en route. The combination of cheap Kanaka labour and Chinese immigration meant that sugar, banana and cotton growing were leaping ahead. Gold was an intermittent fever that flooded the colony with waves of prospectors. The vast inland was gradually being converted into sheep and cattle stations.

The Townsville of 1884, in fact, must have had points in common with the early towns of America's romanticized Wild West. Hotel bars were filled with miners boasting about gold dust, cane cutters and cotton workers spending their pay cheques, squatters stocking their store sheds, drovers being outfitted for their long and dusty inland treks.

But for the young Daisy O'Dwyer, product of an Anglo-Irish upper-class education, guest of the Bishop of North Queensland, the people in the streets, like the flora and fauna, were of touristic interest only. The parties to which she was invited, the homesteads she visited, belonged to "her own kind".

Of such there were plenty. Young Englishmen of public school backgrounds, like Biddulph Henning of *The Letters of Rachel Henning*, had pioneered the grazing country of the South Kennedy district. The log huts with which they began were by now creeper-covered homesteads, flanked with outhouses for servants and stockhands and provisioned by a store maintained by the manager. Family friends, only too delighted to renew contact with the world that they had left behind them, swamped Daisy with invitations to "come and stay".

This was not always so easy. To reach them sometimes entailed a two-day journey on horseback for which tent, billycan and food must be carried as well. Apart from the normal hazards offered by snakes and insects, Daisy could be faced with unbridged rivers over which she must swim her horse, regardless of damage to boots and riding skirt. But this was the kind of challenge she gloried in. She accepted the invitations that came her way, finding in each visit a new experience. She went to Mary

Vale Station, run by the brothers William and Frank Hann, and watched William's wife and daughter help him to muster, draft, even to kill and skin the cattle, returning at night to cook the evening meal. She was a guest of a Derbyshire family of noble descent about whose identity she was reticent but whose homestead was furnished with tables made out of deal cases, curtained by cretonne at a penny a yard. The family had upholstered their furniture themselves, using rags and newspapers and sometimes dried grass.

During this stay a strike of hands occurred and Daisy learnt to milk. Although she admitted that her arms had to be fomented with bran mash between milkings, she helped the four sons of the family to keep the farm as a going concern long enough to ensure its purchase by city financiers.

Not quite so successful were her attempts to "wheel the wild scrub cattle in the yard", but as she continued to ride side-saddle in the manner considered suitable for young ladies of her day, this is not altogether surprising.

Queensland was wonderful, but there was an entire continent to be explored. It was not long before Daisy's nomadic instinct was reawakened.

Why she went south is not clear. Perhaps, as Hester Cayley said, it was to join Philip Gipps. Just how serious was this affair we shall never know, for Daisy omitted all mention of it in her memoirs. One thing is certain. It was in those early months that her abiding admiration for the white pioneers, at this stage practically all of British descent, was born. She was consumed with a desire to take her place among them and it was obvious that to do so she must leave the protective wing of Bishop Stanton.

To travel in those days was not a simple matter. Between Sydney and Melbourne the brand-new railway-line was in operation. To reach New South Wales from Queensland she would need to travel by road.

The monopoly of coach travel had already gone to the famous Cobb & Co. By 1884 their coaches harnessed six thousand horses a day and covered a distance of twenty-eight thousand miles a week. They forged a real as well as a romantic link with America's West. Rutherford, the company manager, was American, the coaches were imported from Connecticut and the drivers trained by Wells Fargo.

Daisy, who did not in the least like being squashed in beside the "three odouriferous Chinese" and the "inebriate squatters" of her description, preferred to ride beside the driver and listen to his tales.

Of such there were many, very often concerned with hold-ups by bushrangers. There was the story of the driver who had whipped his horses right through the hold-up because he objected to the tone of voice with which he had been asked to "stand and deliver". Of another who had persuaded the robbers to return the cheques they had taken from the passengers for the eminently practical reason that no bank would accept them. The story went that the bushrangers had been arrested for their magnanimity: the driver had memorized the detail of their clothing during the course of conversation.

They merited their princely incomes, these drivers of Cobb & Co. There were even more dramatic incidents, such as the time when the brake-band snapped as a coach was hurtling down a hill towards a gorge. On one side of the road was a precipice. The driver did not hesitate. He capsized his coach onto the hill and the only casualty among his thirty passengers was one broken arm. More romantic still was the story of a coach carrying a ton of gold and a woman giving birth to a baby. The driver raced eighty miles over a waterless track to reach the hospital. Only then did he turn his coach and deposit the gold.

Daisy found each new colony rich in such histories, some heroic, some frankly lawless, like the story of the three body-snatchers which she learnt from R. H. White, the banker, in Sydney.

On her arrival in Sydney, Daisy stayed with the White family, at Milton in Ashfield. R. H. White, known as Hoddle Doddle White because of the fortune he inherited from Hoddle Dryberg, a relative, had, she said, borrowed money from James O'Dwyer to finance his claim to the estate, and the welcome given to his daughter was understandably warm. Relaxing in what she called the "tomboy" atmosphere of a household consisting of daughters of her own age chaperoned by an indulgent "Aunt Cooper", she extracted from the banker the story that she was later to publish in the *Australasian* under the title of "The Murderer's Head".

In November of 1867 Thomas John Griffin, assistant gold commissioner of Clermont, was arrested and later hanged for the murder of his two assistants while they were escorting gold to Rockhampton.

According to Daisy's account of it, three friends, White, a surgeon called O'Callaghan and an editor called Thaddeus O'Kane, decided that the skull of so callous a murderer would be worth dissecting. O'Kane put forth the unorthodox suggestion that the surgeon be given a chance to do so.

Griffin had been buried that morning, so there was no time to waste.

"The three conspirators left their separate residences quietly after dark," Daisy wrote, "the tall banker carrying a spade hidden under his overcoat; the surgeon carried the necessary instruments for decapitation. The editor, like the true Irish conspirator that he was, had his lantern handy."

The deed was done, and after "a bath and a change of clothes, the three decorous gentlemen met as usual for evening whist."

For all their precautions the beheading was discovered and O'Callaghan himself was called in to examine the body. He pronounced that "it was the work of an amateur." The three men entered into animated discussions with their friends, exchanged theories as to how it was done and escaped with no breath of suspicion attached to them.

"Finally," Daisy observed, "the incident passed into the limbo of forgotten things."

Australia was evidently a land where convention was second to daring and in which the future belonged to the brave. Daisy did not merely rise to its challenges. Because of them her life took on a new dimension. Above all, she responded to the realities of primitive living.

"There is," she wrote, "that sort of primitiveness in one that makes one eager to tackle primitive conditions."

Nor was she at this time referring to the Aboriginal community. Hers was still a world of white settlers who were braving an alien nature in an alien land. For them the "blackfellow", as he was called, was, in general, just another obstacle or hazard. Even as enlightened a woman as Rachel Henning, who emigrated to Queensland some twenty years before Daisy, could write without emotion in her fascinating *Letters* that the police had offered to "clear Biddulph's land of wild blacks"; and she described them as "the queerest looking mortals, with their long lean legs and arms without an atom of flesh on them, more like spiders than anything human".

There is no indication in Daisy's memoirs that at this stage she did other than accept the white settlers' point of view. She was young enough and egotistical enough to be immersed in life as it presented itself to her. Until she discovered the job she was looking for, her restless energy found its outlet in picnics, parties and balls.

Nor was there any lack of intellectual stimulus. Books were a link with the world left behind, and knowledge of them was widely disseminated. One local newspaper is said to have printed Ruskin's *Unto This Last* in its leader columns. Navvies and drovers attended lectures on such subjects as Darwinism, French poetry and Henry George.

Dodd Smith Clark, editor of a Townsville paper, had given Daisy an introduction to J. F. Archibald of the Sydney *Bulletin.* Archibald, a man of wit and vitality, was renowned for his encouragement to writers, and Daisy joined the circle who gathered round him. Of her personal popularity there is evidence in abundance, if only in the disapproval of her female acquaintances.

"The trouble with Daisy is that she likes men too much," was an acid comment from her future sister-in-law.

She might have put it the other way round, as did another young friend of this period.

"Whenever Daisy came into the room, the conversation became more animated. Even as a child I knew that the men of the district found her attractive."

A photograph taken at the time tells us why. The habitual seriousness with which she confronted the camera is misleading, for "without the Irish grin this is none of you", as an admirer told her. But there is a suggestion of the provocative in the young face, and in repose there is sensuality as well as wilfulness in the pout of the mouth. There is, too, more than a hint of the driving force that compelled her to follow her own star.

Her friend Hester Cayley put it more brutally. "Obstinacy was Daisy's besetting sin. She was a wayward girl, as stubborn as Paddy's mule, as I told her to her face."

The warward girl had corrected her with an Irish grin.

"Say 'determined', dear. It sounds better!"

Obstinate or determined, there can be no disputing that at twenty-one Daisy O'Dwyer was a young woman of many parts. A Victorian with a taste for the primitive, an intellectual who loved to dance, a witty conversationalist with a flair for exaggeration, an excellent rider with a reputation as a flirtatious beauty —such a girl could spread her net wide. According to Miss Cayley, she became engaged to Philip Gipps. "Then," she wrote, "Philip died and Daisy married Bates."

The implication is obvious. An explanation must be found for the unsuitable marriage that happened so soon after her arrival.

Daisy's reaction is interpreted as the impulse of the broken-hearted—to give when there is nothing to gain—in other words to marry the first man who proposed to her.

Miss Cayley's was the judgement of hindsight, her opinion prejudiced by failure. She ignored an important factor—Daisy's emotional reaction to the country of her adoption.

"What heroines those pioneer women were!" she wrote. "In this young country British women of all classes set their hands to all and every kind of work without loss of prestige, for there is no social bar other than dishonesty and immorality."

She described cockney and Irish families who entered "the primeval wilderness a thousand miles larger than Hampshire New Forest", driving before them ". . . the few sheep or cattle which were to found the herd, a dray drawn by two or three horses carrying their year's stock of provisions . . . their tent their first home in the unknown country."

Intoxicated by the freedom from social restraint, secure in the knowledge that in Australia work was no disgrace, Daisy saw an advertisement for a governess and answered it.

One of her introductions had been to the Bates family, dairy farmers at Pyree on the Berry estate, ninety miles south of Sydney. According to Daisy, they were connexions of Sir Everard Bates, a friend of James O'Dwyer's, but by the time she visited them Hugh Bates had died and his widow Catherine was struggling to educate her six children and to maintain the farm. Daisy writes that she was walking towards the Bates farmhouse when she saw a notice pinned up on the paling fence, advertising for a governess, and advising applicants to "apply milk cart in the street". Daisy offered herself for the job and stayed on at the farm, teaching the younger children and helping with the hard work.

The job was never intended to be other than a transition between her status as guest and her future as pioneer. Already she had planned to invest in a leasehold of land offered so temptingly by the Queensland Government.

Whether or not she was conscious of doing so, she would have been looking for a partner suitable for such a project.

Who better than John Bates, man of action, breaker of wild horses, capable of throwing a steer by the horns and of driving a mob of cattle through the trackless inland? In other words, an indigenous Australian?

CHAPTER THREE

They were long and wiry natives from the rugged mountain side,
And the horse was never saddled that the Geebungs couldn't ride.—A. B. Paterson.

The Drover's Wife

They met at Christmas time at the end of the year 1884 when Jack came down from the north to pay one of his periodic visits to his mother on the farm.

They knew each other already by reputation. The family, studious on the whole and fervently Roman Catholic, regarded their eldest brother with a mixture of admiration and disapproval. They referred to him as their "wild colonial boy". He didn't think much of books, but there was not a brumby in the country that could throw him. After all he had been chosen to play polo with the Geebungs, the toughest team in the colony.

Daisy's curiosity was aroused. She found him pleasing to look at: lean and graceful, tall enough to top her by a head, his face broad across the cheekbones, the weaker triangle of mouth and chin ornamented by the fashionable moustache. There was no hint in those early days of their first meeting of the purposelessness in Jack that was to divide them. The "heavy uninteresting man" that he was to become in middle age was foreshadowed perhaps in his quietness, but that seemed no bad thing since Daisy's personality was enough for two. When he did speak he talked of a world that intrigued her if only for its novelty. Daisy was too interested in all he had to say to be critical.

Jack's curiosity had been stimulated by his brother Charlie, who had written with such enthusiasm about their Irish visitor who could dance and laugh and teach, and milk the cows when necessary. In Charlie's eyes, Daisy had everything: looks, brains, and a passion for all things Australian. Jack was intrigued. It was obvious that his younger brother was infatuated, but then young Charlie was still a student, in the midst of his teacher's training course that he was doing by correspondence. Jack was already twenty-nine, with his thirtieth birthday only a few months away. It was time he had a wife.

The young Daisy, in the full flush of her "wild Irish youth", much preferred riding to Charlie's earnest discussions on the future of Australian education. Charlie Bates was left to sigh over his books while Daisy went exploring the countryside with his brother.

Jack showed her the extent of the Berry estate on which his father had taken a leasehold for the farm. He took her to Terara where he was born. They rode down to the banks of the beautiful Shoalhaven River and hired a boat so that they could drift along its green reaches and admire the fertile country awaiting development. He told her about his struggles to get established; about Tyson the cattle millionaire who had been his first employer; about the men with whom he had gone on droving trips. For Daisy his tales were glimpses into Australia's pioneering past. She saw him as one of its heroes and cherished the romantic illusion that with a woman to believe in him he could achieve great things.

Jack, though not a talkative man, could not resist the flattery of her interest. He boasted a bit as most men do in the presence of an attractive girl, making a lot out of the difficulty of procuring his first job, at the age of seventeen, from the redoubtable Jimmy Tyson.

Tyson was already an Australian legend. He had been one of the first to exploit the land abandoned during the Ballarat goldrush and left his butcher's shop in Campbelltown to buy while it was going cheap. By 1884 it was said of him that he could "travel by horse and buggy from Queensland to Victoria and camp every night on his own land." As this represented a distance of close on a thousand miles it was quite an achievement even in the Australia of the day.

An eccentric and compassionate man, Tyson was a bachelor who affected the ragged clothes and unkempt beard of a swagman. He did not scruple to use this to his advantage and, at one of the many cattle sales at which he was the biggest buyer, he sat on the rails while his competitors brought down the price, looking so convincing as a down-and-out, that he was offered, and what is more accepted, a pound with which to buy his lunch. The discomfiture of the donor can be imagined when Tyson then bought the remaining cattle at the rates lowered by the morning's bargaining. On another occasion his drovers were confronted by a river in flood over which they must take a herd of his cattle. A swagman camping on the banks offered to show them how to do it. When reporting for payment a few days later, the head drover confessed that his losses would have been considerable but for the help of this wayfarer who had borrowed a horse and led the herd through the swirling currents.

Needless to say the swagman had been Tyson.

A generous man, capable of financing a church when asked for a donation, he was renowned amongst his fellow pastoralists for his protective attitude towards his Aboriginal employees. Because of it, Jack Bates lost his first job.

Before this happened his promotion had been spectacular. Tyson was quick to appreciate his abilities as a horseman and sent him to Tinnenburra, one of his Queensland stations, in which brumbies were rounded-up out of the bush and broken for use as cattle ponies. This took courage as well as skill and, young though he was, Jack was promoted to the position of overseer of the station.

Two years later Tyson dismissed him out of hand. He had been accused of ill-treatment of an Aboriginal and Tyson, protector of Aborigines, gave him his pay and told him to go.

In the eyes of his contemporaries, Jack's action was not only excusable but justified. Although shortage of labour compelled the pastoralists to employ the Aborigines, in white terms they were unsatisfactory. The timeless philosophy of the blacks was not merely incomprehensible, it was a positive irritation. Few employers bothered to understand the difference in cultures and so had no patience with what was generally considered the irresponsible laziness of the Aborigines. Money was seldom offered to the Aboriginal, and if it was, he did not know what to do with it. He liked the white man's tucker and 'bacca, but not enough to prevent him from dozing in the midday sun or from going walkabout when he felt like it. The white man would find himself without a stockman for weeks at a time. Since he was very often feeding the stockman's horde of relatives, this was a source of grievance. Those rare white men, like Durack and Tyson, who made the effort to understand the black mentality, found that a working arrangement could be arrived at. They discovered that, treated well, the native Australians were an endearing people, capable of sustained friendship or even devotion to the "white man boss". But to the young and unimaginative Jack Bates the Aborigines working for him seemed little better than animals.

Of such was Combo, come to Tinnenburra with a reputation for killing two whites in the Gulf country farther north and spirited enough to answer back when given an order.

The sun was high and Combo was lethargic. Jack, who was branding cattle, told him to "get a move on."

"Get a move on your plurry self," Combo retorted.

This was to dare the white authority with a vengeance. Jack's iron was sizzling the hide of a calf. He lifted and swung it in one movement and Combo dropped where he stood. He did not recover consciousness until sundown.

Jack had no further trouble with his black employees but his action was reported to Tyson and judged as a betrayal of trust. Tyson's attitude was the exception rather than the rule, and Jack's dismissal enlisted considerable sympathy for him. A few months later he had branched out as an overland drover.

"Overland" in those days meant a journey that might begin at the Gulf in Queensland and end at Wodonga in Victoria. It could take the driver between six months and a year to complete but it was still the most economic way for the cattle barons to sell their beef in Victoria. The gold boom had created a market lucrative enough to pay the expenses of the road and the tax needed to cross the Murray. The drovers could return with an interesting profit to swell the pockets of their employers, always provided that the cattle arrived at their destination in good condition. Everything depended on the men, chosen for their proven skill and endurance.

On these long and tedious journeys the drovers must be tough enough to sustain immense periods in the saddle, broken by a four-hour sleep-shift round the campfire. They must be experts, capable of judging the distance between feed and watering-places, so that the animals be kept at the pace required to maintain condition. They must be able to swim the cattle across rivers and prevent them, when thirsty or frightened, from stampeding. To the pastoralists they were all-important.

Drovers were, in fact, the heroes of their age. To see Jack Bates as Daisy saw him in 1884, we must attach him to the group of men as important to the development of Australia as the astronauts are now to space.

Living close to nature at its most ungenerous, their values, like their philosophy, were based on survival. The drover could be illiterate to the point where he must sign his name with a cross, or he could be an educated man, travelling with a classic in his kit-bag; but above all he must be enduring, for his road, often enough through trackless and sparsely watered country, was long and hard. Theirs was a brotherhood with its own rules and its own etiquette.

To this community of men, Jack Bates had given his allegiance. He courted Daisy O'Dwyer as a seaman courts his girl on shore, with the knowledge of separation yawning ahead. His talk inflamed her imagination. There was the fascination of the exotic in his accounts of cattle bellowing through nightmare passes to the sound of distant native corroborees; of dawn awakenings to the discovery of footmarks beside tell-tale spear trails encircling the camp.

He told her of disasters that could befall a drover on the track. Of a friend who had been speared by the Aborigines in the lonely outback. Of another who had left his herd to go on a drinking bout: he thought he was safe enough, since there were plenty of hands to look after his herd; he warned them of the only possible danger, the proximity of a watering place, forty thousand yards across and already half dried by the sun. But the hands were too inexperienced to judge the distance at which cattle scent water. The herd stampeded and five hundred of them were sucked into the quagmire.

His friends were as exotic as his work. There was Tom Mortimer, the quiet, lean man who had the distinction of having boxed with no less a champion than Ed Sullivan. A drovers' rendezvous was Lambert's hotel in Bathurst. At the bar appeared an Irish wrestler, spoiling for a fight. To throw down a challenge in droving terms was to upend your glass on the hotel bar. The wrestler upended his glass, Tom Mortimer took up the challenge and ended by depositing the wrestler in an empty beer barrel.

Another was the Irish squatter on an outback station who hired a cook by whom he had six children. The years went by and there was no hint of a ceremony to legalize the union, until the visit of an itinerant priest. The cook used the opportunity to confess her sins in the hope that the priest would shame her man into marriage. But she was betrayed by her own children who overheard the confession and reported it to their father. The ceremony was delayed for another twenty years, when thoughts of mortality prompted the squatter to clear his conscience.

Jack's proudest boast was the game he played with the famous Geebung Polo Team. One of his droving trips had taken him to Muswellbrook on the Hunter River and he claimed to be one of the "long and wiry natives" immortalized by "Banjo" Paterson in the match against the "cuff and collar" team from Sydney. It was a match that resulted in such carnage that the poet marked the event with "a row of little gravestones" and warned passers-by that

> . . . *on misty moonlit evenings, while dingoes howl around,*
> *You can see their shadows flitting, down that phantom polo ground.*

Whether or not Jack played polo with the Geebungs, it was apparent that he could ride anything. On horseback Daisy felt the awe of the novice for the master. The world he described promised adventure for the price of endurance. Daisy went towards adventure confident of her capacity to endure.

Jack's was a courtship in movement in which each day offered a fresh novelty. They covered considerable distances in which they came upon the remains of old homesteads, or penetrated undiscovered bushland. There was no time for boredom; no static moments that might have indicated their future incompatibility.

The superstitious, on the other hand, might say that they were warned.

Friends of the family had invited them to their station thirty or so miles from the township of Crookwell. One day when they were out riding there, "a thunderstorm" Daisy wrote, "suddenly broke on the slope before us and the lightning struck a dead tree trunk. The tree trunk seemed to divide in half and there appeared for an instant the upright skeleton of a man with a spear . . . even as we gazed, thunderstruck indeed, the skeleton tumbled into a heap."

Warning or portent? The skeleton was that of an Aboriginal hunter. Eighty years later, carved on a rock face, an Aboriginal drawing was discovered. It was of a white woman, dressed in the clothes of the young Daisy O'Dwyer.

In this moment of their lives, with youth to provide an appetite and adventure as a daily fare, neither Daisy nor Jack was in the mood for caution.

On 17th February 1885 they were married. According to Daisy it was in true Wild West style. Jack suggested a ride in order to inspect the old Anglican church at Nowra. In the meantime he saw the minister and filled out the necessary documents. Arrived at the church they got off their horses and walked down the aisle together in their riding clothes. Confronted with the Reverend Best and his wife, Daisy accepted the challenge and went through with the ceremony.

Whether or not her account was exaggerated, it is probable that their marriage was kept from the family as only Mrs Best and one Frederick Thorpe were witnesses to it.

For this there are two possible explanations. One was that Jack, as a member of a Roman Catholic household, agreed to marry Daisy in the Church of England, a sacrilege for which he would be unlikely to be forgiven. The other was his almost immediate departure on a droving trip that was to take him away for the next six months.

If the more romantic version is the true one, then Jack Bates was gambling on Daisy's impulsiveness. He won the gamble and gained himself a wife.

And Daisy O'Dwyer made what she was to describe as "an error of judgment" that was to throw its shadow very long across the years of her life.

CHAPTER FOUR

We cannot obtain what we think constitutes the most desirable form of life and we are therefore discontented.—Daisy Bates.

It Never Really Worked

It never really worked. There was too much to divide them. Too little reality on which to base the future they were committed to share.

The happiest time was the first six months when Jack was away on what Daisy fondly imagined to be the last of his droving trips. Separated, they could dream: Daisy of "the strong man who only required some desired object of attainment, some stimulus, to become one of life's great successes". Jack's dream was simpler. It was of an Irish colleen waiting to welcome him when he got back. It had been a feather in his cap to secure such a prize. He was the envy of his mates. True, she would take some handling, but Daisy's spirit was part of her attraction.

Daisy, the activist, occupied herself by planning their future. Jack would buy a property with the money she would give him. Together they would work, establish a family, prosper and grow powerful. Theirs would be a name with pride of place on the roll of British pioneers.

It would be pleasant to think that they managed to salvage a month or two of happiness out of the disaster of their marriage. But even this is unlikely. They might have achieved it, if only because of Daisy's ability to shut her eyes to what she did not want to see. But their incompatibility was brought home to them as soon as he returned.

The men she had known and admired, such as her father and Bishop Stanton, had dominated her intellectually even though they indulged her whims. She had rebelled against them but condemned her own "female individuality" as she called it, in the process. The male remained for Daisy the superior species. Her husband was unforgiven, not for his refusal to submit to her will, but for his inability to dominate her.

Daisy was true to the Victorian tradition in more ways than one. With no mother to turn to, separated from her sisters while still a child, her knowledge of the sexual act and of its consequences was of the vaguest. Ignorance had enabled her to incorporate marriage into the fantasy world of her childhood. It would have been difficult for any man to have imposed the physical reality over the romantic dream without disillusion. For Jack Bates, that nervous refugee from an all male world, it may well have been an impossibility. An indication of his failure was Daisy's profound dismay when she was told that she was pregnant.

"But I don't want a baby," she told the surprised and no doubt disapproving doctor.

From one whose love of children was the abiding joy of a lifetime, her reaction spoke for itself. The few months of Jack's return had convinced her that their marriage had been a mistake. A child for Daisy "sanctified the home". Like the birds of Ostend she was in a cage and her code of ethics permitted no escape.

In her own eyes Daisy had done all that she could to make their marriage a success. Disappointed in her husband as a lover, she turned her energies towards the realization of her ambition, making over to him a large sum of money, amounting, according to her own testimony, to several thousand pounds, the major part of her inheritance. With this he was to purchase a property. When she could not be with him she urged him by letter to select a site and finalize the deal.

Somehow it was never concluded. His excuses became weaker with time. At first he reported "bad luck" that lost him the land. Other negotiations had "fallen through".

It became apparent to his impatient young bride that, if he had ever shared her enthusiasm, he did no longer.

She did not give up without a struggle. She tried every tactic in the feminine book: attack, coercion, tears, temper and, finally,

Jack Bates

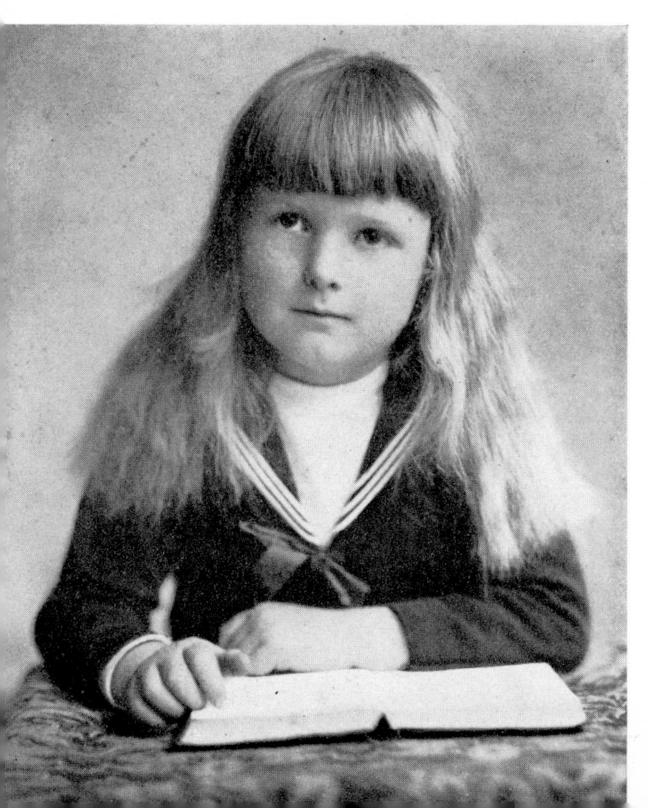

Arnold Bates, 1891

W. T. Stead (*Photo*: *Radio Times* Hulton Picture Library)

Bishop Gibney, a photograph taken by Daisy Bates from the Treasury veranda, Broome, W.A.

departure. Every move on her part was met with resistance, no less effective for being passive.

She had not reckoned on his tenacity. Tested and tried on those long overland trips in which days lengthened into weeks and weeks into months, pitted against the perverse and stubborn will of his herd, obstinacy had hardened into the fibre of his character. Away from his wife the "forceless man", as she came to describe him, rejoined the brotherhood on the wide and dusty plains. The trail led far away from the responsibility of family, from the social life that Daisy enjoyed and in which he had no place. Back with his "cobbers in the outback bars", he could re-establish his self-respect.

At no stage of her marriage was Daisy faced with Jack's problems of adjustment. British immigrants had brought with them the British class structure. Daisy's clothes, her speech, her terms of reference, established kinship with the social élite. Able to hold her own in the bush, she was in her element at Government House. Though headstrong enough to bend the conventions to her will, she was never prepared to disown them. Daisy remained the lady of fashion who became, accidentally, the drover's wife.

This was the core of the differences that arose between them. To her husband she appeared to be able to skip, with chameleon ease, from one to the other of her two selves, but in reality she remained as rooted to her background as Jack was to his. Proof of this was the discipline of dress and behaviour that, even in those days, she maintained against the fiercest opposition from nature because the lack of it was "fatal to self-respect". The indigenous Australian, on the other hand, discarded formality with the city streets. He liked to loosen his tie and relax over a schooner of beer. His grace was revealed in the saddle rather than on a dance floor. His perceptions were attuned to the reins in his hand, to the smell of water on the wind.

To find that his spirited little Celtic bride was a cast-iron Victorian snob must have come as a shock to bushman Jack Bates. His reaction was to retreat back to the environment of which he was master.

At first she went with him. Eager for the adventure promised by his courting, she took her place by his side, a drover's wife, though never admitting to the title.

If the truth had a ring of vulgarity about it, Daisy preferred to refine the sound. Her husband was referred to as a "cattleman" with whom she "travelled extensively in Western Queensland". In evading the issue she did less than justice to her own resourcefulness that enabled her to meet the challenge of this raw existence. Nor did she credit her husband with the help he gave her. Over and over again she was to extol the virtues of the bush, attributing her feeling for it to "the vein of mysticism in the Celtic character [which] attunes it somehow to nature in her loneliest and most solitary moods".

The wall of silence that she erected around her married life prevented her from acknowledging her debt to Jack Bates, that experienced bushman, for teaching her how to become attuned.

What she learnt was important because it became her equipment for the life she was later to choose. Much of it was basic. Since she never shrank from physical work, Jack showed her how to pitch her own tent, to haul logs that would keep the fire alight all night, to manage with a kerosene tin of creek water for her toilet.

He taught her the importance of available water in selecting a site. Fires were easily enough lit with "black-boy" kindlers, but to prevent a scorched nose the billy must be placed so that the flames blew in the right direction.

The kitchen was never her province, but she did learn how to bake damper, made with flour and water like a scone and the staple diet of her desert life. As regards the niceties, Jack spread her tent floor with dried rushes and produced a roll of white paper from which her tablecloth was cut. Above her camp-bed he hung a mosquito-net, an essential for a peaceful night's sleep, warning her that by day she must never be without a face veil to protect her from the flies.

All this was bush lore at kindergarten level. On her first expedition in Queensland's north-west Daisy was no part of Jack's team. She rode at her leisure, inspecting the countryside, collecting wildflowers and noting bird-calls.

If Jack discussed the Aborigines with her, she left no record of it. In her memoirs she went so far as to state that she "did not remember seeing any blackfellows nor thinking there were any in Australia". But by the time she wrote this the selective memory of her old age was at work. According to Jack's nephew Charles Carney, the Aborigines, from the first, were a bone of contention between the drover and his wife.

There were others. For Daisy to think was to act. Jack preferred to take his time to make a decision. The inactivity forced upon her by his protracted negotiations chafed her restless spirit. She left him to go south as guest of Dean and Mrs Marrett in Bathurst. Her pregnancy provided excuse for separation, but it was a temporary respite only. Divorce was now out of the question. The one compromise that offered a solution remained the property they could work together.

Instead, Jack continued on what Daisy now called his "aimless wanderings". As her pregnancy advanced he got her a room at his friend Lambert's hotel in Bathurst. The one as obstinate as the other, their marriage became locked in an embrace of wills that kept it at stalemate. Jack drowned his sorrows on the stock trail. Daisy pursued her independent life in the south, too proud to admit failure even to herself.

Their son, Arnold Hamilton Bates, was born in Bathurst on 26th August 1886.

In fairness it must be said that it is doubtful whether any marriage on which Daisy had embarked at this stage of her life would have succeeded. The urge towards self-realization was strong. She might have escaped from it earlier than she did, but her conflict lay in her traditionalism.

Husband and son belonged to the destiny of women as decreed by society. Daisy approved of the decree even though compelled to seek her own destiny. One thing is on record. After Arnold's birth Jack was refused his conjugal rights.

Daisy did not put it like that. "I had rather a hard time of it with baby," she is reported as saying, "and Jack, the best of men, never came near me after that."

Instead, he installed her in a house in Sydney's North Shore, complete with companion and nurse. This, her one and only attempt at becoming a householder, was not a success, since the companion was not congenial enough to ensure the "perfect equanimity" that Daisy demanded.

"I never have been able to stand a 'hard' atmosphere," she explained. After this, when not staying with friends, she preferred hotels. The atmosphere might be no less hard but at least there was no threat of personal friction. Jack returned to the trail. They met, at intervals, at such towns as Bathurst and Muswellbrook.

"In the meantime," she wrote, "my baby son and I travelled happily through stations, cities and States."

The sentence was left to cover a span of eight years. They were by no means entirely unhappy. She was young, high-spirited and blessed with a cheerful disposition that could banish past disappointments in favour of present pleasures. If she had a headquarters at all it was the Marretts' home in Bathurst. Daisy weeded the Dean's garden and, as soon as she was free to do so, plunged again into the social life that offered her so many "stimulating contacts".

Chief among these was that giant of Australian politics, Sir Henry Parkes. Impressed by his gift for versifying, she found him a "cultured statesman". Since she could afford a nurse for Arnold, she was free to pursue her literary as well as her political interests. She read her papers, Australian and English, chose the *Bulletin* as the outstanding Australian publication, and crossed swords with Archibald on the controversial subject of Australian literature. Archibald was more interested in her views on that still comparatively new writer Charles Dickens. He may well have pointed out to her the inconsistency of her attitude. While railing against the pioneers of socialist reform, she proclaimed her passion for the writer who succeeded above all others in bringing about social reform.

When not thus engaged in literary or more often flirtatious discussion in her friends' drawing-rooms, Daisy visited their country properties.

Like most young girls of the period she kept a diary, but Daisy's was different in that it was an external rather than an internal record. In those fragments that remain to us, dates, places, temperatures, are punctiliously set down. The condition of crops, the quality of soil, even its mineral content, are described. Out of such details emerged her later articles.

From one, written ten years later, comes an account of a visit to Tupurupuru Station on the Lachlan River.

Since rabbits were already the major pest of the Riverina district, she was invited to take part in a rabbit drive scheduled for the rainy month of July 1892.

In the article the conditions of travelling, as well as the plague of rabbits that was the scourge of the pastoralists, are described in vivid and sometimes amusing detail.

The first step of the way was an eighteen-hour train journey from Melbourne to Hay, after which she found herself "on the box seat of one of Cobb & Co's coaches", driving over bush tracks which, because of the rain, were "rivers of mud".

The country was flat, covered by saltbush and rabbits "so perfectly at home that they merely cocked their ears at us as we passed and continued their gambols." Rain forced the passengers to take shelter in one of Cobb & Co's huts and Daisy woke to the welcome sound of the station buggy, come to bring her to the homestead.

The real difficulty lay ahead. To reach the station they had to cross the Lachlan River and several creeks "all of them bankers".

"Our host, like Paddy the Pilot, knew every stick and stone in the creeks," she wrote, "but like that historical personage, he often struck them before he could say 'That's one on 'em!' "

By "hanging on by the eyebrows" they managed to reach the banks of the Lachlan. Here a dinghy was moored ". . . two posts fixed at either side of the river and a wire rope stretched across these. When we got to the bank we descended from the buggy, got into the dinghy and pulled ourselves with the aid of the wire rope to the opposite bank. The harness was carried over piecemeal, and the horses swam across." After that, ropes were fastened to the shafts of the buggy and it was pulled through the water.

To the rabbit hunt itself were bidden squatters within a distance of ninety miles. Since the rabbits were "as thick as autumn leaves in Vallombrosa", the job of the hunters was to frighten them into a fenced-in enclosure. Each rider was provided with a dog and given instructions to "make all the outcry of which his lungs were capable".

"We screeched, we yelled, we laughed, we cackled, we crowed," Daisy wrote.

Four thousand rabbits were enclosed and demolished and first prize awarded to one Dick Forrest "whose expanse of mouth favoured the issue of a volume of sound that left us all far behind in the contest."

A year later came the visit to Tasmania that was to prove to be the turning point of her life. At the end of it she presented Jack with the ultimatum that led to her (temporary) return to England.

Arnold, now a serious little boy of six, went with her to Tasmania. In the photograph taken of him before he left, his hair is fair and worn shoulder-length in the fashion of the day. His expression suggests that he had inherited his mother's ability to dwell within his private world, but the shyness, amounting to timidity, with which he faces the camera, did not come from Daisy.

About her son, Daisy was almost as reticent as she was about her husband. Only when time had sanded over the hurts and the shame, do vignettes appear in letters to her friends that offer glimpses of domesticity. We know, for instance, that at the Manse in Muswellbrook she encouraged a fight between Arnold and his friend Andy Bowman although urged to stop it by the vicar's wife. To stand up to your opponent was part of Daisy's creed and she reported with approval that "the two boys came back with bloody noses and their arms around each other." But aggression was no answer to insecurity. That her son suffered, as she had done, from constant uprootings is apparent from the comment made by his cousin Charles Carney, two years his junior. Arnold remained in his memory as a withdrawn, self-contained boy, lacking the spontaneous warmth that earned for his mother the circle of admiring friends with which she was surrounded.

Had more affection been generated between Daisy and her son, her marriage might have been saved. From the scanty evidence she left us it seems that this need in her nature awakened no answering response from either husband or son.

Tasmania in 1893 was "an island of whites that had been an island of blacks". Since most of Daisy's contacts stemmed from Bishop Stanton, her host was the Bishop of Hobart, a man with a wide circle of friends whose families dated back to the first free settlers who braved the hell of Van Diemen's Land in 1816.

The "witty lady with the vivacious personality and the beautiful Irish eyes" remembered by Constance Vickers, a child of one of these families, was an immediate success. Invitations poured in, amongst them one from the MacKinnons of Dalness, in Evandale. The family consisted of old Mrs MacKinnon, her widower son Donald, and her two grandchildren. Daisy, content to sit at the feet of a pioneer, listened to the "grim histories" of the early days when Dalness was built by convict labour and Jessie MacKinnon furnished it by milking her own cows, churning her own butter and walking the seventeen miles to and from Launceston to sell her dairy produce. When she had wanted a garden she dug it herself, even preferring to cook her own meals rather than to trust the convict labour, filthy with lice and ready to "rob the gibbet of its chains" in order to get money for the rum that was still the currency of the colony.

This was one side of the story. At Dalness was a portrait of Truganini, the last survivor in Tasmania of the first Tasmanians, who died at Hobart in 1876 at the age of seventy-three.

Although, Daisy said, "It was neither tactful nor kindly to ask too many questions", the bishop, a compassionate man with an interest in anthropology, told her the tale of extinction of Truganini and her race: the virtual extermination of this population of some 1,200 Aborigines in "The Black War" which began in 1804 with an unprovoked massacre by the military of a group of men, women and children who were hunting kangaroos. Between 1831 and 1835 some two hundred survivors of the "war" were exiled (for their protection) to Flinders Island in Bass Strait where most of them sank into apathy and soon died. Those who lingered on—forty-four of them by 1847—were taken to Oyster Cove, near Hobart, where the race, except for a colony of hybrids on another island in Bass Strait, died out.

Daisy left Tasmania with the story of two women, one black and the other white, implanted in her memory. Old Jessie MacKinnon was to be "one of the guiding forces" of her future. Truganini was the symbol of doom, representing nature's inexorable law. Regardless of right and wrong, the whites had survived and the blacks succumbed.

In the meantime Daisy was young enough to enjoy the admiration she not only gave but received. That "quiet fine man", Donald MacKinnon, showed his feeling for her by allowing her to ride his dead wife's Arab mare, unmounted since her death. He walked with her through his wooded grasslands while she chanted her version of an old poem:

With stumbling feet did onward press,
To thy lone mountain home, Dalness.

"In your case it should be dancing, not stumbling," he corrected her.

Donald MacKinnon was with her on a trip to Ben Nevis in search of the elusive Tasmanian Devil. Their hosts were the Talbots of Malahide, and to reach Ben Nevis they had to cross the River Esk. Daisy, whose horse "plunged in up to his neck", led the way chanting "The joybells are ringing in gay Malahide" in her "best reckless Irish". The party captured a "Devil" and Daisy an admirer. When she left, Donald gave her his copy of Henry Drummond's *The Greatest Thing in the World.* As they had both agreed that it was "the most beautiful book ever published", he decided upon it as a worthy tribute. From Jessie MacKinnon she received *A Golden Treasury of Verse.* Daisy kept both books with her until the end of her life when she sent the *Golden Treasury*, but not the Drummond, back to the family.

She returned to the mainland to find that her one hope for the future had been shattered. Jack's "irresponsible driftings" had postponed the moment of decision too long. The country's depression had reached culmination point. By 1892 forty-one banks in Melbourne and Sydney alone had closed down. Daisy returned to the news that what remained of her capital had been swallowed up in the eighteen-million-pound liability left by their closing.

There was now no alternative to her future as a drover's wife.

She became ill with anxiety. The doctor diagnosed "nostalgia" and recommended a voyage to England.

Jack offered to supply the passage money but there remained Arnold to be considered. The voyage alone would take the better part of six months. The minimum period she could stay away was a year, and a year was a long time in the life of a seven-year-old boy.

But Daisy's endurance had come to an end. With the precedent of English public schools to fortify her in her decision, she put Arnold into a Catholic boarding-school in Campbelltown. Catherine Bates was near enough to be able to look after him. His holidays could be divided between his father and his grandmother.

To Jack she presented her ultimatum. He would be free to run his life as he wished but she would not come back until he had a home to offer her.

On 18th February 1894, nine years almost to the day after her marriage, Daisy boarded the sailing ship *Macquarie* and left for England.

CHAPTER FIVE

Your true gentlewoman does not sit down and weep and say "I've never done such things"—she simply "does" and no more about it.—Daisy Bates.

London Interlude

If Daisy's action is to be judged, it must be judged in the context of her times. She entered marriage with the Victorian ideal of a future to be realized through her husband. When that future did not materialize, the sheer energy of her personality demanded freedom to create its own outlet.

Hers was not so much a running away as a running towards. She was escaping from domesticity not because she was unable to face its challenge but because it offered no challenge. The resources of her nature, dissipated during the nine years of her marriage, badly needed to be channelled.

No doubt her vitality had proved too much for those closest to her. Scorched by the fire of her mental activity, their personalities lessened by hers, husband and son were most probably united by a mutual feeling of inadequacy. They countered it with apathy, an emotional quicksand that bogged her into a forced inertia and gave her time to contemplate her own unhappiness.

She escaped from it, as always, in flight.

The lack of a sexual bond to unite her with her husband, and a growing separation from her young son had made her conscious of her loneliness before she left for England. That she suffered from Arnold's absence is on record. That the child suffered more, his children bear witness. Those years in Campbelltown gave Arnold a resentment towards both his parents that he was never to lose and for which, in the years of his manhood, he was to seek a subconscious revenge.

In Daisy's defence it must be remembered that her love of children was based more on her feeling of affinity with them than on any maternal protectiveness. She could write and mean that "my deepest and best love goes to children", for the child was the keeper of innocence, responsive to the fantasies that Daisy herself had never quite grown out of. Sadly, her son's unresponsive nature lessened rather than strengthened this affinity.

Even so, she made herself ill with worry about him. But Arnold was the victim of the deadlock between herself and Jack. Her condition of return had been a letter from Jack to tell her that he had a home for her to come to.

In five years that letter never came.

Daisy had, perforce, to learn the discipline of mind that is an essential factor of independence.

"I don't dwell too much on you," she wrote, "as that way of thought does not make for ease of mind or heart."

Instead, she threw herself into the present. Her sigh of relief is almost audible in the gaiety of her account of the voyage. For fifteen weeks she lived in a floating island, separated from all responsibility by the sea she loved so much. To each one of her moods the sea provided its answer. It was "restless and turbulent and stormy, placid and gently rippling, or brilliant like a phosphorescent lane of Aladdin's jewels".

A wool clipper, the *Macquarie* had a capacity for fifty passengers who "lined the Sydney wharf one hot February day to wave goodbye to their friends." They were a varied lot, ranging from "Colonials returning home" to six "prentice middies, one of whom was an Australian, already nicknamed Wallaby". Daisy's chosen companion was a young girl called Vera Lough. Together they divided the congenial from the uncongenial, avoiding in particular a Croatian Count and his pretentious lady friend.

In her determination to forget her private unhappiness Daisy threw herself into the ship's activities. The worst of weather was treated as a joke. She wrote that she and Vera Lough "borrowed trays in order to toboggan down the slippery decks as the ship plunged and reared on the crest of the great mountain waves." When the conditions were too rough for the passengers to go on deck Daisy amused them by bringing out the family portraits.

"The passengers pretended they were notorious convicts and of course I fell in with the joke," she wrote. But "that very night seas broke in and in the morning all my lovely old memories were floating round my cabin utterly ruined."

Sometimes the wind dropped altogether. In the Sargasso Sea, like the Ancient Mariner, they were becalmed and Daisy persuaded Captain Goddard, "a genuine old salt whose penthouse eyebrows formed deep eaves over the grey blue eyes", to allow Vera Lough and herself to be rowed out in a lifeboat in order to appreciate properly "the moonlit picture of a full sailed ship resting on the dark, motionless ocean".

Her zest for experience was finding fresh outlet and her courage rejoiced in the challenge of fog and ice that threatened the worst moments of the voyage. Her goodbye at Tilbury to "the beautiful ship that had carried us so steadily and sturdily through calm and storm" was a sorrowful one.

Her London reception no doubt added to her sorrow. The passengers were met with the news that there was a cab strike. They had to walk to their hotels.

Daisy chose the Arundel, one of the more expensive hotels in the Strand, where her father and grandfather used to stay on their London visits. She arrived with three shillings in her pocket and, as the tariff even in those days was a pound a day, she paid an early visit to the bank.

Here a second and more serious blow awaited her. She had made arrangements before she left for such funds as she still possessed to be available in London on her arrival. Whether Jack had failed to make the necessary arrangements or whether the official explanation she gave was true, that these funds were also swallowed up by the bank crash, the result was the same.

Daisy's embarrassment can be imagined. Fortunately she was still confident that she had only to "demand" for the world to "aid and abet her". Captain Goddard came himself to vouch for her, and Daisy's first London bank account was an overdraft sufficient to take her to her relatives in Ireland.

As the census of 1891 listed eight thousand O'Dwyers in County Tipperary alone, these were not in short supply. She was welcomed back into Dublin's hunting set and then moved on to a cousin's country house. It was one of the remembered ruins, with a façade so unbending that "it seemed to uphold a long line of proud ancestry."

Reality was not yet finished with her. She was greeted with the news of a death in her family. This appears to have been that of her beloved oldest sister Marian, who, as the keeper of her confidence, she had relied upon to come to her assistance. Too proud to allow anyone else to guess at the state of her finances, Daisy remained in the country. In spite of "damp rooms, draughty passages, doors that refused to shut and windows that would not open", she accepted the privilege of being a guest at this historic family manor-house. Although "patched up obtrusively and clumsily and withal so ineffectively as to make it even more ruinous and woebegone than if it had never been repaired", the house was decorated with distinguished cousins from foreign parts. "Relationships," she wrote, "were counted in centuries." It was not unusual to encounter a Spanish admiral, a French colonel or even an Austrian diplomat shivering down the corridors in the cause of family history.

Daisy had become something of a talking point in such circles and found herself arguing, probably to her own surprise, in favour of life in Australia compared with the "circumscribed existence" of Europe. But her penniless state made it impossible to remain for long in Ireland. "In grief and suspense", she boarded the ferry for her journey back to London.

Even to a young woman of Daisy's courage, her situation was daunting. Alone in a vast and ruthless city, she found herself an outcast within the claustrophobic ranks of unyielding Victorian frontages. Though not given to self-analysis, she could not escape their condemnation because it was her own standard of values that she had betrayed. She had abandoned her husband and was now abandoned in her turn. Had she thought of appealing to Jack for help, she could make no contact within four months.

Daisy sold what jewellery she had and added up the days paid for by the proceeds. It was obvious that if she was not to end up in one of Dickens's workhouses she must find a job.

Against the pride that compelled her independence she could set two assets: an optimistic temperament and a niche in the upper stratum of Disraeli's "two Englands".

"Happening by chance" on General Brownrigg, a relative by marriage of her sister Kathleen, Daisy told him of her financial straits. Brownrigg's answer was to take her to see W. T. Stead, editor of the famous weekly *Review of Reviews* and renowned as a champion of women in need.

Daisy, who never despised a cliché if it were apt, must often have reminded herself that "it is always darkest before the dawn." From a state of lonely penury, homeless, husbandless and broke, she found herself living in the genteel haven of the Countess of

Meath's hostel in Cavendish Square working for the man whom she was later to describe as the greatest influence in her life.

Her report of the interview with which she got the job is as follows:

> "Mr Stead, I want work."
> "What kind?"
> "I don't know. I once got ten shillings for one poem and fifteen shillings for another from an editor."
> "We don't accept poems for the *Review*."
> "No, but you have a library and office. I'll dust the one and scrub the other until I can learn enough to fit in somewhere. Try me please."
> "Immediately?"
> "I can pay my way until Thursday. No longer."
> A young man looked in.
> "Go with my son Willie, will you? He will fit you in."

Willie Stead arranged for her to do the library dusting and "sundry other jobs sufficient to feel that £1 a week was earned". He gave her a typewriter to practise on and, with "every other girl and woman on the staff to help and laugh", Daisy started work.

So began what she declared to be the two happiest years of her life.

One of Brownrigg's friends arranged for her accommodation at St Gabriel's, the home reserved for "gentlewomen suddenly thrust into the world of London to earn their living".

Since she could afford no other form of transport, she walked the distance each day between Cavendish Square and Mowbray House. She lived in the same house as twenty-five other women whose ages ranged from twenty to fifty and paid out 7s. 6d. weekly for board and lodging.

Daisy, who was used to being the centre of attention, the favourite guest at a dinner party, the reckless rider at a county hunt, became the "daily" in a newspaper office. And loved it.

Here was the chance to prove her capacity; to take her place as a novitiate at the altar of power. Stead's was intellectual power, used with humility and integrity. But it was power. In 1894 his influence was at its height. World leaders came to his office to seek advice. Daisy, through hard work and natural aptitude, advanced rapidly from office cleaner to office associate.

She was greatly helped, she said, by the "sweetness of congenial companionship" that she found at St Gabriel's. After so many years spent in battling with the difficulties of communication between herself and Jack, she could relax in relieved recognition of "her own kind". Amongst the many contradictions in Daisy's nature was the war between the nomadic instinct and the traditionalism that recognized only one set of values. The women at St Gabriel's, united by their mutual misfortune, products of the same social attitudes, abided by the same code of behaviour.

If a relative should send a hamper, it was the done thing to put the contents on the table for all to enjoy. On Sundays and holidays when the maids were given their days off, it was accepted that each should take her share of the work. If a new member was seen to be unhappy, bunches of flowers or of grapes would be put in her room as an anonymous gesture of comradeship.

It was "not done" to bring one's troubles back from work. The "petty peddlings of the day's struggles", whether they led to "glory or despair", were walked off on the way home.

Daisy settled as comfortably into this world of women at St Gabriel's as she was later to settle into the Aboriginal world, and for much the same reason. The well-bred Englishwoman, like the Australian Aboriginal, was careful not to "trample on the sensibilities of the other".

Her basic social attitudes were not changed as are most people's by misfortune, but her horizons were widened and her character given depth. "Example is worth a ton of precept" was one of her favourite sayings. In London Daisy had before her the example of two men to show her the meaning of compassion and to teach her how to make a virtue out of poverty. The latter was a necessity. Hers was too positive a personality to indulge in self-pity. She needed a concept to which she could attach and so redeem her struggles. It was through James Grun, composer and philosopher, that she discovered Bohemia and the Bohemians.

"Happy is he," she wrote, "who has been born in Bohemia and who has never been able to find his way out of it."

She was careful to define her terms. The true Bohemian might never make money but he belonged in that ". . . enchanted land whose boundaries are aspiration, dreaming, enchantment and pluck. Where the finest poems, pictures, novels are conceived and achieved in the space of a smoke."

"Beware of the false Bohemian," she warned, "who rattles on about this or that impressionist, writer or actor about whom he has probably not the faintest knowledge."

James Grun wrote German operas and lived in one room that was usually occupied by the homeless. He was almost always hungry. When paid for a work, he walked the streets of London distributing his money to the needy. Stead had seen to it that Daisy's office was stocked with such sundries as biscuits and tea. James Grun would wander into Mowbray House at nine o'clock, partake of these with Daisy, who was usually at her typewriter, and walk her home. This occupied his evenings until midnight when he could claim his bed, offered to some unfortunate during the day.

"Gaunt and cadaverous, long and lean-faced, his large blue eyes bright with consumption", he discussed Schopenhauer and took her to hear sermons in Westminster Abbey. Their mutual enthusiasm was Dickens, and James Grun would escort her through ". . . Dickens's London—every street of which he knew as well as Dickens himself."

When they could afford it, they went to concerts and to poetry readings, sometimes with Lottie Royce, future wife of Willie Stead and the third of the "Bohemian trio". With James Grun, Daisy discovered a new kind of relationship. Theirs was neither a flirtation nor a love affair. It was a friendship that neither of them forgot. Years later he sent her a poem "in memory of October 16th 1895". From James Grun Daisy learnt to "love humanity in the rough".

But the "glory" and in the end the "despair" of these two years between 1894 and 1896 she owed to W. T. Stead.

A colossus among journalists, he bestrode the hemispheres, convinced of his mission to regenerate his world.

This "journalistic genius with a multitude of grails", as he was described by a contemporary, was born into the Congregational Manse at Embleton in Northumberland. His career rocketed to the heights in eleven years. At twenty-two he was chief editor of the *Northern Echo*. In 1883 Lord Morley promoted him to the editorship of the *Pall Mall Gazette*. In Stead's opinion, the greatest compliment of his career was Cardinal Manning's comment that when he read the *Gazette*, it seemed to him that Oliver Cromwell had come to life again.

By 1885 he was to shock the entire English speaking world with his "revelations" about the sexual iniquities being practised in London, in particular the slave traffic in young girls.

Gladstone had been on the verge of bringing in a Bill to amend the laws of protection for women when his Government fell. Stead knew full well that the Bill would go the way of the Government and determined to do something about it. In the process, Daisy wrote, he became "the most abused and misunderstood man in England".

First, Stead consulted four dignitaries of the land, all of whom drew back in horror from his plan. He then went, disguised, into the East End and procured a young girl of thirteen for the sum of £5 paid to her mother.

He told the story in a series of articles entitled "The Maiden Tribute of Modern Babylon" and roused a fury of abuse that reverberated in every newspaper in the country. The consensus of Victorian opinion was that the story was not true. If it were, it should not have been written.

A rival paper decided to call his bluff and conducted its own investigations, managing to ferret out the damning fact that Stead has neglected to obtain the written consent of either mother or father. Such was the animosity against him that he was brought to court on a charge of abduction and not even a plea on the part of the Archbishop of Canterbury was enough to save him from a three-month prison sentence.

Stead, while admitting his mistake in neglecting such an important precaution, went to prison rejoicing. He conducted his paper from his prison cell and had the immense satisfaction of seeing his Bill passed under the pressure of public opinion that had condemned him.

This was the most notorious but by no means the most significant of his crusades. He made a stand against conscription and worked to produce a better understanding with Russia. At the salon of his friend Madame Novikoff, Russia's unofficial representative, he talked with General Kireef her brother, and obtained permission to interview both the reigning Czars of the day. He believed that the British navy should be strong in order to keep the peace and edited a weekly called *War against War*, while launching his new venture, *Review of Reviews*, "an attempt to render accessible to all, the best thought to be found in the periodical literature of the world".

His "new journalism" brought a revolution in the newspaper world, the outcome of which was the sensationalism of which it is more than doubtful that he would have approved.

When Daisy joined his staff, Mowbray House was a centre for such men as Carlyle, Rhodes and Gladstone. Stead's imagination knew no limits, and he was fond of quoting a comment of his father's:

"You would do better, William, if you would occasionally leave God to manage the Universe in His own way."

But William had his own ideas about what God wanted. Not content with temporal matters, he turned his attention to the infinite. Believing, with Einstein, that "science without religion is lame and religion without science blind", he decided to apply scientific methods to the study of psychic phenomena, the "borderland" between the finite and the infinite. Encouraged by the discovery that he had the gift of automatic writing, he brought out a new quarterly, based on letters from a dead girl called Julia. He was later to publish his *Letters from Julia* in book form, but they appeared first in the quarterly called *Borderland* and dedicated to Joan of Arc.

In the eyes of his contemporaries *Borderland* proved fatal to Stead's reputation. Certainly the life of the quarterly was short, a fact for which Daisy claimed a degree of credit, since she made no secret of her dislike for it.

But Stead was not a man to worry about his reputation. Sustained by the certainty that "the faith of the materialist is absolutely and demonstrably false", he set out to explore in depth, "the incalculable powers possessed by our subjective selves". The quarterly was prefaced by a quotation from Isaac Newton: "We are but children playing on the seashore while the immense ocean of truth lies unexplored before us."

Borderland invited records of every facet of psychic phenomena, from palmistry to Annie Besant's occult science. The evidence was sifted through a staff headed by Miss Goodrich Frece, a member of the Council of Psychic Research, who wrote under the pseudonym of Miss X.

When the offices of *Borderland* were moved into Mowbray House, Daisy was made "stand in" to Miss X. Willie Stead, as a joke, used to call her the "Sub-editress", chiefly because he knew how heartily she detested the quarterly.

The "practical little Irishwoman without a ha'porth of spiritualism in her make up" received her journalistic training in a cause that she rejected.

Her work on *Borderland* was the beginning of a career that was to support her through life. It was also the issue that was to separate her from her adored "Chief", W. T. Stead.

CHAPTER SIX

In the London Clubs, literary and social, I always held my peace, a difficult task for any woman, but one requiring superhuman effort in an Irishwoman.
—Daisy Bates to the Karrakatta Club, 1900.

The Journalist

For the first six months she was called upon for anything, from delivering messages to filing library books.

"The whole world of my new life was so novel to me that its details stand out," she wrote. "I was the odd man out; the little blue-serged, sailor-hatted maid of all work."

A staunch reactionary in a progressive newspaper office, she "ribbed" the staff for their "advanced views" but "they took my Irish ragging in an Irish way" and sent her to dispense tea in the Chief's sanctum because she was so "mild looking".

Mild she was not. Prejudiced, gallant and gay, her lightness of touch invaded the earnest idealism with which she was surrounded and drew sparks guaranteed to brighten the atmosphere. These first were "days of hard work, jollity and niceness always". Attacking the typewriter with her usual vigour, she practised until her finger-tips were raw, bound them up with rags and practised some more.

Based in the library, she came under the supervision of Willie Stead, oldest of W. T.'s large family. Willie, in Daisy's opinion, was the son who most resembled his father. In her memory he remained as "a male Joan of Arc" because his idealism found its apotheosis in the future saint.

Always decided in her reactions, Daisy's prejudices, like her enthusiasms, could be more feminine than logical. To Cecil Rhodes, for instance, she took an instant dislike because "there is something so juggernauty about a man with a heavy jowl." As a public figure she admired him, paying him the compliment of a comparison with Stead, both being "Manse bred boys, with that quaint Puritan training that led to hardihood, self-reliance and clarity of vision, united by their sensitive love of England and of poetry."

About Bernard Shaw she made no such concessions.

Her position as tea-maker enabled her to be present at the early meetings of two of Stead's "grails". One was the Anglo-American Arbitration Society, destined to become the English Speaking Union, the other "a society that calls itself Fabian". The latter, in Daisy's opinion, was "the genesis of all the rebellious gatherings that have taken place in England since then." Fabian ideals were expressed "with Irish eloquence and jerky vitality" by the "rough unwashed looking, sandy haired Irishman", Bernard Shaw.

Daisy refused to be impressed. She compared Shaw's speech with a current *Punch* cartoon lampooning Redmond. The politician was depicted as pleading to an Irish ancient for "freedom from the Sassenach yoke".

To the cautious question, "and what'll we do for our pinsions then?" came the answer, "Oh shure, we'll go on takin' their dirty ould money."

As a political traditionalist, Daisy might be expected to have disapproved of the young Shaw. Rhodes was another matter. His contribution to the Empire should have earned him her support. In 1895, on his first trip to England after the Jameson raid, he was the man of the moment. When Daisy met him he was barricaded behind the closed doors of his suite at the Burlington Hotel, with reporters waiting in hordes in the lobby below.

Stead had not allowed his personal friendship to influence him and had already condemned "the inexplicable desire of Mr Rhodes to attain Bechuanaland as a jumping off place". Even so, Stead was the only editor in England to whom Rhodes would answer. Daisy was sent to the Burlington Hotel with a list of questions and instructions to wait for the answers. She reported that she "marched confidently" through the crowd of newsmen, as unsuspecting as they were of the responsibility entrusted to her.

According to Daisy, Stead was "as great an Imperialist as Rhodes". Certainly Rhodes was the first to acknowledge Stead's influence. They were introduced in Madame Novikoff's salon when Stead was editing the *Pall Mall Gazette*. After a few minutes of conversation, Stead exclaimed that he had "never met a man, who, on broad Imperial lines, was so entirely of my own way of thinking."

"That is not surprising," Rhodes replied, "since it was the *Gazette* that influenced me."

It was on this visit in 1895 that Rhodes announced his decision to found educational fellowships only. Stead, as executor of his will, approved the change, but pressed for them to be made available for women as well as men. This Rhodes refused, and in the end removed Stead's name from his list of executors.

It might well have been to exemplify his attitude to women that Stead chose Daisy to be his messenger on so important an occasion. That he encouraged her to express her point of view is obvious from Daisy's account of Jameson's visit to Mowbray House.

Since Stead considered that Jameson's act of aggression was indefensible, his greeting was stern. His tea-maker, on the other hand, dared to register approval.

"All power to your elbow Dr Jim," Daisy said. She reported that Stead "threw a book at her" but that her impertinence relaxed the atmosphere between the two men.

According to her own account, Daisy was the only member of the staff who dared to "fight the Chief over an article".

This could well be true. As confident as she was courageous, Daisy was, by the time she arrived on his staff, an independent personality, ready to defend her point of view against all comers. To the man who was congratulating women because they had at last discovered that they had souls, this would have been a cause for admiration rather than annoyance.

Her prejudices he would have recognized for what they were, a product of an upper-class education, as identifiable as her manner of speech. To challenge them, he drew her into his campaign of encouragement to women writers. *Review of Reviews* had already declared its support of the new novels written "by women about women from the standpoint of women".

Daisy was sent off, as staff representative, to attend their meetings.

In an address she gave to the Karrakatta Club on her return to Perth five years later, she confessed that, although ready to be impressed, she had found women writers a disappointment.

"Because of the great awe and respect I entertained for authors generally," she told her audience, "coupled with a desire not to miss one word of the sparkling dialogues I was quite confident they indulged in, I hung about Mrs Humphry Ward, my mind full of *Marcella* and *Robert Elsmere*, Sarah Grand, remembering *The Heavenly Twins*, Mary Cholmondeley, author of *Diana Tempest* . . . but to no purpose. I could not remember one of them uttering anything that reminded me of their books and came to the conclusion that they had left their respective muses at home!"

Olive Schreiner was "carping and envious", Marie Corelli, "with her tricky little vanities, her pale gold hair and ordinary little face", was positively disliked. Filled with a conviction of her own importance Marie dared to be contemptuous of *Review of Reviews*. She sent a message to say that if Stead wanted to review her latest book, *The Sorrows of Satan*, he must buy it.

This was heresy of the first order. None the less Marie Corelli must have won the day, since Daisy was given the job of "scissoring" Stead's review. "Which was all I remember of Satan and his sorrows," she wrote. "I tried to make a bet with the Chief that her next book would invade heaven . . . *God's Good Man* followed in due course."

The 1890s marked the birthpangs of women's emancipation. Her time in Mowbray House forced Daisy to acknowledge the fact but never to accept it. Women writers were a disappointment, but the New Women were an object of ridicule. Although she liked Stead's secretary, Nellie Grace Bacon, she strongly disapproved of her advanced views. Prior to Daisy's arrival on the staff, Miss Bacon had just completed the first bicycle tour of the British Isles to be made by a woman wearing the knickerbockers of the New Women.

W. T. devoted an article to his secretary congratulating her on an achievement of which, he wrote, he was justifiably proud. The newest member of his staff, on the other hand, dared publish her disapproval. In one of her early contributions to *Borderland* Daisy went so far as to describe the New Women as "public nuisances". History does not relate whether or not she was reprimanded for her disloyalty to office policy, but it provides abundant proof of her tenacity in clinging to her concept of womanhood. For the rest of her long life she resisted the changes demanded by fashion in women's clothing. Ironically enough, her accusation that these pioneers of modern dress were exhibitionists who "for the sake of notoriety donned a garb that . . . caused them to be the laughing-stock of every man in the street" was later to be repeated, almost word for word, against her.

It seemed Daisy's destiny to live in two worlds. Away from work she retired to the country houses of family friends, managing to "look rich" and to make a good story out of her vicissitudes. Her admiration for Stead did not succeed in superimposing his values over theirs; but that she was capable of opinions contrary to those popular in social circles she proved by her loyalty to Madame Novikoff.

In the eyes of the Victorian upper classes, Madame Novikoff was no more nor less than a "Russian spy". She was a revolutionary, a nihilist. It was even whispered that she was Gladstone's mistress.

Daisy denied the charge. Madame Novikoff was "fascinating", a "charming but unaffected hostess" with the good manners and the graceful movements of the Russian aristocracy; but, she wrote, "one could no more associate sexuality with her than one could with Florence Nightingale."

Gladstone, she maintained, was too "wife tended" to indulge in affairs. On official functions held on rainy days, Mrs Gladstone would produce a pair of socks out of her capacious bag and insist the great man put them on before mounting the platform.

As an example of Madame Novikoff's tact as a hostess, Daisy described an occasion at which the Bohemian trio, Lottie Royce, James Grun, and herself, were bidden to the famous salon in Symonds Street. Grun's wardrobe was limited to one disreputable suit, as befitted a philosopher. Daisy bought him a new shirt and enlisted Lottie's help in turning up the ragged ends of his trousers. The result was disastrous. The improvements only emphasized the tatters. Madame Novikoff took one look and led him straight to the piano. Her guests, bemedalled and bejewelled, forgot his appearance in admiration of his music.

With no money sense to help her, Daisy did not find it easy to manage on her £1 a week. It was not long before Willie Stead took control, reserving the amount needed for board and necessities and handing the rest to Daisy.

By her own description she was a "horrible and incurable giver" who admitted that "it has always been a weakness of mine to do some little thing for the underdogs of the world." A stew kitchen in Fleet Street called by the tantalizing name of "Peace and Plenty" cooked its "atrocities" in the window—"the smell going up to high Heaven as well as into the nostrils of God's failures". Daisy, hurrying by with her "handkerchief to mouth and nose", would very often see a starving wayfarer whose "poor face was all one wateringness with desire".

According to Willie Stead, who watched the proceeding with interest, Daisy would stop short in her tracks. "You're hungry," she would say, "come and have a meal with me."

The stew cost only fourpence a plate but the fourpences mounted up. It was not long before she was taking on extra typing to pay for them and also for her protégé, a girl she wrote about simply as "Lady Mary".

Lady Mary was Daisy's "staff". Stead's latest lame duck, she was a refugee from a rich and dominating mother and she too was given employment in the library.

The story of Daisy's attachment to this girl, young enough and pleasing enough to act as a substitute for the child she left in Australia, is worth relating if only because of the version she wrote, years later, for the *Western Mail.* The truth was unhappy and ended in failure. Daisy's fiction radiated content and ended "happily ever after".

Her sympathies were roused by Lady Mary's admission of a romantic attachment to a young peer. The peer had not proposed marriage. Daisy, scenting danger, paid him a visit and the young man left obediently for Egypt. She then went to persuade Lady Mary's mother to grant the girl financial independence. This time she was not successful; in fact, Daisy wrote, "She came close to slapping my face, so hard did I plead with her."

Lady Mary was even less able than Daisy to manage on her salary. In spite of the warning jaunts that Daisy organized into prostitute land, she became what was technically known in Victorian parlance as a "bad girl". Daisy maintained her faith in her innocence long after her office colleagues had whispered their suspicions. Not until the Vigilance Society had presented her with a hotel registration in which Lady Mary had given a married name was Daisy forced to admit defeat. Her disappointment was keen. Some time later Lady Mary wrote asking for a renewal of friendship. Daisy refused it. The girl had deceived her on the altar of Victorian respectability. This was unforgivable.

But her defeat rankled and found an outlet, eventually, in fantasy. "Lady Mary's Camp Cure", written more than a decade later, was the happy ending that Daisy grafted onto the story.

Her patronage had proved expensive, a fact that her colleagues registered with sympathy. For Christmas of 1895 Stead sent her a guinea "instead of a Christmas Goose".

In 1896 she was given a rise in salary and promoted to assist Miss Goodrich Frece, editress of *Borderland.*

CHAPTER SEVEN

If life is manifested independently of the body, it cannot be supposed to terminate merely because the organs of sense are no longer in use.—W. T. Stead.

The Spirits of *Borderland*

Borderland was a product not only of Stead's inquiry into spiritualism but of the intellectual climate of his day.

To the privileged Englishman, the Victorian epoch offered a security firmly based on the social and philosophic order of his universe, not yet untidied by self-doubt. His community was boned by an accepted morality, his Empire, a hierarchy with a temporal and spiritual head. Within such a framework all things were possible.

The white-anters were there. Shaw, T. H. Huxley and Bertrand Russell had already begun asking their very awkward questions, but the First World War was still a long way off. Incredulity was not yet demanded as a component of intelligence. The English ego, fed with constant demonstrations of earthly power, looked to the power of the unknown. The more conservative members of society were content with a weekly demonstration of faith. Braver spirits, like Stead, hoped to establish closer contact.

Daisy, for one, was contemptuous of their efforts.

"The educated of those days," she wrote, "liked to dabble in the glorified magic called spiritualism."

She recognized Stead's scientific interest in the subject and removed him firmly out of the ranks of the "dabblers".

"He was no more of a spiritualist than I am," she stated—to the annoyance of his daughter Estelle, who had reason to doubt her.

By her own definition, Daisy was right. Their approach to *Borderland* was based on the same foundation of faith, though from opposite poles. Stead regarded all manifestations of supernatural power as innocent until proved guilty. Daisy regarded them as guilty until proved innocent. To Stead, doubt was an intellectual presumption. Spiritual phenomena existed and so needed investigation.

For Daisy the issue was simpler. Spiritual phenomena were the territory of the Almighty. When genuine they should be left alone; when not genuine they were the final blasphemy.

From the moment that she moved into the office of Miss X, Daisy's ambition was to "squash the spooky little quarterly". She maintained that her attitude was shared by Stead's wife and son Willie, who gave her the courage she needed to resist—for his own good—her adored Chief. Whether or not she needed their support is another matter. She had already given proof of her ability to defend her point of view. A more probable incentive was her dislike of Miss Goodrich Frece herself. In her capacity as Miss X, the editress held seances with Isabel Burton after the death of Sir Richard. According to Daisy's account of them, these were too well rewarded to be genuine. Certainly the report of Miss X herself, written for *Borderland*, contains a strange contradiction.

In one of the seances held in the mausoleum in which Lady Burton spent so much of her widowhood, Miss X admits that she was the medium when messages came from Sir Richard, one predicting his wife's death. Yet, for reasons unexplained, she ended her immensely long and detailed article with the statement that in her opinion it was not Sir Richard who had directed her hand, nor had she been "in telepathic communication with him".

In view of what had gone before, this suggests that Daisy's suspicions were not without justification. Such a disclaimer indicates that Miss X, though prepared to take part in them, was not anxious to be held responsible for the goings-on at the musoleum.

Daisy learnt the craft of journalism with the determination to spike the guns of Miss Goodrich Frece and her like. In the article she was later to write for the *Australasian*, the contributors of *Borderland* were lumped together as fakes, bent on exploiting the gullibility of that Don Quixote of the spiritual world, W. T. Stead.

Part of her job was to attend the meetings of the many little cults that attached themselves like barnacles to *Borderland*'s scientific prow. Each one equipped with its own priestess and its own form of worship, their seances provided Daisy with her ammunition, as well as material "heaven sent" with which to brighten the dinner-tables of her friends.

Principal targets for attack were the mediums, very often illiterate women.

"Who in their saner moments," she exclaimed, "would believe that the spirit of a dearly loved wife, husband or child, would come from the other world, enter the body of a frowsy medium . . . and only talk to them through the medium's cockney or provincial dialect!"

Heaven, she inferred, would have a greater respect for the Victorian class structure.

Not for one moment was she prepared to suspend her disbelief. It was a custom at these seances for the hands of the devotees to be placed on the table in contact with each other. According to Daisy, in the fraction of time after the lights were turned out, mechanical hands replaced the medium's.

In the "reverential silence" that followed, "the spirits moved noisily round to the sound of music and to the rattle of chains." If the medium had the additional gift of double-jointed toes, the spirit rappings were impressive. For those who remained unconvinced there was the gentle caress of the spirit-veiling against the cheek.

"Sometimes," she wrote, "spirits of friends and relatives who were then alive and hearty had apparently stepped over to borderland in order to talk to me . . . of their blessed state."

Her scepticism found triumphant vindication in the exposure, in 1896, of the famous Italian medium, Eusapia Palladino.

Palladino had been declared genuine by no less an authority than Sir Oliver Lodge and the newspapers made the most of the "fraudulent practices", which included the manufacture of false manifestations of sound and movement, discovered during a house-party at Cambridge. But seances were by no means Daisy's only avenue of investigation. She visited palmists who, she wrote, "prophesied marriage with a fair man and a resultant offspring of seven." Planchette boards spelled out "fairy tales of wealth and happiness". Maskelyne and Cook demonstrated their miracles to their awestruck audiences.

Spirit photography was in its heyday and photographs were sent in to Daisy for publication in *Borderland*. In each one "spirit forms" were visible behind the sitter. To these Stead gave careful consideration and, in fact, published some, until confronted by proof positive of dark-room deception.

A clergyman wrote asking for investigation of the "nebulous spirit forms" seen floating around his church. An amateur and a professional photographer were pressed into service. In due course the professional, a "spirit photographer" well known to *Borderland*, came up with plates on which the nebulous forms were clearly visible. The amateur, on the other hand, could produce nothing but the interior of the church. The professional then gave the show away by hinting to the amateur that he might make better use of ammonia in the developing process. After this no more "spirit photographs" appeared in *Borderland*.

Another fraud that Daisy claimed to have helped expose was the "spirit double"—another version, she said, of "the old Irish fetch". In this case the deceived person was Stead himself.

He wrote his own account of the incidents. On two occasions he saw what he thought were women of his acquaintance and found out later on that neither had been present in the flesh at the time. Since the likeness was unmistakable, and since he refused to doubt their word, he assumed that he had seen a spirit double.

Stead's faith in womankind was by no means shared by Daisy. In the first instance the woman in question had appeared at Stead's church on the Sunday morning. When he went up to speak to her she had vanished. He called round to see her and she declared that she had not been out all day, a statement verified by her servants. That same afternoon Daisy and James Grun had visited Westminster Abbey. Both saw the woman riding by in her cab. "At the sight of us," Daisy wrote, "she drew back guiltily and covered her face."

She deplored Stead's readiness to believe, which, she maintained, could lead to unpleasant consequences, especially in his investigation of "satanic obsessions".

Epilepsy came under this general heading and the visit of a genuine sufferer to Mowbray House was both unsuccessful and disturbing. In due course, she said, a fake was presented who foamed soapily at the mouth while the evil daemon answered Stead's questions. Since by this time she was contributing regularly to *Borderland*, Daisy seized the opportunity to insert a warning about "that most dangerous of all obsessing ideas, the idea of self", and suggested that the victim of a satanic obsession might try mowing the lawn, taking a good walk, or even studying the cookery book as a cure.

Although her articles were unsigned, her brisk, often dismissive, always witty style is unmistakable, blowing like a fresh breeze through the 1896 editions of the quarterly.

Her first contribution was to a series entitled "Haunted Houses Up to Date" in which she related an Irish ghost story told by Allie about Leap Castle in King's County.

The tale lost nothing in the telling but if asked to give her opinion, Daisy decided firmly in favour of natural rather than psychic causes for phenomena.

In one case where there was doubt as to whether a disturbance had been caused by poltergeists or teenage girls, Daisy wrote that the phenomena were silly and degrading, but "As I know nothing to the discredit of spirits and a good deal to the discredit of girls, especially at the hobbledehoy pig tail age, I feel an *a priori* inclination to believe it to be girls."

Making a valiant attempt to laugh *Borderland* out of circulation she kept handy a pamphlet entitled *Sources of Subliminal Consciousness*. A glimpse into its pages, she said, never failed to result in "clean healthy laughter". With its help she "sheered off a Judge, a General and shoals of women ennuiantes, idle and occupationless", searching the deep waters of spiritualism for an outlet for their neuroses.

Some of these women were genuine sufferers. One, an Australian widow, came to her office after having lost her money to an unscrupulous medium in the hope of communicating with her dead husband. Her return to Melbourne was financed by that Galahad of womankind, W. T. Stead.

Many were "exaltées" who had resorted to alcohol or drugs to induce the desired state of "ecstatic receptivity". One of these, a "brandy smelling little podge", clasped Daisy to her bosom and hiccoughed a breathless promise that she would precipitate letters to her from the ceiling; her dawn awakenings would be edified by the sight of them floating down to her.

Daisy never missed an opportunity to inform the Chief of these fakes, but to no avail. Confronted by the most absurd of frauds Stead would shake his head and comment gravely that "it was the wrong spirit accompanying the inquiring mind."

She came to the regretful conclusion that the one omission in his make-up was a sense of humour.

It is possible that Daisy was right and that *Borderland* did more harm than good in the short three years of its life. But there is much in its issues to make fascinating and instructive reading.

It is said of Freud that he "expressed in scientific terms many phenomena which before him few had dared to consider and none had been able to explain." Stead was one who had "dared to consider". In an early article on Stevenson he cited *Jekyll and Hyde* as a "foreshadowing of the most startling scientific discovery to be established in the twentieth century, that the disintegration of personality is not merely possible but of regular occurrence". His articles on the therapeutic use of music, and of hypnosis, are well in line with the modern school of thought. One issue contained the startling report that "Mrs Besant and her Theosophical friends, the Occultists of London Lodge, have divided the indivisible and analysed the atom."

Daisy saw the "noble souled Stead" as the "patient editor hoping that some convincing experiences would come out of the ruck of falsehoods". He showed her that it was possible to exploit his material without losing his integrity. Years later, when her journalism alone provided sustenance for herself and for her Aboriginal protégés, Daisy attempted to do the same.

She continued to wage unremitting war against *Borderland* and all it stood for. In spite of Stead's manifesto that the quarterly sought "the verification of that life and immortality that were brought to light nineteen hundred years ago", she came to regard it as anti-Christian. The obstinacy of her conviction and her resultant lack of tact in dealing with her contributors brought things to a head between Miss Goodrich Frece and herself.

Daisy resigned her job. Since she did not know what it was to compromise, her answer was to withdraw. Her library experience had fitted her for a similar position. She went north to take up the post of librarian with Jarrolds of Norwich.

She had the satisfaction of witnessing the demise of *Borderland*, the last issue of which was published in October 1897, but she never revisited Mowbray House. Stead remained her Chief who had rescued her in "stressful times" and taught her a craft with which to maintain her independence. He had earned her lifelong gratitude but from now on it was at one remove.

The reason she gave for the change was ill-health brought on by worry about Arnold. This was true enough. The years in London, though enriching her life, had proved to be indigestible fare. Jack's silence added greatly to the strain. Norwich offered a retreat that enabled her to recover an equilibrium of mind.

Daisy joined Norfolk's hunting set, relaxed in the soothing circles of her own kind, and met Carrick O'Bryen Hoare.

After two years of freedom she was ready to fall in love. Having had a chance at last to establish her own identity, she knew by now what she wanted.

Besides, time was running out. These were the crucial years that bridged youth and middle age. At the end of them she would be faced with the ranks of unpartnered women for whom no place had been allowed in the hierarchy. Her pride rebelled against the prospect.

The barrier of husband and son remained. Jack's silence may well have tempted her into an engagement. It was not enough to justify a second marriage. Nor would divorce obliterate the existence of her son.

An affair, on the other hand, was out of the question. The young woman who had refused to forgive "Lady Mary" for her promiscuity would hardly have contemplated it on her own behalf. Carrick Hoare remained a chosen companion and "dear friend".

Charming, intelligent and, that essential, a first-class horseman, he offered the security of a similar background—rather lessened, it must be admitted, by the insecurity of an all too similar bank balance. But this was the last factor to influence Daisy. She agreed to an engagement but it was never publicly acknowledged. Any hope of happiness with him was a dream of the future that dissolved before the reality of the wedding ring she already wore.

There seemed no way out of frustration. She could neither go forward nor back, since she could not afford the return fare to Australia. Worry about Arnold increased. She wrote that she was "haunted by fears that assumed dreadful shape", in which her son was alienated from her "and growing up with a character aimless and lax as that of his father".

Her remedy, as always, was to plunge herself into activity.

Being, in Victorian parlance, well connected, she had been accepted into the closed circles of that most exclusive of caste systems, the English County. It was regarded as unfortunate of course that such an entertaining little creature had to earn her own living. There were rumours of a husband somewhere in the background; dead, no doubt.

Good manners prevented the question direct. It was presumed that she was a widow and Daisy did nothing to discourage the fiction. The life offered her was the life she wanted to lead. Her conflict lay in the fact that it could not be sustained without a breach of the ethics by which she abided.

If she regretted her departure from journalism she did not admit to it. From this, the Indian summer of her youth, she was determined to extract the last ounce of enjoyment. Nor was Carrick Hoare the first man to offer remarriage. Before him she had refused Richard Attwater, owner of Ratfin Hall.

She had met Attwater at Avon Castle, home of one of her innumerable cousins, John Turner Turner. The pursuit of pleasure at weekend house-parties normally consisted of hunting and fishing during the day and dancing at night. Avon Castle offered a trout stream, a stable and ballroom. It also offered hard work.

Turner had established a precedent that was to become all too familiar among the English country houses. Faced with a reversal of fortune, he had converted Avon Castle into a hotel. Daisy, who enjoyed the challenge of manual labour, weeded the landscaped terraces as she had weeded the dean's garden in Bathurst. At night she acted as a hostess to the guests, mostly weekenders from the Hurlingham Club. Among them was Richard Attwater, and for a short time after their meeting, Daisy's country house alternated between Avon Castle and Ratfin Hall.

She admitted gaily that "if I had not been married I would certainly have married Dick Attwater for Ratfin", giving as her reason the delight of "climbing up two steps into a bed and immediately becoming lost in a feathery drift". But feathered luxury offered no serious temptation. Ratfin Hall remained in her memory as a symbol of the world she had chosen to leave. Years later, depressed by the scorched brown monotony of the Nullarbor Plain, she jotted down a nostalgic description of this house that might have been hers. Green and rainwashed lawns framed cloisters dignified by history. The interior was a museum in which cabinets were filled with curios, shelves lined with Wedgwood. Everywhere were servants, hovering like guardian angels, available, unobtrusive. Like Ashberry House, Ratfin Hall was woven into the fantasy world that was her link with the past.

Carrick O'Bryen Hoare was, on the other hand, a very present reality. A connection through the O'Bryen side of both families, he was as impulsive as she was. Together they were approaching a decision that became more painful to contemplate as time went on.

In the end it was forced upon her. The National Bank of Australasia offered to refund her deposits to the extent of a shilling in the pound. Pitiful recompense though it was, it was enough to pay for her fare back to Australia. While she hesitated, a letter arrived from Jack to say that he was in West Australia with Arnold, prepared to look for a property in the developing North-west.

Daisy was faced with a choice between her lover and her child. She chose her child.

In August of the year 1899 she booked her passage on the *Stuttgart* for Perth. Proof of the cost of her decision was the name she gave her property, bought two years later. It was the realization of a long cherished dream. She called it Glen Carrick.

Daisy Bates in the evening dress in which she was presented to the Duke and Duchess of York in Perth, 1901 (*Photo*: West Australian Newspapers Ltd)

Peak Hill, W.A., 1908. A caption in Daisy Bates's handwriting says, "Every one of these women killed and ate her new-born baby, sharing it with every other woman in her group."

The camp at Eucla, W.A., 1912

CHAPTER EIGHT

The people of the dream watched the people of the clock come out of the sea and strike their flagstaff firmly into the sand . . . the clock was not a toy but a way of life as the dreaming was a way of life.— Mary Durack: *The Rock and the Sand.*

Discovering the Aborigines

In the difficult weeks before departure, Daisy cast about for an interest to help her face the future. She found it in the drawing-rooms of Bournemouth.

She had gone to the resort to stay with yet another cousin and was introduced to those residents with connexions in West Australia. Of such there was a surprising number, and Daisy found that the conversation tended to drift towards pioneer relatives and their problems of behaviour in relation to the Aborigines. The accusation of exploitation, levelled against the white settlers of the North-west in 1892, had never been forgotten. The press kept it alive, publishing fresh scandals that appeared at intermittent intervals, usually in the form of letters from correspondents abroad.

Daisy, whose pioneering ambitions had been in no way affected by her sojourn in London, took up the cudgels in favour of the settlers. According to her own account she called on *The Times* and offered to investigate the situation. Since there is no correspondence to mark the occasion and as nothing under her name appeared until her long letter written in 1904, it is unlikely that, as is so often stated, she was an accredited correspondent of *The Times*. But her experience with Stead and the topicality of the subject would almost certainly have ensured interest.

Her cousin decided that she should consult an expert and took her to meet the eccentric and famous Dr Cunningham Geike, scientist and author of such erudite articles as "The Evolution of Climate" in which he revealed much learning about West Australia.

The meeting was of significance, not because of the doctor's statement, repeated so often by Daisy as a conversational shock tactic, that "all embryo babies have tails", but as a preparation for her future.

She wrote her own account of it. The doctor, she said, greeted her as "gracious lady" and led the way through an intricate maze of books into his smoky little den. Clad in a fez and a long coat "half cassock, half dressing gown", clutching a hot water bottle to his stomach, he discoursed to the accompaniment of singing birds.

The issue, he told her, was not and could not be limited to the question of exploitation. Discovering that she was to sail on the *Stuttgart* he referred her to a fellow passenger, Dean Martelli, an elderly Catholic priest who had worked alongside Matthew Gibney, Bishop of Perth, in his lifelong campaign for the Aboriginal cause. The voyage would give her ample opportunity to find out what she wanted to know. He would arrange an introduction.

On the *Stuttgart* Daisy acquired the foundation on which her life work was based. The voyage was shorter but the days were emptier than they had been on the *Macquarie*. Daisy, older now and fighting the pain of parting from England and her English friends, was only too glad to listen to the dean on the subject of the West Australian Aborigines. A cultured man with terms of reference incorporating civilizations past and present, he was able to give her the facts and yet maintain the perspective of the historian. From Martelli, she learned the history of the white invasion, dating from the military occupation (to circumvent the French) of King George Sound in 1826 and, more importantly from Daisy's point of view, the arrival of Captain James Stirling and his band of British immigrants in 1829.

Settlement had begun well. The white immigrants were only too anxious to live in peace with their Bibbulmun hosts. Nor was there any show of spears when the detachment of soldiers pitched camp amidst the tangle of trees, scrub and swamp that was Perth in 1829.

Ngal'goong'a, leader of the tribe, as Daisy was afterwards to write in "Oldest Perth", an article published in the *Western Mail* in 1909, "stood up in his native dignity to receive the white invaders, bid them welcome and quietly removed himself and his belongings to another camp."

Ngal'goong'a believed, as many others of his race had believed, that the white-skinned strangers were the spirits of his ancestors. It was part of legend that when he had crossed the seas to Konnarup, his heaven, the black man would wake to find himself white. Ngal'goong'a's action was motivated by fear of the *jangg'a*, or ghosts, returned from the island of the dead.

He could afford to be generous. The word Bibbulmun is said to have meant "many breasts". His land was rich in woods and water and provided much game. The Swan River groups, numbering at this time about 1,500, were well fed on roots and fruit, kangaroos and emus. When these were in short supply they fell back on the *wai'en*, or crane, who came to fish on one leg in the estuary. They wandered from spring to spring in splendid nakedness, the men equipped with their spears and boomerangs, the women following meekly behind, carrying household goods and the babies that swung in their *gootas* (kangaroo-skin bags).

Captain Stirling returned the courtesy of the natives' greeting by incorporating them into the family of the British Empire. This was not merely a gesture of conquest. It was an honour bestowed by a people convinced of the superiority of their culture.

These early West Australians had braved unknown seas and were building their homes in unknown territory because of their belief in themselves and the way of life they brought with them. The inferiority of the "naked savages" was proved to them beyond doubt by their stone-age implements, their lack of clothing, the absence of technology, even to so simple a form as the wheel. Some of the whites reacted with revulsion; only the exceptional settler appreciated the peace and simplicity of the way of living of this ancient people whose lives were ordered from within and without, who were bound by laws of consanguinity, their roots in the earth, their spiritual life knowing no boundaries, before or after.

Trouble began as it had in other parts of Australia wherever the two cultures met. A white man was murdered by the natives, another severely wounded. In 1834 a third man, young Hugh Nesbit of the Royal Scots Fusiliers, was attacked and killed about fifty miles south of Perth. Sir James Stirling, as he was then, led a punitive expedition which clashed with a band of some eighty natives in what came to be known as "The Battle of Pinjarra", and some twenty of these were killed.

So began the warfare which was to continue sporadically for many years and, in sad counterpoint, the history of disease and despair which afflicted the Aborigines when they came into contact with the whites.

From the beginning attempts were made to counteract it. But Francis Fraser Armstrong's attempt to fuse the two cultures, though it met with response from both black and white, failed as the Protestant and Catholic missions of George King and Bishop Salvado were to fail for the same reason.

Enclosed, even in huts, the "naked savage" drooped and died.

They complained that, "The smell of the white man is killing us." It was as though the weight of civilization was pressing them out of existence. Salvado called it a "sickness of the soul" that was a form of nostalgia.

Children entered the mission schools and died from such ailments as measles. Adults developed bronchitis, pneumonia or tuberculosis, diseases that killed them even more effectively than the syphilis they contracted from their white conquerors.

What was also serious, the white man's cures were very often as fatal as his diseases. Doctors began to warn the colonists that the Aboriginal could not stand up to their remedies.

"With grief I admit," John Forrest acknowledged, "the native race is disappearing."

Not, it seemed, fast enough for the more aggressive element in the European community up north. A manifesto drawn up in the Geraldton area was headed by the question, "Are we or the natives to be masters?" The myalls, as the wild blacks were called, kept up a guerilla warfare that roused their opponents to a fury of retaliation.

Things had come to the point, Martelli said, where even educated men believed that if the whites were to survive, the blacks must be exterminated. Any talk of humanity was regarded as sentimental, the charge thrown at Bishop Gibney in the controversy of 1892.

In Perth this took the form of a correspondence that occupied columns in the newspapers and continued for months. In it Bishop

Gibney defended the "gentle and docile" people who had led him to safety across the Pindan of the north, neither stealing his provisions nor killing him as they might well have done. Against him were those pastoralists who condemned them as "brutish, irresponsible and treacherous".

Both attitudes had their foundation in fact. The Aborigines could be docile and brutish, gentle and treacherous, depending on the treatment meted out to them.

Daisy, whose values were those of her compatriots, interpreted what she was told as the dance of death between new and old. The superior energy and adaptability of the British, able to accustom themselves to Arctic cold and tropical heat, was, as Daisy was afterwards to write, "a signal for the disappearance of the indigene". Martelli's belief that the Aborigines were doomed roused her scientific as well as compassionate interest. She asked if anything had been done to record the language and customs of the tribes that were left?

Martelli told her that the French abbot of their Beagle Bay Mission in the far north had been compiling a dictionary of the Broome district, and that the present acting abbot, Father Nicholas, was a keen student of their customs.

Daisy glimpsed the hobby that she had been looking for. The dean added that he hoped to accompany Bishop Gibney to the Beagle Bay Mission in the following August. He could not, of course, be sure of gaining the bishop's consent but if he knew of her interest he might be persuaded to agree to her going with them.

It was an enthralling prospect but it was still twelve months away. In the meantime she must adjust to life as Mrs John Bates, mother of Arnold, who had celebrated his thirteenth birthday while his mother was on the *Stuttgart*, learning about the Aborigines of her adopted land.

CHAPTER NINE

Because a man eats with his knife, one must not visibly shudder at the circumstance . . . the extra two pence, thanks to your good luck, were paid for your manners, but that does not entitle you to boast your superiority, otherwise the two pence have not been well laid out.—Daisy Bates: "Lady Mary's Camp Cure".

Reunion in the West

The five years had left Jack pretty much where he had been on Daisy's departure for England.

Without her to prompt him, he had seen less reason than before for changing his profession. He was a good drover. He liked his work and was respected for it—if not in the drawing-rooms of Perth, then in the cattle stations of the North-west.

Among bushmen he was popular. Among pastoralists he had the added reputation of being one of the few men in the country who knew how to inoculate their cattle against the dreaded pleuro. It was, in fact, an outbreak of the disease and not the lure of gold that was his reason for visiting this, the most isolated of the colonies in the Federation.

The gold discoveries of 1893 had brought a surge of new life to the West. The "hardy yeomen" with whom John Forrest had dreamed of filling his land, arrived in their thousands to brave the sun-scorched sands of Coolgardie. Jimmy Withnell's stone, picked up to kill a crow and found to be veined with yellow, brought a second contingent north to Roebourne. The new prosperity was reflected in the demand for more cattle and Jack was one of the drovers prepared to risk the rough seas of the Bight with a cargo of bellowing beasts.

A wire from the McKay brothers sent him hastening up to their Roy Hill station in the Nor'-west.

Sam McKay, Daisy's future sponsor, was one of the richest cattlemen in the West. Son of "Bunga" McKay, he owed his fame as well as a good deal of his fortune to his father, who had endured a three day siege from the myalls at Battle Hill where he had been ambushed. Equipped with a rifle and ammunition, and the tenacity that was part of the make-up of these early pioneers, old "Bunga" McKay had managed to hold off the Aboriginal attacks until relief came. In the end he died in his bed, leaving his sons a vast area of land in the monsoon country near Ethel Creek.

Grass was abundant at Roy Hill but tended to be sour owing to humidity. Cattle flourished and grew fat but became prone to a lung disease that was as infectious as it was deadly. Pleuro was one of the many hazards that faced these early cattlemen and Jack, as loyal as Daisy to his own kind, went up to inoculate the remaining herd.

The virus was obtained from the fluid taken from the lungs of a slaughtered beast and injected into the tail. Sam McKay had imported a veterinary surgeon from England to instruct him in the art and been left with a supply that he used as he needed it.

Jack Bates took the cork off the bottle and buried the contents as quickly as he could. The fluid had gone bad and such cattle as had not been killed by pleuro had died from ptomaine poisoning.

Jack got to work. He obtained fresh fluid, injected the healthy beasts and stopped the spread of the disease.

Sam McKay showed his gratitude by an offer of help in getting Jack established in the district. He pointed out a leasehold available twenty miles from Roy Hill. It was over 180,000 acres of excellent pasture close to Ethel Creek. Any man prepared to work it could make money. Jack had saved him a fortune in cattle, he would finance the purchase.

Jack decided that this, or something like it, could be the answer to his future with Daisy and went East to collect Arnold. In due course they went down to Perth to await the arrival of the *Stuttgart*.

It is not difficult to imagine his state of mind as he waited. He was not a particularly imaginative man. But he was not unintelligent. Reason must have warned him of the difficulties ahead, but his hopes lay in his wife's decision to return. Surely she would not have done so if not prepared, at last, to settle down to family life, perhaps even to become a wife to him again?

That Daisy, the optimist, was entertaining similar fantasies, is apparent from her own account of their reunion. Prepared though they might have been for differences in the other, neither of them seemed to have bargained for the changes in themselves.

The little lady who stepped off the pier at Fremantle on a spring day of September 1899 neither looked nor spoke like the girl who had left on the *Macquarie* five years before. The general outlines were the same. Her clothes were still the height of fashion, though more restrained as became her additional years. Her travelling suit was grey, she wore a blue tie around the high collar, a "gem" toque on her head. Her colouring was as vivid as ever but there was a taut look of purpose that narrowed her mouth and relaxed only when she laughed. This she continued to do, but with others rather than with her husband, whose sense of humour was not hers.

Her voice was now more English than Irish. The soft brogue remained, but her sentences were punctuated by a clipped "don't y' know". If she approved of a plan it was "jolly". Her condemnation of a man was that he was "no gentleman", of a woman that she was "no lady". The "little niceties of behaviour" that separated the classes were all important. Whereas, in her youth, her high spirits might get the better of social decorum, she was now its dedicated apostle.

Jack, who had jettisoned distinctions of class in the cause of his profession, found himself as irritated by Daisy's prejudices as he was ignorant of her subjects of conversation.

His feeling of inadequacy returned. To counter it he fell back on the stubborn streak, as obstinate as hers.

For Daisy's reactions to their meeting we can quote her own account.

In the form of an autobiographical short story that seems to have become too personal to complete, this escaped her censorship of her private papers. It was written in the third person and remains as a fragment among her notes.

> God what a shock the meeting was! A series of shocks, coming tumbling upon each other in the first month of their reunion! This creature with the weak hanging underlip, the man who was to win success for her! This unkempt untidy soul, the

man in whom she thought great possibilities lurked! This enervated body, the strong energetic man of her thoughts and dreams.

Why, his fingers were so slack that he could not hold a plate without letting it fall. His mind had been so little exercised that to follow a thought sent him to sleep. His very form and features had moulded themselves to his character and had become loose and flabby and common—above all common!

Reunion with her son affected her with even profounder dismay.

"The horror of her first sight of him! Dirty, unmothered, neglected, incongruous . . ."

So much for the selective memory that had clung to her dream of the indigenous Australian with whom she might yet build a pioneer outpost of her beloved Empire; of the son who could be a reflection of the "intelligence and clear thinking" of a race that she had compared so often and so favourably with her countrymen abroad.

Again fantasy was at war with reality. For Daisy, manners, if they did not make, then certainly marked, the man. The man she had married and the son she had borne had sacrificed their manners in pursuit of their manhood. Daisy could not forgive them for the sacrifice.

She set about "to take up the years of her life", grappling with each of her problems in turn.

Her first task was to find a school for Arnold. To do so she paid a visit to Dean Martelli, now in retirement in Bunbury. Martelli proved his friendship and found a place at the Christian Brothers College in Perth. Their difficulties of adjustment had not prevented Daisy from considering Jack's plan for a station in the Nor'-west. Since she intended to spend at least six months of the following year in search of it, she looked for a household in which she could board her son.

She found the Brewer family, numerous and good-natured, mothered by a woman prepared to accept Arnold as Daisy herself had been accepted by the Outrams. Determined to remove the "taint of laziness" from her son's character, Daisy encouraged him to work for a future career. To her disappointment Arnold was not literary. His love was for music, his talent lay in engineering. Reluctantly she apprenticed him to an engineer, ready to take him on as soon as his schooling was finished. He would then come under the supervision of Harry Gregory, Minister of Mines, and one of her new friends.

These stemmed, in the main, from the Karrakatta Club. This most exclusive of Perth's women's clubs, consisting mainly of the wives of northern pioneers and southern leaders of Government, offered her immediate membership. She had arrived with the status of an "English Lady Journalist" bestowed on her by Perth's *Morning Herald.* Her tales of *Review of Reviews* and *Borderland* were fascinating. She was invited to give an inaugural address on the subject of London's literary lions and became something of a lion herself. Possessed of the two essentials of a born lecturer, a carrying voice, deep toned and pleasant to listen to, and a bubbling wit that prevented boredom, her lecture was a success.

Club members invited her to their homes. Daisy, enjoying the forward-looking thrust of Perth's leading citizens, dragged a reluctant Jack to the Pindan, home of Magistrate Robert Fairbairn, to the Fairbridge experimental farm, and, of course, to Government House. He had arranged to go on ahead of her and to prepare for their journey in the Nor'-west, but he could not escape until the New Year. The Governor had planned a celebration that was to be worthy of the new century and the Colony's new affluence. The country's future as a Commonwealth was already decided upon. The twentieth century promised great things. The Governor's reception would include those men and women who were to shape the destiny of the West. Chief among them was the Premier, Sir John Forrest.

Nothing would have persuaded Daisy to miss such an occasion. While Jack went to sleep over his glass of beer, she talked to the twenty-stone giant who had forged his own path towards leadership. In Forrest, as in Sir Henry Parkes, Daisy saw the embodiment of her ideal. She spoke the same language, shared the same loyalty. Forrest talked of the "crimson thread of kinship with the mother country". He regarded the Empire as a "symbol of triumph of freedom, justice, civilisation and progress". She respected him as an explorer who had dared to follow in Eyre's footsteps and to walk the waterless plain from Eucla to Fowler's Bay, thankful to quench his thirst with the blood of a hawk. She admired him as a man of vision, who, with the help of engineer O'Connor, was realizing his dream of a pipeline to bring water across three hundred and thirty miles to the thirsty diggers of Kalgoorlie.

Nor was he interested only in the community of whites. As a boy he had played with the Bibbulmun children and been accepted as a member of the tribe. Like his friend Matthew Gibney he deplored their fate. Only the Federal duties that were to monopolize his energies after the birth of the Commonwealth prevented him from taking more action on their behalf. When Daisy talked to him he was already planning his new Aboriginal Protection Act, to come into being five years later.

As Martelli said, Forrest had made rueful acknowledgement of the decline in the numbers of the black Australians. Conscious of the need to record their language and customs before it was too late, he discussed the possibility with Daisy. According to a letter she wrote to the Commonwealth Government many years later, it was Forrest who encouraged her to take up this work and even gave her some initial instruction in such matters as social and marriage laws. But he was equally aware of the difficulties of assimilation. The black people were his trusted friends who had proved their loyalty and earned his gratitude. About their chances of survival he was as pessimistic as any other man of his generation.

The festivities over, Jack left for the North. Daisy waited to see Arnold settled in to his new home, bought some bush outfits and armed herself with notebooks in order to record all that she saw of black as well as white settlement.

Her spirits had improved. Once again the challenge of this new country had fired her imagination. Perth's welcome had been as warm as its climate. Daisy felt at home and decided to purchase, with the remains of her capital, the leasehold of two blocks of land as a security for her old age.

From Bunbury she caught a coastal steamer bound for Cossack. As instinctive a nomad as any Aboriginal, she found it easier to face the crises of her life on the move. Adjustment with Jack became easier because of the thought of the long journey ahead.

The urge to "abandon home and friends and wander somewhere, anywhere" was not just to escape from the "interminable sameness of houses and streets and people", but also from herself.

CHAPTER TEN

Nor can it be imagined that the splendid women who work beside their husbands in those far off stations . . . would callously look on while their husbands vented brutal tempers on unoffending natives.—Lecture by Daisy Bates, 1907.

Nor'-western Travels

Leaving her "squeamishness and fastidiousness safely stowed away in her Perth hotel", Daisy boarded the s.s. *Sultan* for Cossack. The date was Friday 2nd March, 1900.

She had been warned. Brown-faced men with calloused hands, down for the Government House festivities, had listened to her plans with disbelief. This little slip of a woman who talked about the Paris tailor she had found in Perth and never took her gloves off if she could help it, all set to wander around the Nor'-west in a buggy! The first puff of a willy-willy would blow her away, husband or no husband.

But what about the flies? they asked. So thick a man's shirt was black with them? That was why the poor devils of natives went round with their eyes half closed. And the blowflies! Big yellow ones, the filthiest creature God ever invented. Laid their maggots wherever they smelt meat.

That was no problem. She could never handle raw meat anyway. She would do without it. A slice of bread and marmalade was all she needed.

Ah, but then there were the ants. The Nor'-west was swarming with them. Not just the little ones but the big fellows, bull-ants. Get a bite from one of those and she would know all about it.

There would be no part of her body exposed for them to bite. She would be wearing a fly veil, buttoned boots, Turkey twill bush skirt, shirt and tie, gloves.

In that heat?

The nights would be cool.

True enough, but then there would be the mosquitoes to contend with. Not just the kind that buzzed round your ears in the South. These Nor'-western mosquitoes were the real thing. Trunks like elephants. Called the "Scotch Greys" because they were so bloodthirsty.

She had her mosquito net ready. She was never one to fuss about the comforts of life. Her requirements were simple: plenty of tea and enough water for a daily wash.

Tea . . . daily washes . . . there would be no water inland for luxuries like that. There were wells in the Pindan where the water was so salty the cattle could not drink it. . . .

Daisy remained undeterred, even by tales of centipedes with a predilection for "playing hide and seek in the toes of one's shoes".

She boarded the *Sultan* in high spirits. One of the passengers, Arthur Blake, remembers her as the centre of gaiety, fascinating the small boy that he was at the time.

Her route was to take her from Cossack to Roebourne, up to Port Hedland and south to Carnarvon, in a line that remained approximately fifty to a hundred miles inland. The entire journey was to be by pony trap, with rest periods of two or three weeks at a time on the stations passed en route.

Her account of it was her first attempt at serious journalism in the West. The *Journal of Agriculture* published a long and detailed article which repays reading if only for the amount of information, minutely gathered, on subjects varying from the mineral potential of the land to the problems of transport. Here is a different Daisy from the "quasi sub-editress" of *Borderland.* There are flashes of humour to relieve the text but in the main the article is of value as an historical record and shows more of her talent for observation than the breezy light-heartedness that characterized her contributions to "the spooky little quarterly".

Surprisingly, she shows little narrative sense, and the drama of her traveller's tales tends to be lost. The "cockeye bob" that sent the *Sultan* scurrying into harbour for safety is disposed of with a passing mention. It remained for E. L. Grant Watson, her future colleague, to provide a description of this fearsome hurricane that could devastate an entire pearling fleet. "The wind," he wrote, approached "in a broad arrow across the sea, beating it to fury until each wave broke with a crash like the report of a gun." With it came the rain so that ". . . what was before a rattle and a scream became a deafening roar . . . thunder burst and lightning streamed in white rivers across the sky."

She met Jack in Cossack and the first step of the journey was the ride to Roebourne in a horse-drawn tram, in which they "jolted along Irish jaunting fashion". The seats were divided from wind and rain only by ragged curtains. The tram boasted of first and second compartments "in all respects similar to each other", and was drawn by worn-out brumbies, "quite eligible for Zoological purposes".

Roebourne, like Cossack, was a depressing sight because of the state of the buildings, "ruinous and tumbledown after batterings from the Willy Willies, and presenting a most hopeless appearance because of the heavy chains thrown over the roofs to prevent them from being blown away."

Out of the town there were no roads, only the tracks of other vehicles to follow. Bridges were non-existent. "Rivers," she remarked, "were negotiated by the usual method of following the buggy tracks into the water." If, as happened when they crossed the Yannarie, the river was deeper than expected, then "we found the horses swimming, our baggage completely under water and ourselves wet to the waists!" To which she adds the rueful comment that, "I will draw a veil over the result of the damage done to my luggage."

Lightning storms were a constant threat. She admits to one that was so close, the green spinifex nearby was set alight. But her code would not allow so much as a glimpse of fear to add spice to her adventures. We see the straight-backed little figure bumping over the rough ground through an alien and empty bushland, broken by giant boulders rising out of the ground "as though they had all hurried to get out of the way of something that was threatening them from below", admitting to no emotion except perhaps irritation with the caution of her driver. Bushmen, she remarked, were the "grooviest" people in the world, capable of following a "road" in a nine-mile circle rather than take a short cut of three miles across. When challenged, their answer was always the same: "We must follow the tracks."

Her descriptions show that lack of fear did not stem from any lack of imagination. The "grotesque brown mounds of the white ant, that crouch ghoul like over the vast bare flat", conveys atmosphere as did one of her rare flashes of humour. The sight of a myriad cockatoos rising with "a sudden and simultaneous frou frou of wings" she compared with "a women's meeting, when all are asked to rise".

Implicit throughout is her great love of the bush.

For Daisy it was full of marvels. There was the beautiful green beetle with a W on its back; the dugong, or amphibious animal "similar to the Manitee of Mexico"; the turtle, captured by approaching it from the rear and flipping it onto its back.

She saw a "mock sun, shining and sending forth rays irrespective of the real sun, which was in another part of the horizon" and heard a "singing glade of birds, their song beginning at 2 a.m. and kept up until sunrise", when daylight revealed only a clump of scrub "with neither sight nor sound of a single bird" to explain the phenomenon.

The snakes, centipedes and mosquitoes against which she had been warned may as well not have existed. She rejoiced in her "leather bound skirt, that was over three yards wide at the hem", her "shoes with decent heels", her "opaque blouse, collar and tie", comparing them favourably with the "weirdly feminine drapings and tassellings of fashion" and maintaining that such practical comfort "even without the added beauty of bush and sky made tent life well worth living."

Nor did she forget the second purpose of her journey. The indigenous Australians were recorded with scientific detachment, but with a detail that shows how closely she studied them.

"The natives of Roebourne number about 200," she wrote, "some of them fine looking men; the women are very inferior looking. They make several articles from spinifex grass which grows so abundantly about here. Netted bags . . . which they manipulate with a small kangaroo bone, beads, rope and a splendid glue, which they use to fasten their glass spear heads on the end of their wooden spears. In cases of sickness [they] take a sharp wooden carved flat stick, one point of which they stick into their stomachs and leave it there to fester."

To this is attached the comment that "They generally recover under this treatment."

Her description of the bullroarer begins with the questionable statement, "The aborigines have no Deity but many devils." To frighten these, she continues, "they have a long carved stick with a hole in one rounded end through which a string made of human hair is passed and they twirl this round and round, making a booming and most depressing noise, sufficient to send any poor devil flying from the sound of it."

She must have been warned, even at this stage, that reports were liable to contradiction, because in each instance she is careful to quote her source.

A witness on the De Grey station gave her details of a native burial:

"Bark was placed round the body and a very shallow oval grave was then dug and the body put into the cavity, and immediately as many jumped on the body as the grave would hold and set up a most unmerciful howling in chorus." In the case of a dead child, "The mother takes the elbow bone of the deceased and carries it about wtih her for a long time."

Auto-bloodletting (watched by a Government official) was a method of celebrating the return of the prodigal son. "The mother, after howling loudly, gets a good sharp conch and proceeds to cut herself with it. When the blood issues from the cut she subsides and her place is taken by a male relative." A woman who had been gathering the roots of a tree "pounded them into a kind of flour, opened a vein in her arm, letting the blood fall on the flour, mixed, baked and ate it."

An important discovery was the sense of humour that, almost more than anything else, helped to establish the rapport that was to exist between herself and her native friends.

Her illustration was a woman of Karratha, "so seized by the humour of Yamba de Rougemont's life that she would lie down, ejaculating, 'Goodbye my husband, I am going where you will follow' then jumping up and dancing to show how juvenile she was."

About the rock drawings on Depuch Island she allows herself the luxury of enthusiasm.

"On smooth faced rock, in every gully, animals, birds, fish and man have been chipped for countless ages . . . the number and variety of the carvings, their undoubted age and the glimpse they give of the native art as limned in the days when the world was young, render them well worthy of ethnological investigation."

"The unhappy shore people who said 'all the gullies are full of them funny things', had no idea how I envied them."

So wrote the ethnologist she was to become. On this journey she remained the investigator. Her article does not include her findings on the controversial subject of exploitation, but that she asked questions is evidenced by the lecture she gave in 1907 to

Daisy Bates

Making ready to cross the Nullarbor Plain from Eucla, W.A., to Fowler's Bay, to attend the Science Congress in Melbourne, 1914

On the road from Eucla

Lord Northcote, retiring Governor-General. Apart from her predisposition in favour of the pastoralists, it was not surprising that her findings should exonerate them, since her information was received from the De Grey, Boudarie and Sherlock stations, three outstanding examples of white settlement.

The De Grey, in particular, was renowned for its success in employing Aborigines. Perth's Historical Society has documents from this time recording that four hundred Aborigines sheared sixty thousand sheep a year. The statistics are accompanied by a comment from the owner who wrote that "the work would have proved more backbreaking and more heart breaking than most men could endure but for the black man."

On the De Grey, Daisy said, black servants were treated as part of the family. Each afternoon the women changed their attire and worked on one of the wide verandas. Every Sunday the men hunted for game. After the shearing season was over they were allowed the *pink-hi* or walkabout holiday. Corporal punishment was used and justified on the grounds that it belonged to native tradition.

To kill, to spear, to club, were the black man's ways of enforcing his law. "I do sometimes give them a cut for their laziness," the owner of the De Grey told Daisy, "but not half so much of a lathering as I give my own boys."

To answer another accusation, that the white settlers "threw offal to their natives like so many dogs", Daisy was taken to watch the killing of a kangaroo.

"Before skinning it," she explained, "they cut it open and extracted the inward parts which they threw on the fire for the first meal."

Her informants were pioneers such as John Withnell and J. G. Meares. Such men did not close their eyes to the problem but set about finding a workable answer. More immediate was the question of adjustment to natural conditions, as unforeseeable as they were heartbreaking.

Daisy was no stranger to the willy-willies that devastated the land. She had seen for herself the results of the wind that whirled across country, whining like a daemonic top, scooping up sand, roof-tops and tree branches and leaving behind a wake of debris like an upturned rubbish bin. Ornamental iron-work from the Church of England in Roebourne had been picked up five miles from the site. Balla Balla, a town on the coast, had been rebuilt five times. Sometimes the wind brought monsoonal floods, as she found out during her three-week stay with the Meares family.

For some reason she was alone with Mrs Meares and her children when a monsoonal storm broke overhead. For four days and four nights it rained. The two women shepherded the children onto high ground above the house to escape the floods. Marooned on their hilltop they watched helplessly as furniture, animals, the house itself, were swept away. At the end of this nightmare endurance test, the baby, not yet twelve months old, developed pneumonia and died.

When the floods subsided the Meares began at once to rebuild their home on higher ground, with a newly dug grave and a new friendship as memorials to the occasion. Understandably, Daisy, always loyal to their cause, became its professed champion. As soon as negotiations for Glen Carrick were completed she left Jack to go South. The first visit she paid on arrival in Perth was to Bishop Gibney, defender of Aborigines.

Since her intention was to present him with her newly acquired facts, their meeting was in the nature of a confrontation.

They got on well from the beginning. Gibney, as Irish as she was, had earned a reputation for courage that could flare into aggression in the face of injustice. Daisy herself illustrated this in her story of the capture of the Kelly gang in which Father Gibney, as he was then, had entered the burning building "fully aware of his danger from fire and bullet, in order to administer his Church's consolation to the dying bushrangers."

Gibney listened to her arguments and countered them with personal experience.

He had seen Aboriginal women forced by the pearlers to dive when in the later stages of pregnancy. He had seen some with hands crushed by heavy tools because they had clung too long to the side of the boat between dives. He had passed native prisoners chained by neck and ankle, working in the blazing heat on roads or public buildings. He had come across the bodies of absconders who had died, still in their chains, beside the dried-out beds of creeks in the bush.

Daisy, come to convert, found herself converted. Very well, she would go with him to the Mission. She knew he was plannng to leave with Dean Martelli at the end of August. This would give her almost a month to get ready. She would write her impressions for the newspapers. The world would be given the truth about the Aborigines.

Gibney hesitated. He explained that the visit was for a purpose. The Trappists must show the official valuer that they had improved their 10,000 acre leasehold to the extent of £5,000 or they would lose their subsidy from the Government as well as the promise of freehold tenure. It was to prevent this from happening that he had decided to visit the Mission himself. The evaluation was only a few months ahead, it might mean hard work for them all.

This was not a prospect to daunt so energetic an activist as Daisy. She assured the bishop that her articles would ensure justice being done to his Trappists.

That Gibney agreed to her accompanying them is proof of her powers of persuasion. To have taken a white woman with him to a Trappist monastery a thousand miles from civilization can only be described as an act of faith.

That his faith was justified was evidenced, not only by the ensuing three months, but by the next fifty years of Daisy's life.

CHAPTER ELEVEN

An ounce of example is worth a ton of precept.— Daisy Bates.

The Lonely Mission

It was to be a crucial three months, beginning with an even longer boat trip of a thousand miles up the west coast to Broome. There they were met by the acting abbot, Father Nicholas, and Filomeno Rodriguez, skipper of the *Sree Pas Sair* that was to take them the extra three days to Beagle Bay.

The *Sree Pas Sair*, like its owner, belonged to the history of Broome. Once the floating palace of Rajah Brooke, it had been purchased by an adventurer who had used it for the early experiments in dress diving. The resultant fifteen years in the pearling trade had transformed the luxury yacht into an evil-smelling hulk, indistinguishable, except for the beauty of its lines, from any other of the pearling boats, "dummy owned" by whites but usually the property of the Japanese.

Daisy, who had a feeling for sailing ships, lamented its past glory but endured the discomfort in a manner that almost succeeded in reconciling Father Nicholas to her presence.

It is easy to imagine his reactions at the sight of her.

A Spaniard of good family, who had studied medicine in Paris, it was for the sake of the black Australians that he had made the sacrifice of his life. Recalled from the useful work he was doing in the school he had established in Broome, the black-bearded little priest was already gloomy about the prospects of the Beagle Bay Mission. He was prepared to fulfil his role of acting abbot but, faced with the deterioration caused by persistent willy-willies and lack of staff to repair the damage, his outlook was not optimistic. Depressed by the facts with which he must confront his bishop, he must have found it doubly disconcerting to see the eager and strangely elegant young woman who accompanied him.

He explained that there was no accommodation whatsoever for her at the monastery; and that, by Church law, no woman except a Queen or the wife of a Head of State was allowed within its walls.

As usually happened, conversation with Daisy had a mollifying effect. Behind the ultra-feminine appearance he discovered an intelligence both inquiring and receptive. She spoke French with him and was attentive to all that he had to tell her on the subject of the Aborigines. Father Nicholas took it upon himself to grant a dispensation. She could have his room. It was very rough, a bag bed, seaweed pillow, an upturned tree stump as table, but, if she were prepared to put up with the lack of comfort . . .

Daisy assured him that she had never been one to bother with the fleshpots and wrote gleefully that she "broke all the rules".

"I slept in the Abbot's bed (he wasn't in it and besides it wouldn't hold two) and I went through their cells and talked and made them talk to me and all through those months they were perfect little gentlemen."

Her account of the visit, according to Mary Durack, strikes "an oddly light-hearted and feminine note in a story of so much zealous masculine endeavour, earnest soul-searching and bewildered study of native customs and psychology".

In her letters to William Hurst, editor of the *Australasian*, Daisy described it as a series of adventures, that began on arrival at the Bay. Rodriguez, who knew the coast as only a pearler could know it, timed their arrival for the turn of the tide so that Daisy had the "extraordinary experience of disembarking from the ship onto the back of a waiting horse". The *Sree Pas Sair* listed to starboard as the water receded, and even the bullock dray could come alongside across the rapidly drying mud. The little party set off with the clothes and provisions they had brought for the Mission; but, she wrote, "the horses were trappists too, skin and bone in their poverty and stopped so often for their meditations and devotions that the bullock team arrived before us."

No sign of life broke the monotony of country "unlovely and

cheerless to a degree", except for a turtle factory, opened, and soon after closed, at the Bay.

Their progress across the Pindan was, in fact, very little different from Bishop Gibney's original expedition, when, led by the Njul Njul people, he had laboured across the parched and prickly bushland to the oasis of "spreading white gums, sparkling spring fed pools, lily covered and set about with palms and ferns", that had been chosen as the Mission site.

Because of the quantity of water, they were greeted by a thousand birds of bright plumage—wild ducks, parrots, brolgas and finches—which rose with a screech at the sight of them.

"They are swearing at us," Daisy informed the bishop, but this was to distract his attention from their first sight of the mission buildings.

Wind-battered and dejected, they were "a collection of tumble-down paperbark monastery cells and a little bark chapel, a community room of corrugated iron, repeatedly destroyed in bush fires and hurricanes". On either side were clumps of bananas, dates and vegetables, all overgrown with weeds. These flourished as readily as everything else. The soil was fruitful, producing rice, sugarcane, pumpkins and arrowroot that was superior in quality to the Queensland product. But Father Nicholas had explained that as the policy of the Mission had been to help and never to exploit the natives, no attempt had been made to sell their products. In those days £5,000 was a great deal of money. To show that this amount had been spent on improvements to the property must have seemed a remote hope, even to an optimist like Bishop Gibney.

A dogged idealist, blessed with an energy that far transcended his sixty-five years, he set about to ensure that his dream for posterity would be realized.

At the end of two months, "every screw and post, every fruit and vegetable, buildings, wells, trenches and implements had been meticulously valued. The livestock was on the run, supplies in the store, the wells cleaned, fences and buildings straightened out. A thriving property existed where there had been only ruin and decay."

So Daisy could write in triumph for the *Journal of Agriculture*. But the miracle spelled hard work. The fastidious little lady was given her chance to prove that she could rise to the challenge of manual labour as previously she had met intellectual demands; and she was able to do this for the same reason: once again she was working for a man who claimed her total respect.

"It was the selflessness of the great Irishman that made everyone ready and eager to help," she told Hurst.

And work they did, the priests in charge of the men, Daisy of the women.

It took her all her ingenuity to keep them occupied, but discovering that they loved to play the child's game, ring-a-ring-a-rosy, she used this as her incentive. They worked and played in shifts, and she worked and played with them. This way they weeded the gardens and dug out the wells, a job they preferred because the results were more dramatic.

On the marshy ground were three-foot-high mounds that the bishop recognized as signs of artesian pressure. He helped Daisy and her women dig a space of seven feet square and then down until the ground became fibrous like an Irish bog. Using their hands, the native women dug to a level of six feet. By the next morning, fresh water was level with the embankment and in a matter of two short weeks had been populated by a species of tiny fish. Connected by trench to other wells, this provided a channel of moving water, ideal for the purpose of irrigation.

The repair work accomplished, there remained the marathon task of surveying the 8,000 acres of land. With no Government surveyor available, the bishop undertook the job himself, together with a ship's compass, a chain, Daisy and some helpers.

"The Bishop and I were the chainmen," she wrote, "walking in steamy heat of 106 degrees at times, sometimes twelve miles a day. Over marsh and through pindan, now lame from stones and prickles, now up to our thighs in bog, the Bishop throwing down a small peg to mark the chain limit, I always in difficulties because of my high heeled footwear. We were always hungry. Brother Xavier . . . would forget the salt or the bread or the meat, or the place where he had arranged to meet us, or that we existed at all.

"On the night walkings, rosaries were chanted all the way home, the natives and brothers responding. I often stumbled and fell in the dark but that rosary never stopped." After which, Daisy set to and wrote the notes of the day's activities.

She deserved the gold watch that was given her by the bishop in gratitude for her help. But that she endured gladly, we know from her letters to Hurst.

Her "real task" she told him, was to keep the bishop in good heart.

"Plodding over swamps, my clothes torn by rushes and the evil thorny bushes, I'd sing to him 'Thro' hedges and ditches I tore me auld britches, for you, Maryanne, for you Maryanne.' "

Miles from the Mission, after a day's surveying over soil baked hard by the sun, they slept in the protection of their wagon, Daisy between the wheels, the bishop on one side, Father Nicholas on the other.

> Asked by Father Nicholas to wake his lordship, I put my hand through the wheel and pulling the rug off his head, I said,
>
> "Get up you lazy lad."
>
> We sat up and proceeded to put on our shoes and stockings. Suddenly the situation dawned on me. I turned grinning to the Bishop:
>
> "Did you ever put on your shoes and socks in bed with a lady before?" I asked him.
>
> The lovely old man grasped it. "Oh lord oh lord, isn't it funny," he said and it quite put him in good heart through the day.

Irish himself, he understood her teasing, although, if she carried it too far, he was quick to tell her.

Knowing that this was likely to be his last visit to the district, he held a service in the little bark chapel in order "to make confirmed christians of all the natives".

"Crowded into that little bark chapel," she wrote in *The Passing of the Aborigines*, "65 men, women and babies, smelling to high heaven, stood before the prelate of the Roman Catholic Church in all his ceremonial robes of lace and purple and mitre, to be anointed with the papal blessing and a little blow on the cheek of the Pax Tecum.

"I tried to maintain a solemn countenance only to explode into choking laughter by the antics of one boy . . . desperately trying to keep his hands clasped in prayer and a rag of decency well pulled down over his rear elevation."

A frown of disapproval from under the dazzling mitre and an impatient jerk of the sacred crook, sobered her, but when she saw Goodowel, one of the corroboree comedians, acting out the ceremony she decided the bishop must join in on the joke.

Goodowel was sitting on a tree trunk with a red-ochred billy-can on his head and a filthy rug over his shoulders. Each of his audience came up to receive a "resounding smack on the ear" and the words, "Bag tak em."

But the bishop, she reported, merely shook his head and said, "Ah the poor craytures".

On his birthday she decided to cook a dinner of celebration which, as one of her proudest boasts was that she could cook nothing more complicated than a boiled egg, was not a success.

The bishop did not spare her.

After tasting the duck stuffed with vine-leaves, her chosen substitute for herbs she did not possess, he advised that it be kept under a glass case as a lesson in what not to do for the nuns who, he hoped, would join the Mission.

At her custard, he only looked, but "his look was eloquent." The cake had burnt on the outside so that "it turned a sort of Wedgwood blue not at all resembling the flour, eggs and butter I had used in its preparation. The Bishop said, 'You're a bright cake maker', and refused it for the plum pudding which was a great success. It was Swallow and Ariels."

But, she told Hurst, "we were all in the utmost harmony and everyone was doing his durndest from dawn till dark." She insisted that, in her account written for the *Australasian*, the bishop be given full credit. "If there is too much me in the article, blue pencil it mercilessly. I want the Bishop's work to stand out. Every moment of his time, every thought in his head was concentrated on one single object—a mission for the blacks."

The valuer arrived, the improvements were valued as high as £6,000 and the Mission was saved. "In much jubilation," she wrote, "we made the first bricks of sand and loam and clay for the new convent of which I laid the foundation brick."

But one last adventure was ahead of her.

Sixty miles across country was Disaster Bay, where Bishop Gibney had secured a further 2,000 acres in trust for the Aborigines. The Mission had been without a priest for some months and the bishop decided that he must pay it a visit.

To reach Disaster Bay from Beagle Bay meant a journey through marshland that bordered about thirty-five miles of waterless pindan. Silverfish had disposed of the Mission's water-bags and after Father Nicholas had made a morning cup of coffee all round, they had a seventeen-hour stretch of blazing heat and no water. The bishop and Daisy, who had been provided with horses, had to walk for some of the time in order to rest their Aboriginal women guides. In the meantime a way must be cut through the pindan for the dray of provisions. Their mouths became so dry that not even the bushman's remedy of chewing eucalyptus leaves could stimulate saliva. Twice they veered off their course towards Lakes Flora and Louisa to find nothing but a "sun baked surface and a saucer like depression of cracked clay".

It was 2 a.m. before the women shouted "*Ngooroo*", meaning

"camp". Although the water in the Disaster Bay well was sweet magnesium, not one of them except Daisy could resist it. With considerable self-control she managed to wait until tea was made and so was the only member of the party who did not suffer from the agonies of stomach cramp.

Her first night of this three-day visit was a short one. Given a bag bed in one of the corrugated iron sheds, she was awakened at dawn by the awed chatterings of some thirty Aboriginal women who had clustered round to stare at the strange being with the white skin while she slept.

As soon as she got up, a number of dirty but friendly hands grasped her bare shoulders and arms. "Intensely curious, although not vulgarly so", they watched her dress.

"I have always," she wrote, "preserved a scrupulous neatness and all the little trappings and accoutrements of my own very particular mode of dress, sometimes under difficulties, but I think I never made a more laughable toilet than that one. Every motion of mine, as I laced my corset and eased my shoes on with a horn, brushed my hair and adjusted my high-collar and waist belt, was greeted with long-drawn squeals of laughter and mirrored in action, though the slim black daughters of Eve about me had not even a strand of hair string between the whole thirty."

The fifty-five natives who assembled to honour the bishop were headed by Benjamin, his friend of ten years previously. Benjamin threw himself round the bishop's neck, weeping, stroking his friend's face and pressing him to his breast, native fashion. All of which the bishop endured, knowing it to be a proof of affection. They were, Daisy reported, "a merry and light hearted people, their countenance intelligent, their expression candid and open". She was also astonished at their honesty. Prepared to find the Mission native "a sneak and a sycophant—a sort of flour and rice Christian", she discovered that the stores at Disaster Bay, left unguarded for six months, had not been touched. Although she found it a "delightfully ludicrous touch" to watch the "Christian" wedding ceremonies when the Spanish wreath and veil were worn "by hairy savages above wild hair and matted beards and no respectable clothing to speak of", she was impressed by their obvious love and respect for the monks.

Summoned by the conch bell, they crowded the little chapel for dawn and evening mass. But the Trappists, who were educated as well as dedicated men, were wise enough not to try to wean them away from the traditional beliefs that provided strength for their society and meaning to their lives. They tried neither to "work" nor "convert" them, and Daisy, who saw for herself the harmony such an attitude produced, noted it for the future. Theirs was an ideal of service and they made it a principle never to interfere with Aboriginal law. They taught by example and, being selfless men, their example had its effect.

There was one occasion, however, when they were confronted by a moral issue that could not be ignored.

Christian men, with an ideal of monogamy, could not approve of the Aboriginal custom of using women as a means of barter. Whenever the natives had contact with the white, or yellow, communities, a thriving trade sprang up. Their women were leased to the Manila pearlers or fishermen in exchange for food, tobacco, whisky. Even the "marriages" conducted by Father Nicholas between Aboriginal women and Manila fishermen were regarded as a kind of lend-lease.

Daisy, horrified to hear from the women that one of these "wives" was being used by at least five of her husband's brothers, decided that the bishop must be informed of it. The bishop took immediate action. All the women must be locked in the storehouse overnight until the Manila men left the bay.

The storehouse was a shed with no furniture and one window, very small and between twenty and thirty feet from the ground. Yet when the door was opened next morning, not one woman was to be found. They had piled up the stores, jumped onto the soft sand and escaped to the pearlers.

An ugly result of these unions was the fate of the half-caste babies that resulted from them.

Mary Durack in her book *The Rock and the Sand* states that Father Nicholas had "spent much of his time in Broome, bargaining with the native mothers for the part-Aboriginal babies that they frequently killed and, according to his and the other missionaries' testimony, often ate as well." In her paper for the Geographical Society, written shortly after her visit, Daisy wrote that she asked the abbot if cannibalism obtained in that area.

"The Abbot pointed to one of the women near us and told us she had recently eaten her new born baby. When she was asked how she could do so, she replied, 'I only ate one, that woman ate three.' "

On this evidence, Daisy was later to base her much publicized and controversial opinion that cannibalism existed among the Aborigines. The reason given her was logical, however gruesome. Before and after the birth of a child the husbands lived apart from their wives. This was, then, the only time in an Aboriginal woman's life when she could eat any or every part of the meat food that she liked. Sometimes she shared it with another child in order to make him strong, though careful to disguise the meat as otherwise the child would refuse it.

She could see no reason to doubt the abbot's testimony. An intelligent and selfless man who had made the effort to speak the Aboriginal language, his knowledge had been acquired, not out of anthropological textbooks, but from his work with a people whose customs, character and legends fascinated him. Devoid of any false pride, he was to be seen "sitting on the ground in the midst of his aged and decrepit natives, making homely jokes as he tended their sores and administered medicines". Because they were sure of his affection for them, he influenced them. But, he warned, it was necessary to think with their mind. In a conflict between tribal law and Christian domination, tribal law would win. Only because of personal respect would the white man's teaching be accepted. Daisy, realist enough to see that he was right, adopted his method as well as his teaching and was judged for her findings as her teacher was judged before her.

Recognizing a fellow enthusiast, he took time off to show her something of their customs. She was invited to partake of wild honey, collected by a species of bee that was stingless and so tiny that the natives had to kneel in the grass below the white gums to detect the tiny corpses that showed the nest from which they had dropped. The branch was then cut off and "honey, bees and wax eaten holus bolus". She went with them, bare-footed into the mud, to watch the capture of a crocodile. She was shown the ritual of bed-making in which the sand was hollowed out, a fire lit in the hollow and covered again with sand. When the time came for sleep the coals were raked out and the warm sand drawn over their bodies.

For the women who were her constant companions, Daisy felt a maternalism, at once protective and permissive. Touched by the sensitivity that showed itself in "a trifling service rendered or a quiet withdrawal from your vicinity if they noticed your fatigue", she responded with the warmth for which, all her life, she had sought an outlet.

"Never once," she said, "were my sensibilities affected by any action of theirs."

Bishop Gibney in a letter written in 1912, put it more strongly: "I saw with my own eyes how devoted you were to them and how attached they became to you. And I know to this day you are known there and elsewhere as their white sister."

Their one fault, Daisy remarked, was that "they only washed when it rained." But, "how many white men have I met against whom a similar charge could be laid!"

By the time she boarded the *Scree Pas Sair* for Broome her life work was decided upon. Following Abbot Nicholas's example she would record the language and customs of this lovable race before it was too late.

Dean Martelli, whose health had been insufficient to stand the strain of their exertions, had been sent to the lugger on the one horse left at the Mission. The bishop and Daisy were faced with walking the last nine miles in the heat of the afternoon, as Rodriguez was anxious to catch the turn of the tide.

Before they had reached the half-way mark the bishop himself had collapsed. Delirious with fatigue, he was scarcely able to walk and they were compelled to camp on the beach overnight.

Alone in the darkness of that deserted shore, in charge of a sick man whose delirium was such that he was calling her by the name of his sister Margaret; surrounded by Aborigines who whispered to her their fear of the wild "pindana" mob whose footsteps they could hear and who were known to attack such small groups, Daisy had to call upon her reserve of courage.

Her last night in Beagle Bay was spent in a sleepless vigil that lasted until dawn, when they were able to manage the mud walk to the boat.

Before they reached Broome the bishop recovered consciousness sufficiently to rebuke the Manila steersman for his nudity. But Daisy had to remain on board until her Broome friends brought her additions to her wardrobe. Her dress was "all patches", her shoes were the seventh pair of kangaroo-skin slippers made for her by Brother John Berchmans. The little lady who could quieten the fears of nervous Aborigines on the lonely beach of Beagle Bay was not brave enough to face her own kind unless equipped for the occasion.

She put on a new dress, new collar, new gloves, boots, hat and veil, and was ready.

CHAPTER TWELVE

There are a few fortunate races that have been endowed with cheerfulness as their main characteristic, the Australian Aborigine and the Irish being among these.—Daisy Bates.

Among the Koolarrabulloo

The seed of obsession had been sown. The germinating process took a further ten months.

This was mainly due to Daisy's success as a journalist. Her long articles for the *Journal of the Department of Agriculture* had established her prestige. Her Beagle Bay experiences were published by English as well as Australian papers.

Between Jack and herself a new impasse seems to have been reached. Either from lack of capital or in order to offer her a home to which she could come at once, he decided to accept the management of a cattle station on Roebuck Plains rather than to work Glen Carrick. Daisy, who had not returned from Broome until March, was faced with leaving Arnold alone for another long period of time.

She compromised by spending the winter in Perth, joining Jack in September 1901.

She had stayed on in Broome in order to help prepare the official report of the Beagle Bay Mission for the Roman Curia of Propaganda at the Vatican, since "Dean Martelli had knocked up and Bishop Gibney could not perform the task."

The respite gave her a chance to draft her own articles

although, from her account of it, conditions were far from ideal.

The Broome of 1900 she described as a cosmopolitan town that was a mixture of Port Said, Singapore and Hong Kong.

The streets, lined with palms and brilliant with poinciana, narrowed into passages not more than two feet wide. These separated the Chinese and Japanese quarters and in them dramas of retaliation broke out between pearlers and their divers that electrified the atmosphere and resulted in sound and fury that reached its climax during the months of December to March, the "lay-up" season for the fleet.

This, Daisy wrote, was "a season of madness, in which white as well as coloured men went berserk."

"Marooned in a dirty room at the one decent hotel the town offered", she had her meals brought up to her "in such moments as the passages were free of howling drunken madmen."

"This is very dreadful," she said to her Singhalese waiter.

Confident of the gulf separating his ancient culture from these hordes of Bacchus, the waiter was indulgent.

"The trouble is they've got no education, Madam," he said.

Daisy escaped to the Residency, occupying the rest of her stay by interviewing the Aboriginal prisoners at the local jail.

In these early years of the century, her attitude towards her new hobby remained ambivalent in that it was divided between her growing sympathy for the blacks and her missionary zeal in defending the white pioneers. The resultant conflict of loyalty did not make for consistency. She tended to find excuses for malpractices such as neck-chaining and presented the bishop with arguments in its favour.

The jailers, she said, had demonstrated the impossibility of keeping handcuffs on Aborigines because of their unusually small and sinewy hands. The prisoners themselves preferred neck-chaining as it left their hands free to brush away "the flesh eating flies". In their leisure time they could play cards, the pastime that helped them to endure confinement, their real punishment.

The bishop, not surprisingly, remained unconvinced. Years later, when the results of her investigations were published, it was the *Catholic Record* alone among the newspapers of Perth that held up her arguments to ridicule.

Who could take seriously the little lady who confronted the tough cattlemen "dressed in the latest fashion, in immaculate raiment, notebook ready and fountain pen poised aloft to inspire reverence and awe, severely and with all the dignity of a Lord Chancellor!"

To such, it was implied, the truth would not be given.

This was to underestimate her, as the bishop himself had reason to know. Their friendship survived their differences and he assured her that his "esteem for her knew no alteration". When the Perth newspapers published a controversy for and against the value of the Beagle Bay Mission, Daisy wrote to the *Morning Herald* in its defence.

Gibney, thanking her for her "charming" letter, no doubt chose his adjective with care. As so often happened when her affections were involved, Daisy's objectivity was lost to the cause. To the accusation that the Mission natives went unclothed Daisy replied that "during the entire three months I did not see one native who was not decently clothed," a statement that she was later to contradict herself by her description of the "slim black daughters of Eve without a hair string between them".

An unimportant detail, it is worth mentioning as it was this fine contempt for minor accuracy that was to provide fuel for the future fire of the professional anthropologists.

The winter of 1901 was a time of social as well as journalistic success. In it a relic, as sacred as her collection of Dickens, came into being.

Perth had been simmering with excitement over the impending visit of their future Majesties King George and Queen Mary, then Duke and Duchess of York.

Daisy, who had been presented to them by Lady Lawley, dropped her umbrella at the garden party held in their honour. The umbrella, black, with a bone handle, rolled at the feet of royalty and was picked up and handed to her by the Duke himself.

From then on, to the end of her life, the umbrella was sacrosanct.

By this time she was a local personality and the Karakatta Club asked for another lecture. No doubt the subject hastened her departure to the North, since the title was "The Influence of Women in the Home".

Daisy gave her talk in August, finished off her articles and, knowing that he was in need of a typewriter, bequeathed her machine to Bishop Gibney.

His letter of thanks is revealing, not only of her generosity, but of her frame of mind at the time.

"I am too much complimented by the present of the typewriter," he wrote. "I would never have mentioned the matter to you had I for a moment thought you would give away your own without any compunction. I forgot to mention to you that you might tell Arnold that should he want for anything while you are so far away I will gladly supply his wants. God bless and protect you. I hope to see you back in Perth with brighter and better prospects."

From which it can be deduced that she did not face the immediate future with her usual optimism. She took up life with her husband, from whom she had been separated for the better part of seven years, sustained only by the bleak satisfaction of duty done.

Jack had done his best. He had staffed his house with a housekeeper, a Japanese cook and one or two Aboriginal helps. The station was the property of wealthy tea-merchants and lacked nothing in the way of amenities. On paper it might have looked like the realization of Daisy's dream. The difference was that the land was not theirs. Nor were they the harmonious unit that Daisy had visualized on that far-off day sixteen years before when she had jumped off her horse to marry him.

Jack had grown older and heavier. Now in his forties, the effects of the beer he liked to drink with his mates at the bar had begun to show. The black hair and walrus moustache were whitening, his shoulders stooped in a slouch of indolence.

Daisy, on the other hand, was more active than ever. Her mind, stimulated by her contacts abroad, looked for further challenges. She began her researches in earnest. Unfortunately for their marriage, her subject was anathema to her husband. For Jack the Aborigines remained "the blacks", a word always spoken in contempt. He complained to his nephew that they had robbed him of a wife. She was never at home. . . .

But Daisy was fascinated by them. "To live among them, to see them amidst their own bush surroundings and to note their everyday comings and goings," she wrote, "is to experience an ever delightful feeling that you are watching the doings and listening to the conversation of early mankind."

The personal rapport that existed between herself and the Aborigines she put down to "an innate racial affinity".

"In their native state the aborigines possess many of the characteristics of the Irish, being light hearted, quick to take offence and quick to forgive," she said. For instance, "it was the easiest thing in the world to start a row in camp—a word, a look, a sneer . . . and the males rush for their spears and range themselves beside those whom they must by hereditary law fight with." But the fight usually began and ended with a war of words, ". . . a babel of sound in which each person talks at the top of his voice, taunting, daring, complaining", after which "the belligerents, getting their grievances thus ventilated, retire in comparative good humour."

Like the Irish, they were warmly hospitable, quick to jealousy but without malice. In their songs and dances she found the "Celtic mysticism" to which she responded. Their magic, though a more powerful influence in their community, bore a marked resemblance to the peasant superstitions believed in by her nurse Allie.

She was brave enough to voice her opinions in a lecture she gave a few years later, after which a spate of letters from her indignant compatriots appeared in the correspondence columns of the newspapers.

She waited, she said, until a comparatively moderate one appeared and replied to it:

"If the writer realised I am even more Irish by descent than he is, he will acquit me of any desire to insult my countrymen."

Her letter won the day. An apology was published by her opponent and she was asked to repeat her lecture for the benefit of "that hot bed of disloyalty, the Celtic club".

At the end of it her Irish audience applauded her for her courage.

Jack's complaints were not without justification. Daisy threw herself into her researches with characteristic thoroughness, reading all the anthropological literature she could lay her hands on and riding off with an interpreter in search of the native camps.

Even in those days she trusted herself without hesitation to the Aboriginal guides who led her through the trackless pindan by means of signs invisible to the eyes of white people.

Since the locality of the camps depended on the season, they knew where to find them. Where the game had gathered or the fruit was ripe, the groups would be camped beside the nearest waterhole. Smoke signals would be sent up to announce their arrival and Daisy would get off her horse to "sit down" among them.

Never for one moment was she afraid of them. Within a few minutes she would have one of their chocolate-coloured babies on her lap, laughing with them as they laughed at her, answering their sallies with the help of her interpreter and the few words she had managed to acquire of their dialect.

Gradually laughter changed to affectionate greeting at the sight of her. As a *jangg'a*, or white-skin, she was believed to have come from their dreamtime and so was expected to know and to respect their laws. Fortunately for Daisy, during her stay with the Meares family she had been accorded her place in the kinship system. Among the Bibbulmuns she was a *tondarup*, with the classification of "father's sister", which might be roughly interpreted as a kind of tribal aunt. She was shown at which fire she might sit, and the people by whom she would be joined.

To these Koolarrabulloo of the North-west, all living things, trees, animals, even grass, were part of the relationship system that divided their universe.

There were no step-relations. When a baby girl was born, all her father's brothers were called "father" and her mother's sisters "mother", their children were "sisters" and "brothers". Her *kordamat* or "husband stock" were the children of her father's sisters and her mother's brothers. To one of these she would be betrothed at birth. He could be a middle-aged man but she would be handed over to his keeping when she had passed puberty, even though, if he were a good hunter, he already had several wives. By law she became his property though he usually waited until she was fifteen before the "marriage" was consummated.

If, on the other hand, a romance should spring up between herself and a "brother", her husband was entitled to beat her, spear her, even to kill her. Thus did the law keep stringent the morality of the Koolarrabulloo. In 1901 the law remained absolute.

As the natives' confidence in her grew, Daisy's notebooks filled. At first only the women were her informants, and from them she heard the *ngargalulla* legend that was to play so important a part in her life.

To these natives of the Broome district it was an accepted fact that conception would be heralded by the manifestation of a *ngargalulla*, or spirit baby, who had crossed under the sea from Jimbin, the home of the unborn, to appear in the dreams of the father. When this happened, the man knew that his wife could conceive his child, even if he were far away at the time. If the *ngargalulla* did not appear, fatherhood was disowned.

For Daisy the legend had the charm of a fairytale. A people capable of believing it were children, their sins to be forgiven as children's were forgiven, because they were the keepers of innocence. At the same time she was learning respect for the tribal laws that put the good of the whole before that of the individual. As a "loner" she could not approve of this "communistic" approach but she acknowledged the happiness that seemed to result from it.

One of their laws, she decided, the white man would do well to emulate. This was the edict of silence, maintained by the power of vanity, that kept son-in-law and mother-in-law for ever separated.

If a man should speak to his mother-in-law, he believed that his hair would fall out. If a mother-in-law spoke to her son-in-law, hers would turn white. On the other hand, these black children showed a sophisticated understanding of the psychological need to give vent to repression. At the initiation ceremonies held once a year, the law was repealed. But it was the mother-in-law who was allowed to give expression to her grievances. Her son-in-law remained bound to silence.

"Her delight then is to worry and annoy," Daisy wrote. "As provider for the family, he pays the price of his betrothal in meat food. 'This meat is no good,' the mother-in-law says. 'Watch me, everybody, I'm going to kill a fish.' Snatching his spear, she aims it dangerously close to him."

Since their civilization could be traced back for so many thousands of years, she declared, the first Australians had claim to an historical superiority over their white invaders.

"When these descendants of a pre-historic people ask the whites for 'chickpence'," she is reported to have said, "they are quite unaware that they are asking favours of an inferior species of the human race."

It is highly improbable that she ever harboured any real doubts of British superiority, but, if so, these would have been settled by the lot of the women, who continued to be exploited by their men as they had been in the early stages of human existence. "She it is who must build the shelter, fetch the firewood, carry the water and the baby and the spare spears and boomerangs of her man," Daisy wrote. "The native woman is today what she was ten thousand years ago—obedience personified. A touch on the shoulder with a spear and she rises at once, whatever her occupation, and goes where she is told."

Her protective instincts roused, Daisy was to fight for the black woman's rights as ardently as any suffragette; but to be successful as an investigator, she had to accept the domination of the male. Access to the more intimate details of tribal customs and ceremonies was possible only through the men, who debarred women from knowledge of all things sacred.

Daisy was not to be beaten by so unimportant a detail as her sex. She noted that "the natives live in an atmosphere of superstition, with unseen forces always at work among them." She decided to exploit the fact, and it was then that she invented her native name of Kallower. She let it be known that she was a *mirrunroojandu*, a magic woman who had been one of the twenty-two wives of Leberr, a "dreamtime" father.

The black men looked at this elegant lady, always immaculate, always without her man; who spoke with some of their words; who could convey authority even while she laughed with them; whose clothes were always the same; who made mysterious marks with a novelty she called a pencil in a more impressive novelty she called a notebook. Such a being could only belong to Yamminga. They began to confide in her and found that she kept faith with them and did not repeat what she was told to their women.

From the old men she learned their history, as passed down by word of mouth through the centuries. Their theory was that their ancestors came from overseas and arrived in the North-west. These first arrivals were uncircumcised but the second horde to arrive were circumcised. The latter drove the former towards the south and created the two major divisions among the Australian Aborigines. Such was the influence of the second horde, that circumcision had become almost a universal part of the initiation ceremony. When the groups met for their first initiation corroboree, Daisy was allowed to be present.

She was later to say that she did not publicize her knowledge of initiation ceremonies for the simple reason that she knew she would not be believed.

She was quite right. Few anthropologists and fewer Aborigines believe that she was ever actually present at this ceremony that belongs to the sacred and secret sanctum of the Aboriginal male. And yet E. L. Grant Watson, zoologist of the Cambridge expedition, confirmed that she was present, ten years later, at a similar corroboree with Radcliffe-Brown and himself.

"They thought we were ghosts," was his explanation.

So Kallower, the dreamtime magician, the white-skinned ghost in the buttoned boots and high collar, thinking with her "black man's mind" and showing "no revulsion of feeling or of levity, no quiver of timidity", stood in the circle of Aboriginal males while the ancient rites that transformed child into man took place.

Compounded of "sex, a communion of blood and a Black Mass of witchcraft and savagery . . . instinct with the pure poetry of symbolism", wrote Daisy in *The Passing of the Aborigines*, the rites were the culmination of the long years during which the nine degrees of initiation were endured.

The man might have a white hair in his beard before he could take himself a wife. But his early childhood had been totally permissive. Adored and fussed over until he was eight or nine years old, he had then become *nimma nimma* and joined the bachelor's camp, his mother replaced by a *yagoo*, or guardian. He had been taught to hunt and to fish, to dance the symbolic rituals of tradition. If he were a Koolarrabulloo his nose had been pierced, first by a small bone from the paw of a kangaroo and then by a turkey bone.

Known as *baglai*, he had then to learn the lessons of self-control. Certain foods were denied him, he must avoid contact with the opposite sex. All restraints were according to the law of the group and the rituals were laid down until the painful ordeal that he must endure to enter manhood.

For the operation of circumcision the groups were gathered at an appointed place. To ensure the time of arrival, they used their finger joints as digits. There was usually more than one *baglai* and, very popular with all the groups, their arrival was the signal for singing and dancing. When the moment came, the *baglai* was rubbed with fat and charcoal, and an insignia of red ochre was painted on forehead, cheeks and chest. He was held by his *yagoo*, equally fearsomely painted.

A male relative performed the operation with a small stone knife.

Daisy wrote to William Hurst that "however small the flint, it will circumcise the boy in one or two strokes. The foreskin is pulled forward and the thing is done. If sub-incision takes place at the same time, the boy, who is on the backs of the Yagoo and his brothers, has his arms and legs held by more brothers, the organ is placed against his stomach and the cut made underneath. It may extend from the meatus to the scrotum but one or two strokes will suffice for this.

"The blood is then stopped with warm ashes and the foreskin may be kept by the operator and placed between the bark and trunk of a tree, not necessarily any particular tree. The operator will do this and will rub the blood off his hands with sand."

Through it all, she told him, "I conduct myself as seriously as if I were in a Roman Catholic church during mass. I do exactly the same as the others do."

The most gruesome of the rituals was the blood-drinking, a ceremony that usually took place a year later. Men, selected from among relatives, pierced their arms with their nose-bones until about two quarts of blood filled a bark vessel. This was poured down the young man's throat, with his father standing by to hold him. If he were to vomit, this would spell death for his close relations.

It was during this ceremony that he was imparted knowledge which, under pain of death, he must keep from his womenfolk.

Final celebration was the *falgoo* corroboree, consisting of orgiastic songs and dances.

"If you are a Celt," Daisy wrote, "you can sense what the singer is unable to express, and feel the varied emotions passing through him. His totem songs, a few words at most, are sung with a wild abandon, the emotions they stir within him becoming stronger with every repetition until finally, from an excess of feeling, the singer will often fall unconscious, when he is roughly massaged to life again."

In this corroboree that crowned the young man's long struggle for manhood, promiscuous sex was permitted.

Finally, each member of the group slept the sleep of exhaustion.

Daisy recorded all that she saw and sent off her reports to the Anthropological Institutions of England and Australia, of which, in due course, she became an honorary correspondent.

In the meantime her personal problems remained unsolved.

Money was needed if they were to run Glen Carrick. Jack's salary was good but there was Arnold's education to be paid for, apart from ordinary living expenses.

According to Daisy, the droving expedition was her idea.

Beef was needed in the South and the cost of transporting it by ship from Broome was £4.10s. per head. If they took a herd of cattle down from Broome, rested them at Glen Carrick and then sold them, their profit should be considerable. It would also be a means of stocking the station.

Arnold, already fifteen and home from his holidays, could join them. It would be a family affair. Jack would be head drover, Daisy and Arnold would be the tailers, responsible for the stragglers of the herd.

Jack began to organize the outfit. He bought four fine draught-horses, thirty-six riding horses and a provision dray. He hired a cook and eight drovers. Daisy purchased an English pig-skin saddle, three pairs of wallaby-skin shoes, three habits and a felt hat, three pairs of riding gloves and "plenty of fly veiling". Her hold-all was placed beside the humpies on the dray.

They set out, after the summer rains were finished, in April of the year 1902.

CHAPTER THIRTEEN

The natural nomad [is] the man who all at once feels that he must abandon home and friends and wander somewhere, anywhere away from the interminable sameness of houses and streets and people.
—Daisy Bates, 1912.

Overland with Cattle

"There is in Perth," the *West Australian* reported, "a cultured, quiet and somewhat frail looking lady who has just completed one of the most arduous trips that any lady has ever undertaken and has established what must be almost a record in the endurance of the 'weaker' sex. This lady is Mrs Bates, the owner of the Ethel Creek station, who, in order to gain a thorough experience of the most arduous part of station life, decided to buy her cattle herself at Roebuck station and travel them down to her homestead.

"When talking to her, as one of our representatives had the pleasure of doing, one would hardly credit that a lady of Mrs Bates's physique could have undertaken such a journey. Mrs Bates computes that during the period of six months which the trip occupied, she travelled over 3,000 miles on horseback."

The *Year Book* was more explicit. "On the 23rd April, 1902 Mrs Bates started on horseback for her long ride of between six and seven hundred miles from Roebuck Plains, eighteen miles beyond Broome, with 770 head of cattle, their destination being Peak Hill on the Murchison.

"Her object in travelling personally with her cattle was to test the capacity of the wells on the Kimberley-Murchison stock route, for watering a large mob, the mob which she accompanied being the largest ever travelled down in one lot from Kimberley."

Two different reasons, both valid, though neither exact, for an expedition that was to break more than one record in droving terms. The £1,000 earned from it, was, in Daisy's opinion, no concern of the public. Nor were the two hundred head of cattle destined for Glen Carrick and lost en route. This failure was a source of bitterness against Jack and accounted for the astonishing fact that, even then, there was no mention of him.

Her complaints to her Perth friends testify to his presence. To them he was held responsible for aspects of the journey which as a whole she described as "gruesome". Years later she was to declare that the memory of it had never left her.

Certainly it marked the end of her attempt at domesticity. Until 1912, when they were finally separated, Daisy pursued her own interests, meeting Jack, as she had done in the early days of their marriage, at appointed places for appointed intervals.

Proof of her reaction was her comparative silence on the subject. By now all her experiences were "copy", but to this journey, that provided her with material as valuable as it was fascinating, she did not do justice until more than twenty years later, when "3,000 Miles in a Side Saddle" appeared in the *Australasian.*

Part explanation is to be found in her notebooks.

"I do not think a romantic account could be worked up of a real droving trip," she wrote, "if the two principal actors, the he and she who make the romance, have been tailing behind a mob of cattle over dusty plains. When no part of the face is visible through the layer of dust that has gathered upon it, except two small slits where the eyes peep out, where the clothes and especially the hat assumes in a very short time a distinctly disreputable appearance, fatal not only to sentiment, but to that feeling of respect which we all know is the concomitant of a decent outward appearance; where the temper, however angelic it may have been at the start, is daily made sourer and more sour . . . where but one meal in twelve hours in forthcoming . . . But why enumerate the causes? It is sufficient to say that I saw myself after a long day's ride through the dusty curly wattle scrub, covered with dust and mud, coat and habit hanging in ribbons, face begrimed with dirt, added to by vexatious tears caused by the vagaries of a mob of the most malignant beings in creation, the so called mild eyed cow that artists so love to paint."

Of all the many trips she took during these years that introduced the twentieth century, there is no doubt that this was the toughest. Some of the drovers were as "inexperienced in the gentle art" as she was. Attempts at retrieving stockwhips from the branches of the trees about which they had wrapped themselves, led to the substitute of the "humble buggy whip". Not one of the team had thought to provide himself with that necessary adjunct to a droving expedition, a cattle-dog. The disused wells in the formidable Eighty Mile Beach led to a break-back of the cattle in search of water and lost them two hundred of their herd as well as the drovers who had to turn back in search. Needing more horses, Daisy had to purchase ten in an area where, thanks to the dreaded poison-weed that killed a horse although it left the cattle intact, they were at a premium. In her account for the Geographical Society she complained that five of them were outlaws, two unbroken and three so old that they should have been retired a decade before she bought them.

The loss of drovers, plus the demands of her job as "tailer" necessitated an eighteen-hour day. Cattle travel in a triangle, the base of which is broadened by the stragglers, usually cows with calves. Riding side-saddle, zig-zagging from one side to the other, Daisy was very often so exhausted that, as she said, "I threw myself flat on the ground as soon as I dismounted." But, "whenever I have horses or dogs we become great pals. However tired I was I used to groom my mount . . . using a grass root, always. The grooming was an additional feed."

Pardoo Creek, where the poison-weed grew, was dangerous to horses in more ways than one. They tended to contract a disease of the eye called pinkeye, in which a pinkish film spread over the eyeball and, if neglected, often led to a permanent injury to the eyesight. Daisy, always resourceful, chewed the leaves of an indigenous vine that contained a quantity of quinine, and blew them into her horse's eyes, keeping this up three or four times a day until the film disappeared.

At first all went smoothly. Rising in the misty dawn of the golden Australian autumn, they travelled slowly over pasture watered by rivers and dams. Not until they entered the Eighty Mile Beach where the grass was without sustenance and wells took the place of surface water, did she encounter the transformation of the placid Herefords into "creatures that surpassed the Irish pig in contrariness, the English fox in cunning and the Scotch sheep in stupidity". Thirst and mother love combined to bring about a perverse and persistent cunning against which Daisy had to pit all her resources of will-power.

"I should like to compare the mob of cows psychologically with a mob of my own sex," she wrote, "but the females of their species, human or animal, and perhaps insect too, are so alike in this respect that I did not venture to write it up!"

Time and time again the cattle tried to break back to remembered water, bellowing their disapproval of the rotten soil of the Eighty Mile Beach, "the dreariest and most desolate portion of Western Australia". The whole length of the area, said Daisy, was infested with short-tailed bloated rats, whose holes made traps for the animals' hooves. Divested of trees, since these had been cut down for firewood by previous drovers, the track was punctuated by wells rendered useless by neglect. The wood of the platforms gave way, the pumps refused to work. Sometimes the water itself was brackish. Seven out of the herd died of thirst and there was a stampede towards seawater when it became visible that was prevented from being fatal only because of the shallowness of the bay.

At Nampeet well, like a macabre signpost to desolation was a "small wooden slab on an upright piece of corrugated iron" recording the murder of a white man by the name of Horrigan, killed by his black companion for three sticks of tobacco. The murderer had been hunted down and hanged and the unpleasant history left as a warning for travellers. Daisy remembered it when, thrown from her horse, she found herself unable to remount because of the pain in her ankle. Alone and helpless, she was rescued by her proximity to an anthill from which she could hoist herself onto her saddle.

The beach was bad magic to the Aborigines and although they kept an eye on the outfit, they remained well out of sight.

"Every day about noon," Daisy wrote, "on our journey over the beach, we saw the smoke of a native fire in advance of us. After a little time this smoke would be answered by one further down. As soon as the second smoke was visible, the first one gradually died out. I concluded that the inhabitants were signalling our progress to their friends. More than once I rode eastward towards the smoke in an endeavour to come in touch with the natives but distances on the beach are woefully deceptive and a two hours' ride brought me seemingly no nearer to the pindan than when I started."

At La Grange Bay and later at Wallal, she did, however, have the chance to make the acquaintance of the black people and made note of two aberrant types, one a hermaphrodite, the other a consumptive of nearly six feet with a child's body and a man's limbs.

"I asked the kindly telegraph master if he would let me know when the man died," she told the Geographical Society, "so that his skeleton might be secured for anthropological purposes. I fear I gave the gentle master a shock, but the skeleton is really worth obtaining. The hermaphrodite looked too vigorous for me to broach a request for *her* bones. It was a woman's face, head and bust that I looked at!"

To one emaciated and isolated group they gave two of the day-old calves that had to be clubbed to death owing to their inability to travel. By next morning only bones remained and happy black faces and distended bellies witnessed to the gratitude of the recipients. Except for the station owners who offered them hospitality, they met few people, black or white, on the seemingly endless trek. There was the occasional prospector digging away in a deserted valley, content with his mug of tea, his damper and the rabbit he had shot the day before. And there was the apparition of the Jewish Pedlar.

Daisy, riding as usual at the rear of the herd, became aware of a disturbance that divided her "vicious herefords" into two groups as though a pencil line had been drawn in their midst.

"Drovers and horses stood like statues as Moses passed through the Red Sea," she wrote, "but the pedlar spoke only once.

" 'Who iss the lady mit the veil?' he asked."

Their faith in the stock route shaken by the fatalities among their cattle, they left it to follow along "Nat Cook's Nullagine Trail" along the banks of the Shaw River.

Cook was a pioneer among the "legion that was never listed" who had blazed a trail through the "weird gorges and desolate barren hills" to open up the auriferous and pastoral possibilities of the area. Following in his footsteps along the bed of the Shaw River, "often going on foot to ease our tired beasts over the heavy, heavy sand", with "tier upon tier, range upon range of seemingly never ending hills rising before our wearied eyes", Daisy remembered him with admiration. When cattle and men took their siesta in the noonday heat, Daisy, who could never sleep in daylight, wandered east and west as Cook had done, picking up geological and botanical specimens, climbing nearby hills in a vain attempt to see where the track led.

Although he was the first man to ride through the Nullagine Gorge, hers was the first dray. They camped, as Cook had done, beside a pool in the gorge, their only outlet the bed of the Shaw River. When they arrived, she had been shown the watermark, sixty feet high, where a flood had swept through the gorge and drowned mobs of Aborigines camped beside the water. That night rain fell. Confessing to fear for the first and only time, Daisy spent an anxious night, wondering if the river would claim a fresh batch of trusting victims. Fortunately it proved to be a local shower and they emerged next morning, the cattle rain-washed and refreshed.

Looking for additional supplies she rode into country that was "still in its period of complete rest".

"Not a sound greets the ear as you climb hill upon hill, seeking vainly for some variety in the landscape. No bird voices are raised . . . for birdlife would seem incongruous in this bit of ancient world. The air is so clear that . . . the little shacks of mining gear are plainly visible though reduced almost to toy size by the distance."

At Moolyella township, built entirely of hessian and "erected in just the spot the owner fancied, without regard to road or street", the miners "ransacked their supplies to give me what I wanted." The "bumboat" that had brought supplies from Marble Bar was trundling back, his cart empty.

"Why does he fly a red flag?" Daisy asked.

"Oh sure, that's so's we can see him a long way off, ma'am."

One adventurous Britisher had opened a store miles from anywhere although he could neither read nor write. His ledger was filled, not with the names of his customers but "by the very ancient system of 'picture' or 'totem' writing. One was represented by a hammer, another an axe. . . . Shin plasters—notes written on any sort of paper—were the only change given to prospector or traveller, the rubbishy paper usually succumbing to heat, wet, or carelessness an hour or two after its receipt."

Along the Coongan where "a prospector named McPhee found his albino aborigine", Daisy discovered caves in which were traces of pre-history. "In one of them a net made of spinifex fibre and some eight feet square had been stored, the net being used to catch emus or kangaroos or perhaps some luckless human being at a deep Coongan pool."

The final crisis came at the Battle Hill well, adjoining Roy Hill station, the home of Sam McKay. McKay had offered them a paddock in which they could rest the herd, now a thousand strong. As it was fenced, the drovers struck camp and prepared for a rest. But the cattle, maddened by thirst not yet quenched by the well, stampeded. Charging through the fences they made back the way they had come, leaving a mere four hundred or so that were too weak to join them. The tired drovers had to saddle their horses and go after them, leaving Daisy, Arnold and one drover to look after the remainder. As this meant that they must haul buckets of water from the well from morning to night, this could hardly be described as a rest.

Sam McKay, out of his gratitude to Jack and admiration for Daisy, did his best to help.

Daisy's attitude towards McKay was an odd blend of snobbishness and respect. "If Sam had called me by my Christian name," she wrote, "I would have killed him." He was, none the less, a pioneer who had grown rich through his own efforts and so deserving of her esteem. She was never in doubt of his admiration for her, and did not hesitate to put it to the test in 1910 when she asked for and received a thousand-pound donation towards the Cambridge expedition.

His presence did not appear to have relieved her of the arduous work of watering the thirsty cows. Daisy reported that she shared the night watches with Arnold, consoled by "the mysterious sounds of nocturnal birds and beasts, reptile and insects, who only waken when darkness enfolds the earth", to vanish with the ". . . grey dawning in which tree and bush, knoll and mound assume the shapes of long extinct mammoths."

In time the drovers returned with the herd. The last twenty miles of the trek was completed and Daisy, worn out by the strain, collapsed. Glen Carrick had only a bough shed to offer her but in it she remained until strength returned. Aged, she said by fifteen years, her hair grey, her body a stone lighter, she was prostrate, unable to eat or to sleep. When the time came for the return to Broome, she travelled the distance to Port Hedland on a stretcher. The boat trip from Port Hedland must have revived her, for, arriving in Broome, she rode out a further eighty miles to see if she could find traces of the missing two hundred head of cattle that had been left behind.

None were to be found and she returned with the dismal knowledge that Glen Carrick must remain unstocked. Haunted by the "white washed" faces of her Herefords, she sailed for Perth to plunge herself once more into journalism.

Gibney did what he could do to help and for a year or so she ran her own page on the *Record*. Her account of the dramatic opening of the Coolgardie Water Scheme appeared in *Cassier's Magazine*. Two more articles were commissioned by the *Journal of Agriculture*. She wrote a long and statistical account of the intended Trans-Australian Railway in conjunction with the Minister of Works at the time, C. H. Rason.

From the spate of material that poured from her pen, it appeared that she found her new métier comparatively easy. In fact she did not. To the end of her life writing was a hardship to her. The drafts of articles that she left behind show that she polished and repolished. Well aware of her tendency to exaggerate, she took trouble to research her subject and prided herself on the accuracy of her written word.

Journalism made independence possible but she never allowed it to take precedence over her studies of the Aboriginal population. Before the year was out she was back in the Peak Hill district, continuing her researches with Boudarie station as her headquarters. She learned to use a camera and published a series of postcards depicting the natives of the Nor'-west.

In parliamentary circles she was acknowledged, though not yet officially recognized, as an authority on Aboriginal matters. Her visit to the Nor'-west was made possible by a commission from the *Western Mail* to report on the mines of Peak Hill, Meekatharra, Nannine and other centres. She left on 8th December 1903. There was still five months to go before she was put on the Government payroll.

This time she took the train instead of a boat, happy as always to exchange the "mess of pottage" offered by city life for her "free nomadic birthright".

CHAPTER FOURTEEN

The pessimists, like the poor, we have always with us.—Daisy Bates, 1909.

The Office Flower

Independence restored Daisy's optimism. Her mining articles bubble with high spirits. The worst of her vicissitudes are treated as a joke, even the first thirty-six hours of her train journey north, in which she sat squeezed into a corner, wedged in between "seven women of bountiful proportions", her feet imprisoned by a surround consisting of her trunk, portmanteau and dress basket.

She was "disinterred" at Crowther, after which her conveyances alternated between bullock wagons and spring drays, both offering a similar degree of discomfort.

"When a bullock dray slumps into a rut you slump with it," she wrote, "and if your body is not comfortably wrapped round with adipose tissue, you very soon become black and blue and green all over like Sophie Squeer's Pa." The spring dray was carrying a load and by clutching at "a bag of flour, a leg of a sewing machine, a case of tinned food", she managed to keep her balance.

"Sitting and clutching, standing and springing, like Southey's Falls of Lodore on dry land", she was taken to whatever she could find in the way of lodging for the night and "only then did I have the chance to sort out my bones that had become inextricably mixed."

With "my natives" at Ooldea (*Photo*: A. G. Bolam)

More friends at Ooldea (*Photo*: A. G. Bolam)

Lubras at Ooldea (*Photo*: A. G. Bolam)

Playmates (*Photo*: A. G. Bolam)

The difficulties of transport were as nothing compared with her descent of the mines, the operation of which was still somewhat primitive.

A lighted candle clasped in hand, she descended two hundred and twenty feet down the Mount Pleasant mine lowered by rope in a bosun's chair, or swing seat.

"Midway down," she reported, "the seat began to tee-to-tum and, as I had not grasped the due proportion of force requisite for the kick which would keep me clear of one side without ricocheting against the other, I received a few knocks on the way down."

The Volunteer South was a mere hundred and twenty feet down, but at the bottom of the shaft she was confronted by passages two feet high which she must "slither up or slither down".

"For a few yards or so, one was compelled to realise the difficulty the serpent of old experienced when for his transgression he made his first journey under the new condition of things," she wrote. "Climbing and creeping, standing and slipping, writhing and wriggling", she followed her guide through a maze of underground tunnels, managing meanwhile to carry her notebook, fastened on her person.

After such "fine bodily mishandling" her optimism knew no bounds.

"Pessimism to my mind is largely a question of liver," she wrote. "Anyone who can boast of possessing a liver after such a mental and physical shaking up would certainly be a *lusus naturae*."

In a mood then, to confront negative doubt with proof positive she began her articles with an attack on pessimists "pastoral, agricultural or mining".

"There be residents and settlers in this Western land of ours who are addicted to frequent pessimistic twinges, pessimism being a malady that is infinitely more baneful in its effect than gout. A gouty man in the claws of his enemy can only . . . shy curses and shoes at those of his household who are loving enough or tactless enough to be within reach of these missiles, but a pessimist in the throes of his malady will do infinitely greater mischief."

To those whose cry it was that "the mines were played out" she offered statistics designed to boost confidence in the mining industry, including her own forecasts of undiscovered riches that were to be triumphantly vindicated in the 1960s.

Special mention was given of the haematite-bearing quartzites traversing the Nicholson and Weld Ranges. The native red ochre, or haematite mine, at Barloweeree Hill was estimated to yield twenty-six and a half millions tons of iron ore.

Daisy's interest in this particular mine had nothing whatsoever to do with its iron potential. Red ochre was Aboriginal "gold", in other words the chief article of native commerce in Australia, and Barloweeree Hill had been mined by its Aboriginal owners for countless centuries. Part of the Mindoola hunting ground, the mine was dug into the summit of a hill lined with iron pebbles and deserted of all life except for an occasional kangaroo. Legend had it that the scratching of kangaroos had exposed the red soil, so precious that it must be guarded by spirits at all times. Aboriginal miners went in fear of their life, especially of Meeril, a formidable ghost to be heard by campers as he ran down his hill, striking his club against his spear-thrower.

For the intruder who helped himself without permission; or the miner who forgot to walk backwards from the entrance, brushing away his tracks as he did so; for the unlucky one under whose feet a twig might snap, the vengeance of Meeril lay in wait, mortal and immediate. To approach the mine, it was necessary to camp overnight in the vicinity. Only then was the Aboriginal brave enough to enter it.

Ever since she had heard of it, Daisy had been anxious to visit Barloweeree Hill, but it was some years before the privilege was granted her. Even then, her escort, by name of Minyoondee, became tense as he approached the entrance.

"Me nothing, father nothing, grandfather nothing when *dooaree* [ochre] first got," he muttered by way of imprecation.

Daisy followed him through an entrance about fifty feet across and descended by a roomy tunnel to a depth of about eighty feet. From here excavations fanned out, dug over the centuries by a diorite hammer such as the ones used by miners of ancient Britain.

Small fires were lit to show them the way and Daisy, conscious of the honour being bestowed on her, followed Minyoondee through the maze of passages that grew smaller as they went on. Hair, hands and face were covered, the cream of her suit absorbed the oily red ochre. She emerged, to the satisfaction of her guide, as a woman in red. Her baptism was complete.

Her articles provided the official reason for her journeys, but she made the most of the opportunity to study the Aborigines of the district. In spite of the limited transport she covered an amazing distance, travelling by horse, by buggy or in the coach that ran from Nullagine to Port Hedland.

Her reports of these journeys belong to Australian history. Nannine, "one wide street along which most of the public buildings are situated", was adjoined by a sandy plain transformed in flood-time into a lagoon on which regattas were held by the townspeople, although the "season might be once in six years."

Meekatharra, possessed of only one well with which to water its population, responded to her request for a bath with the outraged comment: "Such a thing as a bath is not known on Meekatharra."

The mail-changes on the Nullagine to Port Hedland route were mere rest-houses built of posts and branches, but Coachman Bell personally cleared them of snakes and spiders before allowing his women passengers to enter. Daisy described him as "a master of makeshift, a squire of dames, a true horse lover and an excellent whip". He saw to their luggage and provided them with a bag bed each, together with a dipper of water and a basin that they had to share.

By the time she had returned to Perth, Daisy was a devotee of the new State that she called the "plain sister" of the Commonwealth.

"As one becomes more familiar with its gaunt gum tree, its apparently miserable attempts at water courses and rivers, its huge plains of sand and scrub, a certain harmony grows on one," she wrote. There was "the fascination of ugliness in the bush scenery of the West as there is in certain types of manhood".

Her feelings were reciprocated, especially after her letter to *The Times*, defending the pioneers of the North-west and published in May 1904.

An investigator by name of Malcolmson had been one of the main accusers of the white settlers. His charges of exploitation had been published by the London *Daily News* in 1902. On 8th April 1904 another letter appeared from him, this time in *The Times*, detailing the crimes of the pastoralists in relation to the blacks. Daisy, who believed, with reason, that she was now an expert on the subject, wrote in answer:

> During my four and half years residence in Western Australia, I have made the native question my special study, the district collectively termed the Nor'West occupying my most exclusive attention in connexion with the treatment of the aborigines.
>
> I have journeyed throughout the whole of the district from Beagle Bay to Perth, giving myself ample leisure to observe the mode of living of the natives in the various districts, of

> their treatment by their white masters on the various stations . . .
> For Mr Malcomson to describe indenturing as slavery and to assert that the aborigines are worse off than the American negro slaves is ridiculous . . . there is no hope of the station owners ever growing into plaster saints, yet the majority of them are humane and will not wantonly ill-treat their natives.

"No State in the Commonwealth," she declared roundly, "is doing more for its aboriginal population than this State is doing at the present time."

With her colours thus firmly attached to the mast of white settlement and her knowledge of the Aborigines thus underlined, the Government could safely welcome her as an authority.

Malcolm Fraser, the Registrar-General, had been nursing for some time an ambition to record the customs and dialects of the Aboriginal population. Influenced by his namesake John Fraser, editor of *An Australian Language*, who had reminded him four years earlier that it was "a pity your colony had done nothing towards a record of your aborigines", he had already made an attempt to collect all available material on the subject.

But the Registrar-General was a busy man. He needed someone to do the job for him—someone prepared to accept the pittance that was all he could squeeze out of his reluctant associates. Money was the last of Daisy's considerations. She applied for the job and was accepted. Her appointment began on 3rd May 1904. She was paid eight shillings a day, given access to Government source-books written by Grey, Moore, Salvado and others, and an office facing Cathedral Avenue. She reported for work each morning, read, noted and compiled, sent out forms to Government employees all over the State so that the local vocabularies might be filled in, wrote indefatigably to every anthropologist of note and to most of the anthropological institutions in the English-speaking world, and compiled a volume of eight hundred pages.

Fraser was impressed. He christened Daisy the "office flower", joked with her, argued with her, and wrote to the under-secretary to suggest that her employment—never on more than a temporary basis—be renewed.

Since she was giving a great deal more in terms of time and energy than her salary warranted, and since she was a recognized member of the "literati", he pointed out that her book might well put Western Australia in the forefront of achievement, ethnologically speaking.

Unfortunately for Daisy, this was not an argument that carried much weight. But Fraser was well thought of and his recommendation accepted. Daisy's period of office was extended.

By this time Daisy herself was becoming restless. Used by now to the freedom of bush life, she found her confinement within the four walls of her office difficult to endure.

"With the exception of the Chief," she wrote, "there was not a congenial soul whom I could rouse to anger or argument." Walking along the narrow balcony that linked the offices she would talk to the men in the windows she passed. "But oh, the groovositiness! I would return to the Chief and tell him what I thought of them all, asking him why he could not employ humans instead of kewpies and golliwogs and then he would 'add fuel' by telling me how highly they thought of the 'office flower'."

More serious was her dissatisfaction with her material.

The more she compiled, the more did she find contradictions in the works of the so called "authorities". Very little in the way of comparison proved to her that the dialects returned from post offices and police stations were far from reliable. By this time she was in regular correspondence with Andrew Lang, noted English anthropologist and former contributor to *Borderland.* An Australian correspondent was R. H. Mathews, author of many learned papers on ethnological subjects. Both warned her to avoid textbook theory and to concentrate on the facts. Mathews urged her to "get out among the blacks herself". So enthusiastic was he that he offered to come himself for the price of his fare from Parramatta to help her.

Luck was on her side. A Labour Government came into power and, she wrote, "room had to be made for Labour parasites male and female."

Daisy's office was requisitioned. This gave her the chance she needed to put to Fraser an unorthodox idea. At the Maamba Aboriginal reserve in Cannington at the foot of the Darling Ranges were many old Aborigines who were the last of their different groups. If the Government would give her permission she would pitch her tent among them and take down information from them at first hand. This way she could be sure of her facts, and record dialects that would die out with the natives on the reserve. She would report regularly to the office and continue to work for her eight shillings a day.

Reaction to the idea can be imagined. In 1905 it was not considered suitable for a lady to camp alone in a tent, let alone among a reserve full of derelict and often drunken Aborigines.

That she won her point is proof that Fraser, at least, recognized the value of what she was doing.

Daisy, well aware that it was a "unique concession" that had been granted her, wasted no time. On a winter's day of July 1905, she set out with a police escort for Cannington. The men remained long enough to choose her site and pitch her tent for her. When they had seen her safely settled in they left her, a lone white woman, her tent a hundred yards away from the Government huts of her black neighbours.

Impressed by the power of this white woman who could dismiss from her presence the policemen of whom they were so much afraid, the black people watched proceedings from a discreet distance.

Daisy stood at the edge of her breakwind and smiled at them. Little by little they came closer. She did nothing to encourage or discourage them. Waiting patiently for her moment, she invited them to visit her.

Then, speaking in the dialect of the Bibbulmuns, she asked them if they would care to join her for a cup of tea.

CHAPTER FIFTEEN

The real bush poetry cannot be interpreted by English poets, but by a true Australian steeped in the charm of it. . . . His poems will issue like Chaucer's from the inborn joyousness that is the heritage of all who are born in this land of sunshine.—Daisy Bates.

A Tent at Maamba

Her new home was surprisingly comfortable. Commissioned from "Adams the tentmaker", her tent was fourteen feet in diameter, supported by a central pole of Oregon pine, with flaps that opened out at back and front. Protected by a lattice work of tea-trees and mallee bushes that she called her "breakwind", the interior had been designed with the economy of experience.

"Along one side of the tent are my hold-all and tucker box and some odd aluminium plates and sundries; under my table, placed across the open 'back door' and covered by study books, tea cups and looking glass, is my portmanteau, which, with the hold-all, carries all the wardrobe I require for a year. The other side is occupied with my Coolgardie stretcher, at the foot of which are the kerosene supply and medicine chest for the natives."

As a carpet, blackboy tops were strewn over the ground and covered by bagging as a protection against snakes. Around her table were pockets in which she put "everything hangable".

Her "kitchen" was outside in the breakwind. Here was her fireplace, an upturned case to serve as table, and inside it, her gridiron and pans. Nails hammered into the trunk of a tree were used to hang tea-towels, washing-up dish and other odds and ends. She liked to write outside and, by placing a packing case against the trunk of a tree, she was provided with a chair. Not, perhaps, the most comfortable of supports, but then, "I wasn't allowed to lean back when I was little and so I do not miss an easy chair."

Her routine was spartan. As six hours sleep was all she ever needed, it usually began before the dawn. In her own account, written for the *Western Mail*, she leaves a vivid picture of the early morning:

"The sun has another half hour before he shows his clear cold face over the horizon. . . . A keen strong wind blows, making sweet music amongst the karugu trees. Out into the bright cool air I come from my tent and probe the ashes of my open fireplace in the hope that some embers have remained alight. I am usually rewarded as I cover my big fire with soft white ash as I have often seen my compatriots cover theirs with turf ash in Ireland."

Careful to readjust her stones to leeward of the morning wind, she set the billy to boil.

Breakfast consisted of a boiled egg, bacon grilled on the gridiron, bread and butter and the inevitable tea. It was, in fact, the most substantial of her meals, partly because of her limitations as a cook and partly because "like Toddie I don't want to be bothered with lots of things."

Much more important to her was the aesthetic beauty of her surroundings. As she ate, she watched the rising of the sun transform her "white canvas wall . . . into the most exquisite frescoed patterning, far surpassing the finest of Grinling Gibbons' handiwork".

No matter how busy her day, these early mornings were peaceful, given to contemplation of "the slow sweet living ways of old time". The bush was an endless fascination. Although commenting that "the adjectives of scenic description are exhausted and moreover the coinage has been too long debased," her notebooks are scattered with her attempts to put down what she saw. Descriptions such as "the elfin fabrics of iridescent gossamer in beaded spider webs of morning", are interwoven with observations about "the marvellous bird the mallee fowl who . . . never knows his parents but can fly as soon as he is hatched"; or about the "vivid wattle that permits the clinging embrace of the clematis and so courts its own undoing, for here and there I notice a dead tree hugged round and round by the soft and subtle tendrils of the vine."

Everywhere she saw evidence of an implacable Nature that "is ever making and breaking with infinitely slow process. She fits her verdure to the soil, her trees to their surroundings, her plants to their environment and no sooner has she accomplished this work than she proceeds to disintegrate [it]."

The breaking up of the native groups she saw as part of this inexorable process. Her certainty of their eventual extinction provided the incentive for the enormous effort she put into the next few years. It was also her reason for risking the disapproval of the Government, believing that it was necessary to give all that she could of care and comfort in order to "mitigate the guilt of one's race", as she put it.

Her neighbours on the reserve were, in the main, a pathetic group. She called them "the remnants of the once mighty Bibbulmuns", reduced by age and frailty to dependence on the white man's bounty.

Daisy behaved with politeness in their midst, never crossing the dividing hundred yards unless invited; because, she said, "you must not go indiscriminately into a native camp if the friendship of the occupants is valued." They returned courtesy for courtesy and answered her questions. Her informants were old men and women, often the last of their groups. One was Fanny Balbuk, and the other, Jubytch, a native trooper and last of the Guildford line.

Stead's influence was beginning to show. Daisy took down all that they told her, used the material for her book and turned their personal histories into stories for the newspapers, "Fanny Balbuk-Yooreel" and "Policeman Jubytch" being two of the more successful.

Balbuk, an aggressive character, remained noisily resentful of her loss of property and prestige and turned towards the white man's drink for compensation. Jubytch, on the other hand, kept his dignity to the end, retaining the beliefs that had fortified the community into which he had been born. Nor did he compete with his friends Monnop and Dool for the favours of Ngilgee, the "rich widow" of the camp.

Ngilgee, one-time nurse of John Forrest, was an old friend of Daisy's. She had been a domestic at the Fairbairn household and was valued as a gossip who entertained the family with the peccadilloes of Perth society. On the Maamba reserve she had been given a Government hut complete with a double bed which she shared, successively or at once, with her "thirty-two dogs, seven goats, a dozen fowls, four aboriginal suitors and one half caste aspirant".

Brought up in a white family, she had been married at an early age to a half-caste called Whitey Brown George and found herself deserted by him for another of his colour.

For Daisy, Ngilgee was proof of the adage that, where a man was concerned, women, black or white, were sisters under the skin. From then on, she wrote, Ngilgee became a wanderer, choosing her own "acting husbands" as she called them. These she got rid of when the time came by the effective method of emptying a bucket of water over their heads. An Aboriginal beauty, she was possessed of a "shapely form, beautiful teeth and eyes, and skin smooth as burnished bronze". Though already sixty years old when Daisy moved into the reserve, she was the source of rivalry among the four elderly "bachelors" who sought for her attentions.

One morning Daisy saw one of these emerging from Ngilgee's hut to the accompaniment of the contents of a bucket and asked what the trouble was. Ngilgee, whose English was perfect, confided in her that, a few months beforehand, she had taken unto herself a new lover, young enough to be her grandson, with whom she had fallen in love. Unknown to her, the jealous four had threatened him with their magic unless he left the camp and Ngilgee woke up one morning to find him gone. She tried in vain to "sing him back". When this didn't work she had consoled herself with old Baabur, one of her suitors.

It was no good. Ngilgee's heart remained with her young lover and old Baabur had been given his marching orders.

Through Ngilgee, Daisy learnt an important lesson in native manners.

One day she called at her tent with a present of a somewhat soggy damper. Daisy thanked her and noticed that Ngilgee's departure was a trifle crestfallen.

Next day she arrived with a second damper. This time she lingered. "Wangallin", as Daisy was called, put down her pen and paper, prepared for the inevitable.

"Wangallin learning all our customs now?" Ngilgee asked conversationally.

"Coming along, Ngilgee."

"Not know all customs yet. When we give a present we get one back."

Daisy registered this. She went on talking for a minute or two longer and then said, as though the idea had just occurred to her:

"Would you like a tin of fish, Ngilgee?"

"Thank you Wangallin," Ngilgee answered, with polished courtesy. "You are kind."

The lesson learned, Daisy's larder, never plentiful, became seriously threatened. Fortunately she found that her neighbours would gladly exchange fresh native fruits for the tinned variety, and that illustrated magazines were much in demand. This was just as well because, even if camp life solved her accommodation problems, eight shillings a day did not go far. By now the papers accepted everything she sent them, but for two articles in the *West Australian* she received only £10. 10s. and for one of six columns in length in the *Western Mail* she received £6, reasonable recompense for the period but inadequate for her needs.

Medicines were a constant expense. Like her first teacher, Father Nicholas, she bound up cuts and sores while asking questions. Fortunately she needed only the simplest of remedies, bandages, antiseptics, fruit salts, olive oil; brandy in emergencies. Her patients responded to psychological rather than medical cures. Dominated as they were by their belief in the supernatural, a *mobburn* or magic doctor could cure them or kill them. Daisy graduated to their ranks after she came into possession of her *nowinning*, or magic stick.

Her explanation for it was that she had been called to the bedside of a dying *mobburn* doctor who had placed his stick between his body and hers and died after pronouncing her the official recipient of his *mobburn*. The stick, four inches long and carved with the figure of a woman, became her "passport". The southern natives believed that there was fire in it. When she left the camp for Perth, she would be told on her return that a light had shone all night from her tent from the *nowinning*. While she possessed it, no native would come near her without permission. She could go anywhere, ask anything. If there was trouble she had only to produce it.

A visit to the Ashburton district added to her reputation as a "sorceress".

Although her headquarters remained for two years at the Maamba reserve, she spent some time visiting the different camps. In the North-west, a signal honour was conferred on her. She was included as a member of the "rain totem". According to traditional belief, Aboriginal ancestry could be traced back to the natural world that surrounded them. A dreamtime ancestor might have been a kangaroo, an emu, a tree, or in this case, rain. Whichever it was, it became the totem of its group. Totem boards were sacred. Ceremonies were held to encourage increase. When Daisy was made a member of the rain totem, she went with the group carrying a wooden bowl of water to the top of a nearby hill. Arrived at the crown, one chosen amongst them filled his mouth from the bowl and squirted himself and his companions. During this rite a "rain song" was sung which, she said, was both plaintive and catchy. One day she was heard "thoughtlessly singing the rain song" and that same night a cloudburst descended on the camp.

"After that," she told reporter Gwen Sargent White, "my reputation was established for ever."

She could never resist making a good story out of her experiences, but in fact she was less contemptuous of Aboriginal magic than she had been of Stead's experiments in spiritualism. Like Grant Watson, she saw evidence of its power. Seldom if ever did she rely on it for protection, for the reason that she never felt the need for any.

"Not one native felt like a stranger to me," she explained. "I seem to have known them ages ago. They are my kin. My poor relations, if you like."

At the Katanning camp, at which she was a regular visitor, her confidence was tested.

One twilight evening, seated beside her fire dreaming dreams of northern gloamings in which she wandered through English rose gardens with her former lover Carrick Hoare, she became aware of a silence that had settled over the camp. Looking up, she saw a group of figures in full war array, watching her. Moving without sound, as only Aborigines can, they had crept close. At the same time she noticed that all the campfires had been extinguished, a bad sign, as fire is a token of welcome.

It was evident that this was no friendly visit. Daisy remained where she was, returning their interest. After a moment she called out to them:

"I don't know who you are, but will you come and have tucker with me?"

They accepted her offer, though with some caution, sitting on the ground beside her fire, spears ready in case of emergency. Daisy ignored the spears, set the women to making damper for them all and gave them supper. Turning their backs on each other, as was camp etiquette, they devoured the damper and drank the tea. She said they "spent a pleasant evening together, chatting like friends." Next morning they were gone. Danger had been averted.

Although she was provided with a revolver as part of her equipment, she told Hurst that she never used it except to kill a rabbit and then "only when I was sure of hitting my target".

The one time when she produced it for disciplinary purposes was for the benefit of white and not black offenders.

For some reason her account of this episode was never published and remains, as she wrote it, in her notebooks:

> One night after a full day I was getting ready for my night's rest. I heard some drunken voices and, putting on my kimono and slippers, took my revolver and went out.
>
> Three drunken men with a sugar bag full of bottles of drink were calling for black gins.
>
> I went over to them and said: "Get up at once and go before me."
>
> The lantern showed my revolver. They got up, staggering, and I called out in native dialect:
>
> "Go into town, one of you, and tell Sergeant Perkins I will guard these bad men and wait for you."

Hoping that she would not have to walk into Katanning in kimono and slippers, she began to march them in the direction of the town. In due course Kaka, the Aboriginal who had done as she asked, appeared out of the darkness with the sergeant.

"The Sergeant touched his cap and went off with the men. Not a word was spoken by him or by me."

Next morning was Sunday and Daisy, who was in the habit of walking to church when she was near a town, passed unrecognized as the sergeant headed the three men out of Katanning.

"I rewarded Kaka with a new pair of trousers," she noted. "They do so hate the dark."

It was while she was at Katanning that she dealt, single-handed, with an outbreak of measles. This arduous and at times distressing experience she transformed into an amusing article which was published first in the *West Australian* in November 1907, and later in *Science of Man*.

Her first invalid was Notuman, an elderly "sister" "who embodied in her bulky form all the cunning and devilment of her race . . . whether it hailed, rained, or the sun shone, I being the 'younger sister' was at her beck and call at all hours." After her came Daddel, a thirteen-year-old boy, Togur his friend, and so on from one to the other as the disease spread through the camp. The Katanning doctor broke the sad news to her that there was no hospital space and recommended "gruel, milk, soup, tea, or any other liquid foods for a few days".

"To begin with I can't cook," Daisy wrote, "cooking and washing having been left out of my itinerary. I had never made gruel and the only soup I could manage was Liebig's extract of Bovril. I had, however, either heard or read somewhere that properly made gruel took four hours in the making. I wish I could put all the native magic I possess into the fiend who made that statement! My fire was an open one, and the winter winds of Katanning are not faithful two minutes, running to any one point of the compass. I sat down by the fire on a kerosene case to make my first billycan of gruel. . . . The wind shifted suddenly and the fire caught a handful of my hair and singed it. I changed my seat but the wind changed too, and blew smoke and flames against my scorching face. I stirred the gruel steadily, discarded the kerosene case and walked round the fire and billycan to the forty-eight points of the compass with which the wind was flirting that dreadful afternoon. I had started gruel making at 2 p.m. and at 6 exactly I took it off the fire. By this time I had recited FitzGerald's *Omar* at least six times . . . it wasn't the words of the poem that brought relief but the way they could be uttered."

Daddel had no sooner recovered than his mother and seven brothers and sisters caught the infection. Living in a *mia* (hut) divided into two, the entire family was housed in a space of not more than five feet in diameter.

"They lay with their heads within the mia, their feet towards the open fireplace between the two huts. To reach one I had to lean over the others, huddled up at either side . . . like peas in a rounded pod. What with the odour, the smoke, and the bodily contortions necessary to reach each patient and spoon feed him or her, it became a matter of constant appeal to emulate Mark Tapley and to be jolly and cheerful during the process."

All but one of her patients got better and her account ends with a paean of approval for the cheerfulness that was her birthright.

"Oh! I do think cheerfulness more than cleanliness is next to godliness and down in that miserable camp where not a single convenience helped to lighten the troubles of sickness for those poor natives, I often thanked Heaven for the light Irish heart I was born with, which went all the way with me and helped them to bear their troubles more easily."

The years 1904-11 were the "Indian summer of her contentment". For the first and last time, life offered itself on her terms. As a representative of the Government she was accorded her place in the ranks of the ethnologists; as a writer she was recognized as "the authority" on the Aborigines. After one of her many lectures she was reported as "possessing the infinite capacity for detail, which, according to a well known philosopher, is the stuff of which genius is composed".

Even her domestic problems appeared to have moderated. Although neither Jack nor Arnold could have seen a great deal of her during these much-occupied years, her Perth friends remember that Jack used to come down to join her at Bunbury for the summer months. Her letters show that her "talkative son" Arnold was sometimes with her in camp.

Amongst her correspondence from this time is an invitation for Arnold and herself to dine at Government House, a visit followed by one from the Governor to her camp. This she regarded, with some justification, as a triumph of recognition for her work. Letters from Sir Frederick and Lady Bedford show that they were both her staunch supporters, believing, as Sir Gerald Strickland, Bedford's successor, believed, that her researches were not only of present worth but would be "of increasing value to succeeding generations".

On the evidence of the press reports that she so carefully preserved, it would be fair to say that during her term of office Daisy did more than any one individual to interpret black to white in the West. Her lectures were greatly in demand, her subject, invariably, one aspect of Aboriginal life chosen to suit her audience. She spoke on Totemism for the Training College at Claremont, and again for the Geographical Society. She lectured on "Our Aborigines" at each of the country centres she visited, for Perth's Historical Society and to the women's political clubs.

According to the *West Australian*, "this well known lady, authority on the manner and customs of our natives . . . is good company for hours on end." Her talks were illustrated by lantern slides and phonograph records; and her audiences, stirred out of their apathy by her ability to project her own enthusiasm, were stimulated and sometimes even conscience-stricken.

Her lecture at the Karrakatta Club for the benefit of Lord Northcote, retiring Governor-General, was of some significance, as he took her text with him to answer the questions still being asked in London on the subject of exploitation.

Her arguments in defence of the white settlers, and the controversy that resulted from them, overshadowed two important items. One was a suggestion from her friend, J. G. Meares, ignored at the time, but later adopted by the Government, that a reserve be established for the use of the natives of the North-west. Meares presented the eminently practical scheme, also ignored, that this be stocked by white settlers to prevent the spearing of their cattle that was the current retaliation tactic on the part of the myalls.

The other was an astonishing statement from Daisy, that the alternative to the extinction of the black race was inter-marriage with the whites. It was not an alternative of which she herself approved but she had the courage to present it and was criticized strongly for having done so.

In 1909 she was given the official backing of the Australian Natives Association and asked to lecture at the Perth Town Hall with the Governor in the chair. Her doings had a habit of finding their way into the columns of the three main Perth newspapers. After this, her starring appearance, their applause reached new heights.

"What Howitt, Spencer and Gillen have been to the vanishing races of Eastern Australia, Mrs Bates has been to the natives of this State," wrote the *West Australian*.

The *Western Mail* gave her a "profile" in which her achievements, by now considerable, were itemized: she was a "Fellow of the Anthropological Society of Australasia", an "Honorary Correspondent of the Royal Anthropological Institute of Great Britain and Ireland", a "Member of the Royal Geographical Society of Melbourne". Her paper on "The Diseases of Native Women" had been read by the Medical Association of Glasgow, another paper on southern dialects had been published by the *Revue Ethnologique*, Paris. The list occupied half a column.

By the time the Perth Carnival was planned for the holiday fortnight linking 1909 with 1910, Daisy was elected "by unanimous consent" as the responsible member on the Aboriginal committee. To her was assigned the difficult job of "mustering in the highways and byways of the bush those aborigines who are still familiar with the use of native spear and boomerang".

She had to produce eighteen members of tribes from the North-west and twenty-two from the South, to take place in a corroboree at Subiaco, to compete in sporting events, and to parade in full war paint. She had to arrange for their transport, house them on the reserve, guard their train tickets, keep them from the liquor they loved to drink, and shepherd them from camp to Carnival and from Carnival to camp, walking ahead of them, red umbrella pointing the way.

To manage at all demanded her resources of patience and guile,

New arrivals at Ooldea from the Musgrave Ranges (*Photo*: A. G. Bolam)

The corroboree seen by the Prince of Wales, 12th July 1920 (*Photo*: A. G. Bolam)

Native women decorated for the Prince's visit (*Photo*: A. G. Bolam)

Native women and children, Ooldea, 1922 (*Photo*: A. G. Bolam)

chiefly because of the rivalry between north and south. This needed only a spark to flame into a fight.

If they threatened each other with magic, Daisy produced her *mobburn* stick. If they accused each other of theft, she herself investigated the charge. In spite of all her efforts alcohol invaded her territory. As a result, north challenged south to a game of *Owt*, a variety of hockey that, she wrote, had been in existence long before the advent of the whites and closely resembled the Irish hurley.

Owt would have provided the excuse for the fight that Daisy knew had peen planned. To prevent it she joined in the game, and so kept the peace.

Her explanation for her influence was their universal acceptance of her place in their kinship systems. She was "mother", "sister", "aunt", "grandmother", sometimes even "wife".

"I worked this for all it was worth," she explained. "The ugliest and liveliest young man was my 'son'. Another calmly told some members of the Committee that I was his *yakkanjee*, 'all-the-same-wife'."

As excited as children, they threw themselves into the carnival atmosphere. Three days it took them to decorate their bodies. Nookar, a young athlete, reported as jumping "a record height of five feet six inches", brought his curling tongs with him. Each day he curled two long love-locks that fell on either side of his forehead.

Like everything else for which she was responsible in these charmed years, her Aboriginal display was the success of the Carnival. The press even complained of the crowding that prevented the corroborees from being properly seen.

January 5th of 1910 was their day of departure. Daisy put her charges onto their respective trains. Their pockets jingled with the money she had raised for them, her white gloves were black with the handshakes of forty none-too-clean hands. Perth housewives, reading in their press about this essentially feminine ". . . womanly Mrs Bates, fashionably coiffured and dressed", speculated on the miracle she had achieved.

"I often heard remarks passed upon the female shepherd," Daisy wrote. " 'I saw her painting their bodies,' said one shocked woman. 'She will even wash them,' said another. 'I'm told she's a great big stout woman. They'll do anything in the world for her they're so frightened of her,' said another. . . .

"She did not know that the 'pennorth-of-God-help-us-on-abroomstick' standing beside her was the great female so erroneously described."

Questions that she was to be asked for the rest of her life began to be put to her. Why? What do you see in them? How can you, a lady, live among them?

The answers she gave have already been given. The Aborigines were law-abiding, light-hearted; they had good manners; they did not offend her sensibilities; they had that priceless asset, a sense of humour; of this she offered a new illustration:

"The spectacle of a small woman rushing about with an infinitesimal bough, threatening to kill them all if they didn't at once prepare themselves, invariably put them into a good humour!"

Summed up, she said, it was simply "the real mutual liking and respect my natives and I have for each other".

CHAPTER SIXTEEN

There is no doubt that you have done more for ethnology in Western Australia than anyone who has preceded you and I am sure you will do a lot more if you are only properly supported by the Government.—R. H. Mathews to Daisy Bates, 1906.

The Virus of Research

It was an answer, but not an explanation.

The reason for her decision to live among the Aborigines and the motivating force of Daisy's actions for years to come was the "virus of research" with which, she told Professor J. A. FitzHershe had been bitten in Broome and later in Perth, and which transformed her work into a "labour of love".

In spite of eye-strain, personal discomfort, and the disapproval of many of her friends, she could still write in 1910 that "I have given up all my social life to my work and am as happy as larry over the 'sacrifice'."

The book, planned by Fraser as *A Short Authentic Historical Record of the Habits, Customs and Language of the Aboriginal Natives of this State*, mushroomed into a project as lengthy as its title. It was to attract the interest of anthropologists of both hemispheres; to provide the incentive for an ethnological expedition planned by Oxford and carried out by Cambridge University, and to result in the Government's offer to send Daisy Bates to England for the purpose of publication.

Although this did not, in fact, eventuate, the offer represented a major victory. Throughout the six years that it took to compile and arrange her data, the official attitude was one of grudging scepticism that grumbled through the files under her name.

To those civil servants who were neither especially academic nor especially interested in her subject, Daisy's work appeared to be as ephemeral as a house of cards, no sooner built than blown away. Twice she completed a bulky manuscript and twice asked permission to begin again from the beginning.

Useless for Fraser to explain that the original project had been amateurish in conception and that "only the energy and zeal of Mrs Bates, for whom nothing has been too much trouble", had been able to place the investigation on a satisfactory footing. The under-secretary demanded constant and detailed reports from Daisy herself, involving foolscap pages of explanation for the contradictions of her source material and the failure of the vocabularies that she had dismissed as "so much waste paper, differing according to the taste and fancy of the speller, as Sammy Weller said".

Fraser's sensible suggestion that her book come under the jurisdiction of Prinsep, Protector of Aborigines, was ignored. His request, in 1907, that her salary be raised to the munificent sum of 10s. per day, was dismissed with the irritable comment that "the work should have been completed long since, or abandoned."

Fortunately for Daisy, her Chief continued to act as a buffer between the suspicions of his colleagues and the enthusiasm of his "office flower". It could not always have been an enviable position. Daisy, unused to knuckling under to authority, was more than inclined to argue the point. "We used to have such words!" she admitted to Hurst.

As the book had been Fraser's idea in the first place, he was well aware of its value. More important, he understood the difficulties with which she was confronted.

These were formidable. The early records, careful and painstaking though they were, had to a certain extent been defeated by the complexities of the subject. R. H. Mathews went so far as to assert that "It would be fortunate if Grey, Salvado and others had never written a word about the blacks", so misleading were their findings. With no reliable precedent to follow, Daisy had, therefore, to "break new ground". Rising, as always, to a challenge, she tackled the job with enthusiasm that was not matched, as she well knew, by method. She could and did make sure that the information she received came verbatim from the natives, but the problem remained of putting her data into correct anthropological order. With the humility that characterized her attitude at this stage of the work, she decided that all she could do was to "sit down like a native and write down all she was told", leaving it to the experts to revise the results.

In order to have a plan upon which to work, she divided her material into eleven headings, ranging from the controversial subject of the origin of the Aboriginal race, to its social organization. These would comprise the sections of her book, under such titles as Totemism, Initiation Ceremonies, Legends, and so on.

At the same time she wrote to fellow enthusiasts and anthropological institutions outlining her project and asking for help.

The response she received was impressive, especially from R. H. Mathews. Hampered by his job as land surveyor that kept him in New South Wales, he had been forced to obtain his information from the West by means of correspondence. Well aware that this was unsatisfactory, he encouraged Daisy to get out into the field, warning her of the "hell of a job" she was tackling.

Definite in his views, he was equally blunt in expressing them. She was to "beware of theories and to investigate without prejudice"; to write down all that she was told "no matter how stupid it might appear"; to be "continually on the watch for new puzzles", very often caused by the Aborigines themselves. Contact with the whites, he explained, had made them conscious that their ideas could be held up to ridicule. As a result, they tended to give the answer they believed the questioner expected.

Daisy took his strictures in good part. For the first two years she was much influenced by him and wrote to confess that, less than twelve months after she had moved, on his advice, into the reserve, she was faced with alterations to her paper, read to the Royal Geographical Society in November of 1905.

Mathews, amused, answered that he had "many times thought of advising you to say nothing at all for a year or two. I was afraid it would discourage you. I thought you would some day say, if it hadn't been for that wooden headed Mathews, you would soon be famous."

At first his letters showed a certain deference to her femininity, but it was not long before he was discussing every aspect of their subject with the candour of a colleague.

"I have been wishing to ask your permission to refer to sexual mutilations," he wrote, "but on account of your being a woman I was hampered by our rules of false modesty."

Assuring her that "a blackfellow has none of our nonsense and would talk about his genitals with the same freedom as he would talk about an ear, a foot, or a finger," he asked if she could throw any light on the origin of the rite of sub-incision.

"One of my correspondents, at my request, has asked a native to let him see the penis during erection and he says the glans spread out on account of being split . . . the same correspondent gathered from a conversation with a black woman that the organ when spread out was more gratifying to the female."

He went on to ask if she could verify Roth's description of copulation in which "the women lies with her back and shoulders on the ground, the man kneels down and the woman throws her legs around his loins." And, while on the subject, to find out all she could about such customs as the drinking of semen.

His letter ended with the somewhat nervous reassurance that "these things may seem horrible to us, but they form part of a blackfellow's daily life and must be reported by someone. You need have no hesitation in broaching the subject to any black man or woman. Don't look horrified and take it all as a matter of course."

Whether or not Daisy took his letter as a matter of course is open to conjecture. She confined herself to remarking that "Mr Mathews has a lot to learn in the refinements of letter writing." Aware of the compliment of his frankness that promoted her from the ranks of Victorian womanhood to the status of scientist, she admitted to "thoroughly enjoying her correspondence with him".

This continued until 1907 when doubts about him filtered through from other anthropologists.

He was accused of plagiarism and for Daisy, whose battle for recognition had been hardly fought, this was a serious charge. Although he wrote hopefully that he would "always be glad to hear from her", she answered no more of his letters, and the correspondence ended.

It was not a charge that could be levelled against the second of her early correspondents.

The Reverend John Mathew, ethnologist, philologist and author of *Eaglehawk and Crow*, proved to be as generous as a friend as he was enthusiastic as a colleague.

Although he himself was later to admit to certain misconceptions in his book, written a decade earlier, to Daisy it was "the work of a cultured man and a deep and clear thinker". She recommended it to her overseas correspondents and used it as a model for the grammar she was preparing for publication with her vocabularies.

Fraser, comprising a diary of her activities, are exhausting even to read, as the following extract shows:

> August 21st. Left Coolgardie 8.45 a.m.
> „ 22nd. Arrived Norseman at noon. Went immediately to native camp outside the township. Worked until dark.
> „ 23rd. Sunday. Went to native camp at 9 a.m. Obtained the Norseman dialect.

At Albany she "walked a mile there and back to the native camp". At Esperance "the postmaster most kindly placed a horse at my disposal and the other residents offered the use of their traps" but she had "walked the distance to Israelite Bay as it is but three miles distant."

Only once did she step off her treadmill and that was to return to Perth to say goodbye to Arnold. Now a qualified engineer, he was planning to leave on 14th November to take up a post in the Eastern States.

Daisy sent in for her return ticket to Perth "since this is the first time my son has left me and I am very anxious to see him and to attend to his personal belongings."

The refusal of her request appears as yet another proof of the parsimony of her Department. A degree of scepticism might, however, be forgiven towards this belated show of maternalism on the part of a mother who had voluntarily absented herself from her son for the previous six months.

In all she was away for seven months, during which time she covered the astonishing distance of 5,400 miles, visited seventy towns and obtained thirty-four new dialects.

She followed these statistics with the announcement that, once again, she must rewrite her book. The chance to find out for herself, she said, had shown her "the variations in dialects and the many changes occurring in the marriage laws and forms of descent". The information she had gathered was invaluable, as in many cases she had interviewed the one remaining member of an otherwise extinct group, but almost total revision was now necessary.

Surprisingly enough these disquieting tidings were greeted almost without protest. Her plea that "I have spared no pains, demurred at no inconvenience during my travels to gain absolutely reliable information", had been backed up by Fraser who added that her book should now "set Western Australia well ahead of the other States in ethnological terms".

Daisy was accordingly allotted a further sum of £200 but with the firm proviso that it was to cover the remainder of the time needed for completing her book.

Full cooperation was now given her and she wrote to Mathew that she had been offered the services of the Lands Department "to prepare a map of the localities where certain marriage divisions obtain and where paternal and maternal descent meet", also "a sort of linguistic map, showing the places where the dialects obtained".

Working in her room at the King Edward Hostel, her headquarters in Perth, she set herself to the task of finishing the book.

Chapter after chapter was dispatched to Andrew Lang who complained that "they pursue me up and down this Island, which is risky." He had already called in the services of Professors Rivers and Hartland to assist with the revision of her material and wrote relieved assent to her suggestion that she come to England to finish the work.

"I certainly wish you would bring [the book] to England and consult the learned," he wrote; adding that it had been "especially unlucky that Mr Frazer's three volumes on the subject were destitute of your information.—I don't agree with a word he writes, but it is bad luck."

If she were on the spot it would be "easy to revise her prima cura . . . to hurry over such a novel and important work would be a misfortune."

This letter provided Daisy with the ammunition she needed.

With Fraser as her go-between, she approached the under-secretary with the audacious suggestion that she be sent to London for the publication of her book. His answer was a request for an estimate, first of the cost of publishing in Perth, second of the journey to London.

Daisy was ready with her figures. Because of the cheapness of publishing in Edinburgh, both estimates amounted to the approximate sum of £700.

In that case, the Government decreed, "the decision should be in favour of England." But permission carried with it the stern condition that a time limit be fixed and that "the salary of Mrs Bates . . . be credited to the Agent-General who would exercise a general supervision over Mrs Bates's operations."

It was, in spite of the caution of their proviso, a triumph of hard work over apathy. Daisy had reason for rejoicing. It was one of her life's tragedies that it was followed by the news—also the realization of an ambition—that an anthropological expedition under the auspices of Oxford and Cambridge was to visit the State in the following year.

There is no doubt that some of the responsibility for the expedition must be laid at Daisy's door. Her work had attracted attention in both universities. From letters received from Marett, organizer of the expedition, it seems clear that she had, at one time, suggested such a venture and had offered her services if it came about.

Plans were already in motion for her trip to England, when Marett wrote suggesting that she join the party as a representative of Oxford University, since Knowles, who had been going to represent them, had dropped out. This was followed by a letter from the lecturer in Anthropology at London University, A. R. Radcliffe-Brown. Spencer had been approached to head the party but, as no reply had been received from him, leadership had been given to Radcliffe-Brown and the expedition placed under the auspices of Cambridge. Hearing of this, Andrew Lang sent him the chapter on social organization from Daisy's book.

Brown wrote at once to say that she had "clearly got together a large amount of very valuable information which will be of immense value to us in the work we propose to do". Urging her to wait for his arrival as, with his help, "the material you have collected might perhaps be published with the Reports of the Expedition", he told her that if finance could be raised, he intended to spend some six years in completing her researches.

His letter concluded with an acceptance of her "kind offer of personal help to the expedition".

Daisy was jubilant. She wrote to Mathew that "it was a huge honour even to be asked to cooperate with such learned professors and I should love it. Indeed I want to accompany them, and, as Professor Brown is a young man under thirty, I have placed him in the Paljeri Division where he becomes my son. (I am Boorong throughout the north so one difficulty is removed as a mother can accompany her son anywhere.)"

Believing that the future of her book was now settled, Daisy lost no time in sending Radcliffe-Brown's letter to the undersecretary. Fraser backed up her request to join the expedition with an argument that, he no doubt knew, would be decisive. If Brown's offer was accepted they would be relieved of the financial responsibility of publication while ensuring Daisy's recognition for the work she had achieved.

This was in February 1910. From then on until October of that year, correspondence went back and forth between Fraser,

Brown, and the under-secretary, while Daisy's future remained in jeopardy.

On 20th September she reported to Mathew that Mr Brown had arrived, had proved to be a "keen inquirer, but whether I accompany the party or not is on the knees of the Gods."

Four days after this letter her impatience reached breaking point. In a three-foolscap-paged memo to the under-secretary, she outlined the benefits to all concerned of collaboration with Brown.

"If my inclusion in the Expedition is approved, the book could either then be amalgamated with that which the expedition intends to issue, or Macmillans would probably publish the book on its merits. . . . Should I accompany the expedition for, say, twelve months, the revision of the book in England would be obviated."

Brown, summoned to confer with the under-secretary, confirmed that he would be "very glad to accept the offer of Mrs Bates's services for a period of six months. I would undertake to publish the work which Mrs Bates has already done by including it in the reports of the expedition."

To this the under-secretary agreed, underlining that "the book . . . in regard to which Mrs Bates had been engaged by the Government for some considerable time . . . will be edited and published by you free of cost to the State. . . . You will doubtless make acknowledgement of the value of Mrs Bates's researches and of her collaboration as may seem meet and proper."

This was going too far. Daisy saw her efforts doomed to anonymity and wrote "to express my regret that the long and arduous labour I have undergone in the compilation of the work has not met with more equitable consideration."

She asked the Government to "urgently consider" that "I should be given the material which [Brown] does not use to publish later on as a popular work, the book to be issued without any further expense to the Government."

The under-secretary, however, did not think it necessary to make "any undertaking at present as suggested by Mrs Bates. The Government may be relied upon to treat her in a liberal spirit with regard to her M.S."

There the matter rested. It could hardly be described as a satisfactory outcome but, as Daisy told Mathew, "The Government want to do the thing cheap and that's really the crux."

As compensation there was the immediate excitement of the expedition. Here was a fresh challenge, beckoning her back to the bushland of her "beloved blacks". She became a nine days wonder. As the first woman to be included in such an expedition, the papers were full of her. For future prestige she traded present glory.

Everything would now depend on her collaboration with the young man destined to be Australia's first Professor of Anthropology to hold a chair at Sydney University, A. R. Radcliffe-Brown.

CHAPTER SEVENTEEN

Daisy was made for Brown's exasperation and he for hers.—E. L. Grant Watson: *But to What Purpose?*

Radcliffe-Brown

In a matter of months it became evident that a work relationship between them was out of the question.

"Anarchy Brown", as he was known at Cambridge, was, at the time of his arrival in Australia in 1910, an astonishingly good-looking and gifted young man in his late twenties whose reputation fluctuated between the "bit of a superman" that he was to his assistant, Grant Watson, and a "fabricator of stories", regarded with distrust by his more cautious colleagues. By this time his political views had been modified from anarchy to socialism, but he was still far from the nationalism that dominated the thinking of his contemporaries. As strongly individualistic as Daisy herself, he carried a sense of style into the detail of ordinary life. His dress was that of a Paris "savant". He had even thought out the best posture for sleep.

It was after his triumphal return from the Andaman Islands that he was offered the leadership of the expedition. He had gone alone into a dangerous situation and shown so little fear that the islanders had regarded him as a god and allowed him to gather invaluable data on their social organization. Anxious to repeat his success in what was still considered, anthropologically speaking, the uncharted territory of North-west Australia, he read Spencer and Gillen and dazzled the impressionable Grant Watson, a newly qualified zoologist, with tales of the Aborigines.

Later writers were to agree with Daisy that collaboration with him was difficult.

Towards women, whether they were students or colleagues, he showed a condescension that was to gall more than one among the now distinguished women anthropologists.

Ruth Benedict, in her letters to her colleague Margaret Mead, quoted in Margaret Mead's *The Way of an Anthropologist*, describes him as "impenetrably wrapped in his own conceit".

"I don't think Brown is fighting for good work over bad, but for work done by disciples over against work done by non disciples," she wrote. Hortense Powdermaker, one of these disciples, made the more cautious comment that he seemed to need to be worshipped. Margaret Mead was more forthright:

"Brown identifies himself with every idea he has ever voiced and any disagreement, tacit or uttered, with his ideas, he takes as a slap in the face."

All three women conceded the personal magnetism to which the young Grant Watson succumbed. Where Brown led, Grant Watson was prepared to follow. The two young men became a unit from which Daisy, a woman and a strong-willed one at that, found herself excluded.

At first all went smoothly. It was not in Daisy's nature to worship, but her letters to Mathew show that she was prepared to learn. She arranged to have an extra desk put in her office so she and Brown could work together on her material; she noted his comments and made the necessary corrections.

In the field it was another matter. Here she was on familiar ground. Experience asserted itself and she was less prepared to follow. Brown, on the other hand, would tolerate no question of his leadership.

Two very different people, they were alike in that they were both egotists with a declared ambition: Brown to occupy the first Australian Chair in Anthropology; Daisy to publish her book. To realize their ambitions, each needed the other. That Brown was successful and Daisy was not, was due, in part, to the generosity of her nature. By giving him access to her material, she was acting in her own as well as his interests. But that the expedition received recognition throughout Australia was very largely due to the power of her prestige.

By 1910 this was considerable. "The epoch-making work Mrs

Bates has done amongst the aborigines," wrote the *Western Mail*, "the interest she has created in those quaint, lovable and primitive people to whom, when all is said and done, Australia really belongs, entitles her to rank among the women who have accomplished great things in this age."

Daisy transferred the accolades to her leader, telling the press that she "greatly appreciated the opportunity of cooperating with Mr Brown". She admitted that "these further investigations must mean considerable amplification of the work I have been doing", and thereby established their relationship as master and pupil.

Brown appeared to accept such homage as his due. In neither of his two long press interviews is there a mention of her name.

What he failed to do, the journalists did for her.

"The interview with the leader of the expedition, A. R. Brown," said the *Mirror*, "will have been read with great interest, all the more so because of its confirmation of the facts and views set out by Daisy Bates in her lecture in the Perth Town Hall on the curious class divisions existing amongst the Australian aborigines."

There is no doubt at all that Brown could have managed without Daisy. As an anthropologist he was brilliant and his ability to pioneer his work had been proved. But to finance his expedition was another matter.

Discovering that it lacked funds, Daisy contacted her old friend and admirer Sam McKay. According to her own account she rang him from her office "and in ten minutes a £1,000 was mine." This, she said, she handed over to Brown.

One of her newspaper cuttings, however, gives rise to a minor mystery.

It seemed that McKay had already donated the amount to the Aboriginal cause. The cheque was in the keeping of pastoralist Sir Edward Wittenoom, "whose attention had been directed towards the Cambridge expedition".

Since Daisy herself had kept the cutting, the inference is that it was she who contacted Wittenoom. To add to the confusion was Brown's story to Grant Watson that McKay had handed him the cheque after a lecture he gave in Perth.

Putting the facts together, the most likely interpretation seems to be that Daisy knew of McKay's donation and took him along to hear Brown's lecture so that he would allow the money to be used for the expedition. McKay was impressed enough to write out another cheque there and then. But, as the paragraph pointed out, it was to cover the amount already placed in the keeping of Sir Edward Wittenoom.

As so often happened when she looked back over the years, Daisy's memory took a short cut. But there seems little doubt that it was she who was instrumental in procuring the thousand pounds—a gesture that she was, in later years, to bitterly regret.

Brown showed his gratitude by asking that she be attached to the expedition for a further six months. Since this was what Daisy wanted most at the time, she considered herself rewarded. He agreed also to continue his revision of her material although, he told Grant Watson, this was becoming more and more difficult.

To Brown, Daisy was an enthusiast rather than an anthropologist. Her book was the work of an amateur. To the man who carried method into every facet of his life, her mind resembled "a well stored sewing basket after half a dozen kittens had been playing there undisturbed". As his own researches continued, to put her book in order represented a waste of time—the one thing he feared. That he continued to do so is apparent from her complaints about the "mutilated manuscript" handed back to her. But by then their relationship had deteriorated beyond hope of any mutual achievement.

Their differences remained a private matter. The press notices that heralded their departure reported Daisy as "anticipating the journey with intense eagerness". As a woman in an all-male scientific expedition she continued to be the focus of interest.

"So far as can be called to mind," wrote the *West Australian*, "the instance is unique, except perhaps for Eve's sojourn in the wilderness."

"Her exceptional and unique knowledge of the natives as well as the mysterious influence she holds over them . . . will be of invaluable assistance to her companions," purred the *Mirror*.

There was one dissenting note in the applause, in a cutting kept no doubt to show the kind of opposition that Daisy was up against. It was a paragraph under the heading of "Larks". What paper it came from is unknown: "Any reader who wants to hear Carr Boyd's opinion of Daisy Bates's proposed exploratory trip into nigger infested mulga, first plug your ears with anti-septicised cotton wool and then ask Carr to write it on a slate. N.B. Please disinfect the slate before handing it back."

On 14th October 1910, two days before her forty-seventh birthday, she set out for Bunbury. There she met the two men and all three continued by steamer for Geraldton, where Louis Olsen, the cook, was engaged. Hiring horses, they rode to Sandstone, pitching camp some miles out of the town near an Aboriginal camp.

Some seven or eight groups had collected for the initiation ceremony which the three "ghosts" were allowed to watch. Work was progressing well until a police raid disturbed it by scattering the natives in all directions.

Just over a month before their arrival, on 11th September to be exact, what were known as the "Darlot murders" had taken place near Laverton. In her report to the Chief Protector, Daisy explained that the murders were spearings demanded by tribal law because of "wrong" marriages. The Chief Protector remained unconvinced and decreed that "Justice be done according to the white man's laws."

As a result, their camp was searched by white troopers.

"Some ten or twelve white Australians came riding through the camp, firing off their revolvers at the native dogs, and shouting and swearing in quite a cinematograph manner," Grant Watson wrote.

Brown was angry. Refusing to budge from his tent door, behind which he had hidden two of the so-called "murderers", he informed the constable that if it were any satisfaction to him, the work of the expedition in that area was ruined. They had no alternative but to cross to the Lock hospitals on Bernier and Dorré Islands. Here the groups were well represented and there would be no fear of interruption.

Daisy approved of his stand but not of his decision to leave. She argued the point. If they waited, she said, the natives would return. Brown listened without reply, his eyes fixed on distance, as was his habit when wishful of putting an end to a conversation. Daisy's arguments trailed off into silence. She confided in Grant Watson that Brown was indeed a very strange young man and "no gentleman".

The next day Brown informed her that plans for departure had been made. If she still wished to stay behind, she was free to do so.

"And so it was that we went our way," Grant Watson wrote, "leaving Mrs Bates to follow how and when she would. . . . [she] did not like to yield and I do not think she supposed that Brown would be so ungallant as to leave her, but he contended that if women claimed the privileges of men, they should be treated as men in like circumstances would be treated."

It was a difficult moment for Brown's young disciple. Daisy had put herself out for him more than once. He genuinely liked her, admiring her "guiding spirit that was not a missionary spirit but one of charity and compassion". The obvious affinity between the county Irish lady with her "neat and dapper appearance" and the "stone age men and women who accepted her with trust and appreciation", struck him as an odd example of symbiosis.

But his loyalties remained with Brown. The party split up. The two men left for Bernier Island, Daisy remained at Sandstone.

This was the first open breach between them. Again, Daisy gave no hint of it, writing cheerfully enough to the Chief Protector that "Brown and Watson have left. I am to follow on Thursday's train."

She was later to claim that she had in fact chosen this particular train in order to travel down with the men captured in the raid. Her reports, she said, prevented the death sentence from being passed on them.

If so, she was to pay dearly for her magnanimity. Her journey became a nightmare that began at Carnarvon. From here she was to take the boat to Bernier Island, but she found out, on her arrival, that Henrietta, the captain, was sleeping off a drunken spree from which no power on earth could wake him.

Daisy was forced to wait. The town, filled with squatters celebrating the yearly race meeting, was as disorderly as Broome and offered no accommodation at all. For one night, at least, she had to sleep on a table top. When it did sail, the *Shark* ran into the tail of a "cockeye bob" and the lugger heaved its way over storm-tossed seas, taking a record thirty-five hours in the process. She arrived seasick and exhausted, blaming Brown for her vicissitudes.

In the meantime the two men were well established in their tents, basking in tropical sun on the sandhills of Bernier Island.

In his first novel, *Where Bonds Are Loosed*, Grant Watson described the conditions under which they lived.

The island, about eighteen miles long and never more than a mile in width, was hot by day but cooled by sea breezes at night. Tent life, however, was prevented from being idyllic by the ants, persistent enough to devour underpants or even toenails. To keep them at bay, their nests had to be dug out and filled with hot ashes.

The hospital itself consisted of three walls of tarred canvas and a corrugated iron roof. In its ten beds were "broken and helpless pieces of humanity who lay still all day and looked out across the bleak expanse of sand dunes under which they were destined to be buried." The scientists carried out their investigations in an atmosphere heavy with death and crackling with tensions. Between the doctor—a young man "more interested in spirochetes than in suffering men"—and the stockman, a vendetta was being fought. They had been seen to stalk each other across the dunes, rifles cocked.

Shortly after Daisy's arrival on 11th December, they crossed to Dorré Island to celebrate Christmas in retreat from a tornado. This time Daisy experienced the full force of a "cockeye bob". The women convalescents were tumbled along the sand dunes. The hospital roof was torn away. Her tent was cut to ribbons and she sent an urgent request for a new one.

In the meantime, she wrote, she had been given hospitality by the "devoted medical staff, so much loved by the patients".

Nothing provides a clearer indication of her change of attitude over the years than her contrasting reports on these "Lock" hospitals, the Government's misguided attempt to put an end to the venereal disease that was spreading with frightening rapidity among the ranks of the Aborigines.

Acting in their capacity of Protectors, police officers were empowered to examine women as well as men for signs of the affliction. After enduring this humiliation, sufferers were then neck-chained and transported by camel buggy to Carnarvon. Their bodies were very often rotten with sores, suppurating and fly-blown, and many died before they reached the shore hospital at Carnarvon. Those who survived were shipped to Bernier and Dorré, the men to the first, women to the second. In his novel, Grant Watson has left us a horrifying account of this method of transportation as he saw it:

"All the hatches were open, and in the shallow hold were standing some forty natives, pressed close together, their heads just coming above the level of the deck. They looked miserable and suffering pieces of humanity and from their close packed bodies came a pungent odour which permeated the whole boat."

"The horrors of Dorré and Bernier unnerve me yet," Daisy wrote in *The Passing of the Aborigines*. ". . . To question the poor shuddering souls of these doomed exiles was slow work and saddening. Through unaccustomed frequent hot baths, their withered sensitive skins, never cleansed in their natural state save by grease and fresh air, became like tissue paper and parted horribly from the flesh.

"There was no ray of brightness, no gleam of hope.

"In death itself they could find no sanctuary, for they believed that their souls, when they left the poor broken bodies, would be orphaned in a strange ground."

So she could write when, after twenty-five years, she looked back on the islands. By then she was "thinking black". But at the time when she stayed on Bernier and Dorré she was still the Government representative, whose duty it was to write objective reports for the benefit of the Chief Protector.

"The work is extremely satisfactory," she told him, "the women being generally very willing to afford all the information required of them. I have visited the camps of the outpatients several times and found the occupants pretty contented with their position." At the Carnarvon hospital, "All looked cheerful and happy."

The only hint she gave of the misery she was later to describe was by her request to act as "postman" or message-bearer between islands.

The Aboriginal had no written language. His "letters" were *bamburu*, short sticks on which were carved pictorial messages. When Daisy crossed from Dorré Island to the mainland, she carried some of these with her.

"I think these little messages and my reports of the sick natives and their friends will bring kindlier thoughts about the Islands, which to many of them do not now seem so far away nor so gruesome," she wrote.

Although Brown had extended her period of service, he had also taken the precaution of dividing the work, and Daisy was free to come and go as she pleased. Permission to carry the *bamburu* was granted, but at the same time she received a stern warning about the limitations by which she must abide in handing out rations.

No bills would be honoured, the Chief Protector warned, except for the list already authorized. She pleaded the case for greater liberality as her "little presents" promoted goodwill. Besides, "one woman on the ration is old and deaf, another is blind. Some have their sons and husbands on the Islands." Wherever possible, she assured him, "those who can work come into town daily and wash, or chop wood."

Her appeals were ignored. The warnings grew sterner. But as compensation for official disapproval was the growing affection of her black friends.

"All those whom I had previously met amongst them rushed over to the buggy to greet me. The diseased natives and their women do not avoid me," she reported with pride.

On 14th April 1911, six months to the day after their departure, Daisy returned to Perth. On the strength of McKay's donation

Brown went north again, this time with two men, his destination "inland from Carnarvon". Daisy returned to her old camp in the Murchison Bush. The decision to split up had restored her good spirits. She was reported as "brimming over with enthusiasm"; and that, "notwithstanding the loss of weight of something like a stone, she had nothing to say concerning the privations and hardships which must have been endured but spoke only of the work that Mr Brown and she had done and of what it was hoped to do. . . . As a student of the aboriginal races of the State, Mrs Bates has perhaps no compeer, and yet she herself acknowledges that she has still so much to learn in the matter."

The pupil was still paying homage to the master. In view of their differences, this showed a magnanimity that the master did not show towards his pupil. He did, however, utilize a press interview to make known his hope that "the Australian Government would follow Canada's example and establish a department of Ethnology."

"For that work," he pointed out, "[the Canadians] have made a grant of over £800 a year." This left Australia as "practically the only place which has not a department of that kind".

The Government took the hint but was slow to realize it. It was more than a decade later before a Chair of Anthropology was created at Sydney University. It was offered to Radcliffe-Brown.

Daisy's explanation for her return to the bush had nothing to do with ethnology. "The dear people, I simply love them," she said. "They are just simple children and I would do anything in the world I could to help them."

Her life resumed a now familiar pattern. She moved from camp to camp, filled in her vocabularies, recorded fragments of legends, noted customs, nursed the sick and comforted the bereaved.

About her book her mind was at rest. One copy remained with Andrew Lang in England. The other was with Radcliffe-Brown. Publication had been promised. The raw material that she had taken down by word of mouth would emerge in the pattern of scholarship. Recognition would be hers.

In twelve short months her hopes dissolved. In July 1912 Andrew Lang died. A Labour Party was in power and Brown was on the high seas, on his way back to England and without her MS.

In a letter to Mathew, dated 5th September 1912, Daisy filled in the unhappy details:

> Dr. Andrew Lang had a copy of the book in typed MS. and Macmillans say they have only received portions of it from Dr. Lang's executors. The late Government handed over the only copy I had to Brown and that was mutilated beyond recovery. The present Government has relieved Brown of the responsibility of publishing the book, returns it to me, but will not pay for its publication. . . . Mr Fraser had promised free copies of the book to several hundred contributors on the assumption that it was to be published by the Government. Mr. Brown could not fulfil these promises if the book was to be published by the Cambridge Press . . . and so the Government released Mr. Brown from his undertaking and has given me the MS., but the mutilated portions are useless. . . . I told Mr. Fraser I feared the whole thing would have to be rewritten and his reply was "Oh Lud!"

There was more to the story. Perhaps in defence of his "mutilations", Brown had showed her a letter written to him by Andrew Lang in which Lang had said that "a red pencil would be needed in [Daisy's] long and wandering work". Outraged, she had written at once to Lang, who broke off relations with Brown but did not deny the charge. After Lang's death Professor Marett of Oxford agreed to take over the job of revision and Daisy decided to take her chance on a separate publication. Brown agreed not to use her material but the manuscript he returned was still in the process of revision and the one in England incomplete.

Her chances of publication were, literally, in ribbons, and Daisy's final comment to Mathew shows that even her apparently invincible optimism had suffered defeat.

"I had hoped to have been able to go home, but alas! That is another disappointment and as there are so many others I won't dwell any more upon them."

Instead she replaced one ambition with another.

The expedition had deprived her of academic laurels but had led to success of a different kind. Her bitter disappointment at the hands of the whites coincided with her total acceptance by the blacks. She understood their needs. As an official representative she could fulfil them.

The first woman to be included in an Australian scientific expedition should be eligible as the first woman Chief Protector of Aborigines.

To achieve such a position she would be up against the prejudice of men who regarded leadership as their right. Daisy decided that her job was to convince them that she would be no rival in their field; that they needed a woman as a doctor needed a nurse.

"The virus of research" remained her chief preoccupation but, though she did not know it, the story of her book had reached its sad and tattered conclusion.

The story of "the life that was service" had begun.

CHAPTER EIGHTEEN

That a woman inspector is needed cannot be questioned for a moment and that the position has not long ago been created is a dishonour to ourselves. That male inspectors should be commissioned to examine native women and children under well known conditions is a blot on our civilization.— Bishop Gibney, 1912.

Protector of Aborigines

"Dear Mrs Bates: In connection with your application for the position of Protector of Aborigines in the Northern Territory, I have very much pleasure in proferring my testimony in regard to the exceptional work done by you during your attachment to this Department, in connection with the personal study of, and compilation of a history of the habits, customs and language of the various tribes of this State.

"I cannot speak too highly of the enthusiasm with which you have devoted yourself to this formidable task and it is evident that the valuable original experience already gained by you in the course of your investigations, together with your natural ability, adaptability and the great personal interest you take in the Aborigines, their wants and their welfare, should eminently qualify you to successfully carry out the work of a position such as the one you seek."

So wrote Daisy's old "Chief", Malcolm Fraser, the Registrar-

General. Bishop Gibney offered an unsolicited testimonial that ended with "the earnest hope that I may soon see the native women and children represented by such a friend and advocate as you have proved to my own knowledge, during the past twelve years."

She was backed by recommendations from Frank Wilson the past Premier, the Minister of Mines, the Commissioner of Police, the Anglican Bishop. Women's societies in Perth petitioned the Government.

Daisy did not get the job.

The reason given her was that the risks involved would be too great for a woman. Her work would be hampered by the need of a police escort.

For one who had lived alone amongst Aborigines, wild and civilized, it was a galling decision, made worse and not better by the honorary protectorship conferred on her as a consolation prize. This was for the Eucla district in the farthermost south-east of the State, and still virgin territory in terms of anthropology. Had it been a paid position, nothing could have suited her better. Unpaid, she told John Mathew, it was "an empty honour" since there was so little that she could do for the natives. Besides, it nullified the reason given for refusing her a salaried position in the Northern Territory.

The Government, she commented ruefully, was "somewhat inconsistent in their consistency".

If there were a reason, other than her sex, for deciding against her, it could well have been her extravagance in the matter of "little presents to promote goodwill". Her habit of extending Government largesse beyond the ration allowed her was to be a cause of unpopularity in both of the two States in which she made her home. But, as the man chosen for the Northern Territory happened also to be a Roman Catholic, Daisy seized upon this as the cause of preference.

From 1912 on, the Church of Rome and the Labour movement were bracketed as joint cause, not only of her personal troubles, but of the downward trend that she saw in the politics of her adopted country.

Such prejudices were by no means new, but until now, they had not been obsessive. After this year of disaster, she seemed almost compulsively determined to voice them, usually in letters to friends. An externalizing of frustration, this was a psychological process that was also the first indication of the influence of her black companions. To them, no misfortune happened by accident.

Their ills were the result of "bad magic" wished on them by the enemy.

To endure frustration, Daisy had to find an outlet for resentment. In other words she had to choose an enemy.

One blow followed the other. The new Labour Government terminated her appointment along with their refusal to publish her book. Scaddan, the new Premier, told her bluntly that her MS. was not a commercial proposition and Daisy admitted, forlornly, to Mathew that "I did rather spread myself through the chapters." She was ready to cut; but, "I am greatly hampered by the Government's refusal to help me along."

In other words, she was not only jobless but broke. The Government's pittance of eight shillings a day had at least allowed her to continue with her researches, provided that she lived in a tent. Her freelance journalism had been useful in supplementing the native rations but had never provided enough to keep her. Nor could she, if she had been prepared to, turn to Jack for help.

By this time both husband and son had left the West. Arnold, who, she said, "had been cutting his life's teeth", had settled at last in New South Wales, and was planning to be married.

Jack had accepted the post of overseer stockman on a property near Darwin with the pantomime name of "Humptydoo" station.

Whether or not Daisy's application had been influenced by his move to the Territory is a matter for conjecture. To say that he had left her would be, in any event, unfair, since their marriage as such had ceased to exist when they parted in 1903. Her Perth friends who remember these years insist that she felt deserted by him, an opinion borne out by the astonishing fact that, from 1912 onwards, Daisy referred to him in press interviews as her "late" husband—a fiction which continued into some Australian encyclopaedias.

A convenient adjective, it conferred dignity on the débâcle of her marriage. Respectably interred, her husband could be the cause of no further awkward questions. Glen Carrick became the property he had "left" her, a talisman to an affection that had been so sadly absent in reality.

Theirs had been the tragedy of incompatibility. To his friend H. L. Richardson, Jack confided that he had done his best and that his best had not been good enough. Daisy conceded to William Hurst that her husband was a "good simple man" but, as a relative had told her, "if a Bates is born within the shafts of a wheelbarrow there he will be when he dies."

A racehorse cannot be confined within the shafts of a wheelbarrow, but the price of cutting the traces, for Daisy as well as for Jack, was loneliness.

In fact, Jack lived until 1935 when he died at Mullewa in West Australia at the age of seventy-eight. His was a rootless old age. After retirement from station life he drifted from one to the other of the properties of friends and family. Charles Carney, his nephew, remembers him on one of his visits to his mother's home. By then he had become a somnolent, irritable old man with an old man's tendency to wake at two in the morning and to sleep, like Combo, through the noon hours. To his grandchildren he remained benign, given to reminiscing about the good old days. Seldom, if ever, did he speak of his wife. Nor did his attitude towards her work become less bitter. Only after she left Perth did he return to the West, to end his days in a hotel room belonging to one of his droving mates, now retired.

By June 1912, with no young pioneer offering to lease Glen Carrick, Daisy was forced to start negotiations for its sale.

Her friends rallied to her cause. Robertson of the *Western Mail* offered to publish everything she sent him, Mathew approached the *Australasian* on her behalf, and a new friend, Georgina King, interested the *Sydney Morning Herald*. J. G. Frazer, writing to thank her for her corrections to material included in his *Totemism and Exogamy*, suggested that she write for the *Journal* of the Institute of Anthropology. Robert Fairbairn, magistrate of the Aboriginal prison at Rottnest, offered her an extended visit to the island. She could live in her tent and continue her researches among the many groups represented among his charges.

Warmed by the affection shown her by the Fairbairns, and especially by their daughter Ainslie, who had become the child companion she had hoped to find in Arnold, Daisy went to work. The prospect of new material revived her hopes for the book but the "bad magic" that followed her through the year 1912 had not yet finished with her.

Radcliffe-Brown had begun to publish his reports of the expedition and she wrote to Mathew that "some of my MS. is being printed as new discoveries by those who had access to it. You will remember that I mentioned the Ngargalulla (spirit babies) of the Broome District natives some years ago. I see in a recent paper that these spirit babies are Mr. A. R. Brown's discoveries.

"It is entirely my own fault for not looking after my own interests, but I am only keen to get the information before the natives will have died out."

Slowing down this race against time was her concern for the

people to whose doom she believed she was a witness. As she gathered her data she became more deeply involved in their tragedy. Her description of prison conditions makes harrowing reading. She looked back on Rottnest much as she looked back on the Lock hospitals, as "another tragic mistake of the early colonists in dealing with the original inhabitants of a country so new and strange to them".

"Just as there was little understanding by the black man of the white man's law, so there was little by the white man of the black's," she wrote. "Natives were thrown together in a cell regardless of group antipathies and evil magics."

Amongst the prisoners were two old friends, Jingooroo and Muri, serving sentences for the murder of a tribal enemy, a blood man of Meekatharra. The cells contained four or five men and one of these was Thurudha, another of the hated "blood" men.

"I did the only thing possible," she wrote. "I arranged with the authorities to have myself locked into their cell for some hours and took both magics away."

There was a sad codicil to her story. Tuberculosis was one of the main killers among the groups of the North-west. Sent down to the cold climate of Rottnest, many of them died of it while serving their sentences. On Daisy's last day at the prison she heard that Jingooroo was very ill and went to keep him company. In *The Passing of the Aborigines* she records:

"Suddenly he stood up and laying his hands upon my shoulders, said 'That blood magic! How strong it was to cross the big water and find me.' A heavy haemorrhage followed and in a short time, Jingooroo's grave was added to the many hundreds on the island."

Her appointment as Honorary Protector made it imperative that she get to Eucla as soon as she could, if only because of the publicity that resulted from it.

Paid or unpaid, she was still the first woman Protector of Aborigines, and the women's pages of the press were not slow to register another triumph for their sex.

As "the link connecting the aboriginal race with the white", she was already something of a legend. Gwen Sargent White, who interviewed her for *Everylady's Journal*, claimed for her "attainments amongst blacks and whites of which no other woman in the world could boast".

Describing her as "smartly and suitably dressed for every occasion", her background a tent pitched in an oasis of green in a desert of sand, Miss White went on to draw a well-observed portrait that is a remarkably faithful record of Daisy as she was then. Her conversation is reported verbatim. Dull fact leaps to vivid and humorous life. The imperious charm dominates the interviewer. Daisy's stories are highlighted with that flair for exaggeration that is the equipment of the raconteur—if not that of the scientist.

From this interview her prestige emerged triumphant. She was presented with a flourish of trumpets, a success in two worlds. That she chose to live without personal possessions, we are assured, was a mere matter of choice. Clothes, manner, speech, hinted at a background of financial as well as social security.

As a contrast there appeared, almost at the same moment though in another and less fashionable journal, an advertisement that tells its own story:

> Glencarrick. Three lots, two at 50,000 acres, one at 83,000 acres. Near Nullagine. Annual rental of house £23. No improvements. Little fencing required on account of Opthalmia Range. Water at 20 feet. Also from Fortescue River. The Estate close to the Goldfields Stock Route. Brand of 200 lost head of cattle. Price 500.

By November of 1912 the Honorary Protector was on her way to Eucla.

Once again a friend had come to her rescue. Beatrice Raine had invited her to her brother's home on a station a hundred and twenty miles out of Eucla. There she would be free to come and go as she chose. It was understood that she would continue her researches and carry out her duties as Protector.

Daisy wrote to the Fairbairns that she was "well beyond civilization, right in the heart almost of the continent. On the plateau formed by the extensive cliffs which so impressed Eyre on his East West journey."

The house itself was set in a treeless plain so flat that "the eye . . . takes in all the landscape at once", and it was shabby enough to be the kind of challenge that Daisy loved. "In no time at all it was comfortable and habitable." Both brother and sister were being "excessively kind" and all was peaceful—except for the "inevitable gramophone that discourses sweet music for us of evenings".

No doubt Daisy, used to the silence of the bush, was glad enough to escape the sweet music. Fragments of her diary show that she spent long periods away from the station "roaming the Nullarbor in pursuit of her subjects", and trusting herself as she had done in Broome to her Aboriginal guides, whose bush lore she respected more than she ever did the "gigglywinks" of civilization.

One of her absences was a "dogging" expedition undertaken with her black friends Karnduing and his wife Nellie.

The destruction of dingoes, the wild dogs of this area, was a humane as well as a commercial exercise. As savage as wolves, they preyed on the herds of sheep, leaving behind them a trail of maimed and suffering creatures. Daisy's terse and uncommitted notes leave an exact, and possibly a unique record of a hunt that lasted for almost a week. They reveal much about the country, and something about her state of mind at the time.

Wednesday April 16th, 1913.

Nellie drove the two camels, Karnduing and I rode Bosun and Hope. The wild dogs had been playing among the sheep, several dead, the rest run off their feet. Went on about a mile and a half to a wattle clump where I just put up my tent native fashion. I could not stand up inside and performed a poor toilet. Put up with inconveniences. Retired early.

Heard Nellie and Karnduing talking and snoring at intervals all night . . . we were up at five and in the saddle before dawn.

Got home late and ran down a kangaroo for the fencers just on the top of the cliffs. Noted the Nala tree in flower, and a tiny little flower of the sorrel species smiling at us from its tuft. Clumps of trees remind one of the Darling Downs. There was a heavy swell on the sea. The cliffs are rubble for a good distance down, then granite or stone, then clay and conglomerate.

Thursday April 17th. No luck again today, though we came upon two newly killed sheep and a poor lamb nearly dead. All day long we saw and followed the tracks but found no dog. Poisoned the sheep and while I lay down an eaglehawk came to eat of it and got poisoned. The waggon had been out and brought me cakes, jam, meat, sugar and a letter from Bee [Raine].

Saw no water today. Found where the wild dogs, having tired of mutton, were trying to obtain wombat. . . .

Friday, April 18th.

A most unlucky day. Karnduing has laid down again "sick" wanting "Mijal". I did not give it to him and he soon got better. I went South East, saw plenty tracks, found one sheep with its neck bitten . . . in the titree scrub I saw my first dog, a brown spotted one . . . he broke cover at a swinging trot, just like a fox. I started Hope after him but she couldn't even trot. I couldn't get near enough to have a shot at him.

Here the diary blossoms into the fragment of an article, becoming at once better humoured and rich in observation:

> Going out in the very early morning over these plains is most interesting. Little trap door spiders make themselves a webbed maia to catch the night walking insects . . . the burn-burn (bellbird) sings from the mallee trees. The night feeding wombats have gone to bed, but about ten or eleven a.m. Mr. Wombat comes above ground for an airing, sitting calmly on his burrow roof and contemplating the world around him. A few cats which have gone feral are out after small birds . . . the dogs are evidently pining for a change of food, preferably wombat, but I don't think they can catch wombat as easily as they catch sheep, as is evidenced by the torn ground about the wombat burrows. The dogs sleep in the burrows too, but choose empty ones.

A flash of irritation, never allowed to appear in her public writing, notes that "Karnduing is something of a fraud. Yesterday he tried for lizard eggs . . . he returned with a hatful of about 30 which must have taken him hours to gather and dig out, so his time for dogging was limited. These blacks are unreliable, no matter how kindly they are treated."

Work went well. She wrote to Mathew that "I am already getting the dialect and the social organisations of the groups." This was a triumph since the native population was rapidly disappearing and, "Some of the classes . . . number only four or five."

Because of this fall in numbers she had "sometimes to cross out all the information I have been at pains to collect, as my informant had married his mother's stock and was too greatly ashamed to admit it. Now after three months they are beginning to realise that I really do not mind their lapses and I know there are not enough women of the proper clan to choose from."

Their information showed a link between the Eucla system and that of the Norsemen, Southern Cross and Eastern Goldfields. Daisy, who could now ride as well as drive that cantankerous creature the camel, wrote to the Department for Aboriginal Affairs to suggest that she lead a new expedition to follow the Aboriginal route through Balladonia. The answer, predictably, was no.

Up against departmental opposition, her reaction was usually to go higher. This time she wrote to the Premier to ask for the loan of camels and supply wagon. She also wrote to her new friend Georgina King.

Miss King, daughter of the pioneer missionary George King,

Deserted *mia-mia* at Ooldea

Medical attention (*Photo*: West Australian Newspapers Ltd)

Daisy Bates with Aboriginal skull, Pyap, 1938

Farewell to "my natives" (*Photo*: West Australian Newspapers Ltd)

had contacted Daisy after the publication of one of her articles on the Protestant missions of the West. They became friends by correspondence. Miss King, like Daisy, combined an interest in anthropology with an abiding compassion for the people concerned. She sent a donation of £50.

As the proceeds for the first of Daisy's land sales had come in, this meant renewed affluence. It was still insufficient to launch an expedition but it did make it possible for her to stay where she was.

In October 1913 she broke the news to the Fairbairns. There was, she wrote, to be "a general exodus from the Nullarbor. Miss Raine is returning to her people as her brother is resigning the management of the station." But, she assured them, "I will be glad to get under canvas again."

It was plain that Miss Raine was not as happy as Miss King about her decision. After her return, offers of work began to reach Daisy from Perth.

"Friends," she told Miss King, "are writing deploring my burying myself in the bush for a lot of ungrateful blacks. They ask if it is worthwhile as if one were doing the work [for that reason]. I am doing it because it gives me pleasure in the same way that hockey and tennis and fox hunting gave me pleasure when I pursued them."

Miss King, on the other hand, was "a true friend of science". Because of her help, Daisy was "more than ever desirous" of doing her best.

In 1913 the ethnologist was still uppermost. But, by the end of the year, a letter came to Miss King, written in a different spirit and setting out what was to become Daisy's manifesto for the future.

"My sole desire is just to live amongst my black friends. . . . I have not a particle of personal ambition or self seeking beyond my desire to impress upon this native race that there is one woman who is absolutely their friend, without thought of self advancement.

"When all look upon me as a friend, when men, women and child come to me freely and confidently . . . well then here my mission lies."

CHAPTER NINETEEN

Our road is the Road of Yesterday and the Road of Today, for Yesterday and Today are still the same.—Daisy Bates: Eucla Notebooks, 1913.

The Nullarbor Plain

At last Daisy had made her choice between two worlds. She had walked for miles along the great cliffs towering above "twice ten thousand caverns" and listened to the sea as it sighed and thundered through them. She had driven her camel buggy into the vast and empty stretches of the Nullarbor. She had felt again the "deep sense of peace" that solitude brings with it.

In the mornings she had awakened to the sound of birds in the bush around her tent and heard again the liquid chatterings of her Aboriginal companions. She knew that she had come home.

When she had arrived at Eucla she was a disappointed and unhappy woman. After she left, she looked back on "an exciting sixteen months" that was "one of the most illuminating contacts with this primitive race I have ever made."

Her choice was no longer a transfer of ambition. It was a way of life.

She continued to use words like "primitive" and talked about her "natives" because these were symbols of communication acceptable to the whites. But it was in Eucla that she learned to "think black". With no longer any personal ties of her own, she adopted the native community as her "family". She had always been conscious of their need of her, now she accepted her need of them.

Her role of Protector had increased her status. The Aborigines called her their "Queen Government" and she saw herself as an administrator of the Empire.

The benign despot of her diminishing black kingdom, she could continue the researches that remained a source of fascination and still serve her subjects as her grandmother, the matriarch, had served the tenants at Ballycrine. She could even supplement the Government rations out of her own pocket and be answerable to no one.

In gratitude, her black "family" laid bare their tribal secrets, initiating her into the inner sanctum of holy tradition by making her Keeper of their Totems.

This happened after her move to Jeegala Creek, a lonely waterhole sixteen miles out of Eucla and seven miles from the South Australian border.

By going there at all she established herself as one of them, since few white men and no white woman entered alone into this arid domain of the black man where survival could depend on water found in the roots of a mulga-tree and food from the nests of white ants. But, Daisy assured Miss King, "No queen is safer in her palace than I in my unfastened tent."

But this was some months later. Her first camp at Eucla was in the backyard of the station master, a personal friend and one of the fifteen or so white inhabitants of the little community that had sprung up around the telegraph repating station.

The town itself was a mere huddle of limestone buildings perched on the level ground between the sea and the great cliffs that, at this point, had receded to form the Hampton Ranges. Eucla was a derivative of Yirgilia, meaning Venus, star of the east, but all connection with the Goddess of Love began and ended with the name. In 1913 it was a desolate, sun-blistered outpost, already yielding to the encroaching sand, and consisting of "bachelor quarters", a recreation centre called Jubilee Hall, a general store and an untidy line of sagging timber that was all that was left of a jetty.

Sea traffic was limited to a quarterly boat from Albany and another from Fowler's Bay. There was neither hotel nor hospital, no Flying Doctor service, no creeks or rivers. The white inhabitants watched the sky anxiously for their ten inches of annual rainfall, and put down wells to tap the artesian water below the surface.

Behind the town yawned the great Plain, named "Nullarbor" by Alfred Delisser from the Latin *nulla arbor* and regarded as fearsome by black and white alike.

Because it had once been under the sea, its limestone formation was riddled with caves for twenty-five miles inland. These mouthed their way to the surface in blowholes that might be only a foot or two in diameter and made eerie music when the north wind was blowing.

Daisy, who had enough commonsense not to venture too far into the plain without her black guides, explored as much of it as their courage would allow. They took her as far as the Goonalda Cave, an underground lake two hundred feet below the surface. Legend had it that an Aboriginal once descended as far as the water by means of a rope strung out of his hair, but the cave was avoided as the domain of Ganba the serpent, who was supposed to inhabit the subterranean channels of the plain. His breath hissed through its blowholes. He was always thirsty and sucked in the surface water as soon as it had rained.

Surveyor Tom Brown's report endorsed their belief.

"I have known a hundred acres of water, two feet deep, disappear in six hours and next day when listening down a blow hole, I heard water rushing through the country like a river," he wrote. He may not have believed in a thirsty serpent but he agreed with the Aborigines that "to be lost in the Plain meant almost certain death".

Daisy's response to this "prehistoric country in which the knowledge of the twentieth century finds itself at sea", is scattered through her notebooks, in descriptions that are an attempt to recreate atmosphere, fragmented like a mosaic and distilled into prose poetry:

> Here there is nothing young that was not long since old. Here there is no germinating potency of nature. The mystery, beauty and freedom of these boundless plains will repel one whose artistic sense demands a more genial scene for its gratification.
>
> There is a solemnity for some, a weirdness for others in this hushed immensity.
>
> There is little travel along these desolate tracks. The mailman, ever anxious about horse feed and water; oddments of humanity [who] pass through on their way to fortune or defeat.
>
> The air is so sensitive that the crack of a whip, the slow

> tread of the camels and the noise of the lumbering, broad-wheeled waggons can be heard for miles. Sometimes there are no signs to indicate that living things have ever drawn breath in this desolate and treeless plain. The solemn all embracing silence . . . is so impressive that one feels as if the moment of breaking will usher in some catastrophe. Even the echoes seem to be dead.

White history began with Eyre, who limped into Jinyila, as the Aborigines called it, nearly dead with thirst and watched by the invisible band of black men who had been following his progress. After him came the Muir brothers who pioneered Moolpina sheep station and lived in total isolation for two years. A black "postman" by name of Karraji became a local legend by carrying mail from Fowler's Bay to Moolpina and back, covering four hundred and eighty miles on foot in three weeks.

In black history Jinyila was part of legend. Through the centuries it had been used as a meeting place along the great trading route that used to encircle the continent.

Chief object of barter was flint, dug out of the Kaldiyerra white flint quarry by the "Wild Currant" or "Nala-tree" totem men. To Jinyila came groups from as far north as Boundary Dam and as far east as Fowler's Bay, to hold their initiation ceremonies by the great salt water.

But the octopus tentacles of white development had established their stranglehold even over the desert. The mild-eyed hordes of kangaroos had been slaughtered in their thousands by white hunters who drank themselves to death on the proceeds. Game was scarce, though beginning to be supplemented by the English sparrow and the English rabbit, both of which had arrived at Eucla on their migration West by the time Daisy got there.

Everywhere the same sad story was being told. The groups were drifting down towards the line. Their numbers were diminishing and the manhood ceremony that took Daisy to Jeegala Creek was the last to be held in the area.

The men bartered their women for food or whisky to the lonely white men working on the line and a new problem of unwanted half-caste children had begun to arise.

The old people had no meat. They existed on Government rations of tea, flour and sugar. When these ran out they drank water until the next supply arrived.

"They are in their wommoos," Daisy wrote, "these old people waiting unconsciously though it be, for the mysterious end they know as 'nalba' (death). Their contact with the whites has destroyed their beliefs and now they are undecided as to whether they are going up into the sky or under the ground—or just becoming Kambu (skeletons) like the animals they have killed and eaten."

This, then, was the territory of the new Queen Government.

On 17th November, she wrote to Georgina King that she had made her first move out of Eucla. She was to picture her in her tent two miles along the line "deep in the bush and close to a storage tank", with about forty Aborigines camped nearby.

"The younger members go out foraging daily and in the evenings the air is full of their voices as they narrate the events of the day. Now that I am here to look after the old people, they have no concern about them. I make their tea and serve them with a couple of meals and at night they always have some native 'delicacy', iguana, sweet roots, or, if the hunting has been good, kangaroo or turkey."

For the *Western Mail* she added to the picture.

Before dawn, "the silence of the bush night is broken by a low mournful wail, like a Gaelic keen. It is the wail of the old women apostrophising the spirit of some recently departed relative." The words of the song might mean anything or nothing and ended in "a long drawn out Oh like the howl of a dingo".

Shortly afterwards the camp was awake, fires raked into a blaze and the remnants of yesterday's food, "if there are any", taken out from under broad pieces of bark, to be portioned in prescribed order, in-laws having first priority, the camp sorcerer second.

Amongst the Eucla district natives, "water never appears to have been over plentiful and so no undue liberties, such as using it for washing themselves—have apparently been taken with it." The first thing the Aboriginal did when he woke was to put on the clothes he had taken off at night, look at the sky to see what he could expect from the day and then, when his meal was finished, go out foraging for food.

After that,

> The camp is mostly deserted, except for the feeble or blind members, the hunters returning at night. As they have probably had a feed and a sleep in the bush during the hot hours they returned home quite lively . . . with game either carried in their string belts or, if happily large, on their shoulders.
>
> Everybody brings something home from his or her day's quest, even if it were but a yarloo full of ngabba (white ants).
>
> As soon as they arrive in camp, the fires are made up and

such chattering and babblement accompanies the cooking as only women can encompass. The men club together and do a living "cinematograph" of any mishap that may have befallen them for the amusement of the others and to while away the time until the women have finished the cooking.

In the evening when appetites have been sated, there is much mirth and singing, men women and children joining in, in perfect unison and harmony . . . the songs accompanied by the clapping of two boomerangs together, the scratching of sticks on meeros or beating of kylees on the ground.

As she showed herself anxious to learn, they taught her some of their skills. The hunters allowed her to accompany them on their expeditions and she observed that "their apparent want of ingenuity is occasioned by the nature of the country and of the climate." After watching them catch fish without need of a rod and kill a kangaroo by stalking him, silent and invisible, until their spear could reach its target, Daisy conceded that their "weapons were all they needed for procuring food and for material of war."

Under their tuition she learned the subtle science of tracking, in which signs, invisible to any but a trained eye, equipped with phenomenal powers of seeing, could be read as a white man reads a map.

"They turn aside to scrutinise every empty camp we pass," she wrote. "Presently one hears them discussing the disposition of every member, the names of those whose footprints are still visible and every little association that this or that spot has, is frankly related. Here Wardura and her man had a row when he clubbed and nearly killed her. There Yargu beat Ngoorgooji very severely because he was so sorry for his brother Boongara who had died."

In the evenings, they instructed her in the mysteries of their zodiac.

These were the moments that Daisy treasured, when the meal was eaten and they sat beside the campfire under the velvety black arc that reached from horizon to limitless horizon.

"These moonless nights," she wrote, "when the stars are at their brightest and even Magellan's Clouds take on a warmth and a shimmer from their glittering neighbours; when you look up into the worlds on worlds in myriads and try to realise that the earth in which you are but the tiniest atom, is one of the smallest of these twinkling planets. On such nights it is good to wander over these great distances in company with the aborigines and listen and hear their wonderful legends of this and that star . . .

and wander with them along the 'Yaggin' (moon) road that was made when the moon was human."

She claimed that she was "never lonely in such company as I can command". No doubt this was true, but the lightness of heart that she said was the bond between herself and the Aborigines was by no means always hers.

This was a transition period in more ways than one. Her outlook, her circumstances, even her body, were undergoing changes that were too radical not to leave their mark. Because of the façade of cheerfulness that her pride insisted that she present to the world, it is easy to miss the unhappiness against which she battled so fiercely. Just how close she came to breaking point her notebooks reveal.

"I have often to feel grateful for the Irish blood in me with the strong tinge of fatalism that is the heritage of the Celt as well as of the Oriental," she noted. "It rescues one from breakdown, calms one suddenly and enables one to lift the burden with unwearying shoulders until action is possible."

In the no man's time of "blended twilight and moonlight", she admitted that "a great sadness overcomes me."

To combat it, she decided on a doctrine of good cheer spelled out by a quotation from Southey: "I make the most of my enjoyments and as for my troubles I pack them in as little compass as I can for myself and never let them among others."

Using her considerable force of will she "crushed and put away" hopes and ambitions that had been centred on the white world. As an extrovert, she preferred action to self-analysis. But she did not entirely escape her moments of looking inward.

"I am two people, one I like and the other I do not know," she observed. And again, "A thing of patches am I—here an exaltation of duty, there a love of fun and frolic and again of melancholy."

Work remained her panacea, for "restfulness is a quality for cattle", as she was fond of quoting. But here again a change was taking place.

The deepening of her understanding caused by her researches led to a deepening of her commitment to the black community.

Since she doubted the efficacy of all organized attempts to better their lot, this was in the nature of personal friendship, a concept she had seen exemplified by men like Gibney, Nicholas and Forrest. To Miss King she called it her "apologia pro vita".

By her presence among them, she said, the black people recognized "that kindly friendly interest in their daily doings and happiness, that readiness to comfort them in sickness and in sorrow, [that willingness] to bear with their weakness" that constituted friendship.

Like Nicholas she relied on example for her discipline. The job of keeping her camp "morally clean" depended on herself. She must live "so much above reproach" that they could accept that she "meant only their good".

But, she pointed out, her standard of values was as much theirs as hers. Few people realized that the white man appeared as decadent to the black, as he very often did to the white. Daisy could allow no man inside her breakwind, since the rules of the camp separated men from women unless the law allowed them to cohabit. Though she loved to dance she "refrained from this pastime" because, if the Aborigines saw her with a strange man's arms around her, they would condemn her as immoral. They kept as strict an eye on their Queen Government as she did on them. Each morning the entrance to her breakwind was examined for tracks.

Because they found none; because she respected their laws, they accepted her as one of themselves, a white woman from their own Dreamtime.

It was, for Daisy, the greatest comfort to be able to write in such personal terms to Miss King, for, "I never talk about my natives in this strain to anyone. Perhaps it is from a rather childish fear of ridicule or contempt. Even as it is, I am called 'rash' and 'foolish' and 'quixotic' and these expressions send me back into myself."

At the end of the year 1913, Daisy made the move to Jeegala Creek. Because of the initiation ceremony there was to be a gathering of more than a hundred and fifty Aborigines, representing the many different "totem clans" of the area. As these included a contingent from South Australia as well as from the West, some fighting would be inevitable but, she told Miss King —"I am always safe whatever tempers may be about."

"Provided you have some friendly authority over them," she explained, and "provided you choose the psychological moment", it was possible to relieve them of their spears and clubs when tempers became short.

That it was not quite as simple as it sounds, she shows in the instance she gives in *The Passing of the Aborigines.*

> Because there were so many factions, tension grew and grew until one day I found a raging crowd, with spears and spear throwers and clubs, ready to fall upon each other. I had gone

over to choose those who would see to the damper making for the day and penetrated right to the centre of the angry mob—a delicate moment.

I looked around. "All you *boggali* [grandsons] bring your spears to me," I said quietly. "I will sit down and take care of them and then you can go little way and have a good fight and come back for food."

To my astonishment old Ngarralea and Dhalja and other totemists of the loudest voices and most belligerent attitudes, put down their spears beside me. The others followed. I carefully arranged every spear in order of tribal eldership in its right totem group. Then I said, "Now go and have plenty talk and a little clubbing. I will wait." They went a little way only and I could hear the shouted grievances and antipathies in a wild medley of argument and accusation. Then, without rancour, they came back, ready for a meal.

"I sometimes think they are rather glad to be put out of action," she commented to the *Western Mail*, "for the after effects of a fracas of this kind are far reaching and the individuals who have wounded some member or other have to pay dearly in food and other gifts."

The initiation ceremonies began and, Daisy wrote, "orgies continued night after night." The excitement became so intense that an old man "danced himself into a frenzy of heat and passion" and dropped dead.

On her return to her camp she saw what seemed to be rain dripping from the branches of the Nala-tree. Her black friends, said Daisy, believed that it was the dead man's totem, weeping tears of mourning; and Daisy, the witness to it, was accepted at once into the Nala totem clan.

A more prosaic explanation for the "miracle" can be found in the reports of surveyor Tom Brown, who wrote that:

"The plain was subject to heavy dews and sea fogs, drenching trees such as the Nala tree. Wild dogs and kangaroos quenched their thirst by licking the water off the trees. It was possible to get a shower by standing under a tree and shaking the branches."

Daisy's rations of tea, sugar, flour and jam made feasting possible in spite of the game shortage. In gratitude the groups bestowed on her the "Freedom of their Totems". It was the highest honour they could give, more than equal to the "Freedom of the City" bestowed on a distinguished citizen.

To be worthy of it, she had first to promise to keep secret her knowledge of the totem shrine and of the totem storehouse. To their women, such knowledge was death, as it was death to tread the ground—even by accident—in the vicinity of the storehouse.

Daisy's vow of silence was to prove expensive.

"Prospectors in search of gold were always headed off from the spot by the natives," she wrote. "Several years ago, one of the writer's Jimari totem 'brothers' brought her a specimen of quartz from some hill near the storehouse. Though an assay of the specimen gave seventeen ounces to the ton, a promise was asked and given that while any Jimari totem men lived, the locality would not be disclosed."

To prepare her for the ceremony, all those natives of the Eucla district collected near her camp. The elders then brought her portions of their traditional totem food, usually cooked and presented in a bark scoop.

Then, one morning, she was awakened by the clicking of boomerangs. Outside her windbreak were a group of men "naked except for their decorations". The camp was silent, for the women and children had already been sent away.

A downward gesture of the hand meant that she must follow where she was led. They moved off single file, Daisy in the centre, her "sober Edwardian coat and skirt, sailor hat with fly veil and neat high heeled shoes" making "quaint contrast" with the oiled nudity of her companions.

Led from fire to fire, she was "purified" in smoke caused by flames beaten with green branches. Beside the file trotted some of the younger men, emitting "long tremolo eaglehawk screams, caused by covering their mouths with their hands".

At length they reached a cleared space some fifty yards in diameter. A great fire was lit in the centre. At a given signal each one took a mallee branch and sat in a semicircle of which Daisy was the centre:

> Then, "Yudi", came a shout from the elders. With bowed heads, in a tense silence, and with closed eyes, the great crowd of squatting natives bent to the ground. I ventured to watch.
>
> In a cleared ground that was used as the altar appeared Wardunda, an ancient tribal father, holding before him a totem board fifteen feet or more high, deeply grooved and painted in red ochre and white pipe clay with the sacred markings of Maalu, the kangaroo. Turning to face the prostrate circle, he lifted the *koondain* in the same manner as the elevation of the Host in the Roman Catholic Church . . . a frenzied chanting rose, the board was lowered until it was flat on the ground, Wardunda prostrated himself upon it and then rose and reverently carried it out as the singing died away.

All now rose to their feet. The men circled twice and then stood with their spears in fighting position while Wardunda approached Daisy. Taking the boards which she held in her arms, he touched her with each one, upon breast, back, shoulders and knees. Finally they were laid at her feet.

The young men who had witnessed the ceremony for the first time then came trembling to be touched in their turn. The totem songs were chanted. Finally the incongruous little procession returned to camp.

Symbiosis had now been hallowed with the most sacred rite of Aboriginal tradition. Daisy had been elevated out of the ranks of women. The trust of the elders had been bestowed on her. From then on the totem boards became her special responsibility, to be guarded and oiled with the care due to symbols of the sacred.

Their significance dated back to the dreamtime. "They hold the mystery of life," she said. "No native knows more than that."

CHAPTER TWENTY

Opinions differ most when there is least scientific warrant for having any.—Daisy Bates: Notebooks, 1914.

The Talking Point of Adelaide

On Christmas Day, 1913, Daisy provided dinner of damper, tea and pudding for fifty-three of her Aboriginal friends. In the hot months that followed, she lived in her 7- by 9-foot tent near the South Australian border, alone in the midst of a hundred and sixty-two black people.

As Keeper of the Totems she swung the sacred boards over the heads of newly initiated boys as they were sprinkled with blood from the arm veins of their tribal "brothers".

In August that same year that "ethnological student", Mrs Daisy Bates, was reported by the Melbourne press as "walking through the galleries of the State Government Reception in a trailing gown of blue brocade and a becomingly arranged coiffure".

Between these two manifestations of her persona, came an invitation to attend the congress of the British Association for the Advancement of Science. It was to include such eminent anthropologists as Professors Bateson and Malinowski, and was scheduled to meet in Adelaide, Melbourne and Sydney.

The invitation was the result of a paper requested by Mathew and read at the Australasian Congress the year before. In itself it was an acknowledgement of status in the scientific world. Daisy saw it as a Heaven-sent opportunity to press for the post of Protector.

To this purpose she had sent copies of her letters of recommendation to Georgina King, and that indefatigable worker for her cause had written back almost at once with the news that Professor Spencer, no less, had offered his "commendation" that her application be accepted. A new friend, Mrs Wordsworth James, "very energetic and a strong society woman", had taken up the matter in Adelaide.

With such support Daisy had reason to hope that, this time, she would be successful.

She could hardly have anticipated that the inaugural meeting of the Science Congress in Adelaide would coincide, almost to the day, with the outbreak of World War I.

Her immediate problem was how to get to Adelaide. The quarterly steamer that could take her would be too early or too late. A suitable ship was available from Fowler's Bay, but between Eucla and Fowler's Bay stretched two hundred and forty miles of waterless coast. To reach what she called the "heaven of contact with my own kind", Daisy was capable of emulating Eyre and of walking the distance, but fortunately another alternative presented itself.

She wrote to Miss King that, "I am trying to go by camel buggy, a journey that will take, under the best conditions, at least 12 days. Should rain come and spoil the camel track, a month or more. The storekeeper is trying to fix up the matter for me. He will lend me his buggy but I must hire the camels from another man."

It was a wrench to leave her elderly patients, but Eucla had been stricken by a drought so severe that the hunters had gone sixty miles north in search of game. Daisy admitted that she was "looking forward to the luxury of fresh milk and butter again".

By 12th May everything was arranged. She was to start in the middle of June, taking the overland route used by the natives. Her boxes had been transferred from Perth to Adelaide, so that, "I shall not be delayed in sartorial matters."

On a cool winter's morning, up the steep and dangerous road to the top of the cliffs, the long journey began. Her diary records that, at the start, "the off camel was refractory. We had rather an exciting time and went hurdling after the waggon. . . . Eventually, however, order was restored."

Her companions were her friend Gauera and Gauera's "latest and fourteenth husband, Balgundra". Balgundra had bought her a few weeks before from his brother Ngallilea for two shillings and a well-seasoned pipe, and when they reached a waterhole forty-odd miles out of Eucla, Ngallilea was waiting to join them.

"We were the happiest quartette you can imagine," Daisy wrote. "We sang songs, drove and sometimes walked for exercise. The men looked for lizards and grubs and edible gum, while Gauera sat aloft in her buggy, cursing the camels and feeling very important."

The road, "stretching hushed and spectral on and on towards the sunset", crossed the oldest existing land surface in the world. It was "a road of legends, the face of the landscape seared with native memories". Daisy put up her own tent each night and Gauera erected windbreaks for them all. But, "such was the sense of honour between these native people, that Ngallilea did not expect her to work for him. She had been sold not lent, and so he built his own shelter and took his meals alone."

They passed through Ilgamba, "an Arabian desert in little, where it never rains nor snows and where the fiery north wind raves and bullies"; through orphan territory, left unclaimed by native law because its inheritors had died. Those groups that were left, drifting "landless and listless" from waterhole to waterhole, greeted them in response to their smoke signals.

At each stop Gauera cooked the game the groups produced in welcome. They ate such delicacies as "wallaby tail with the skin left on, thrown into the ashes", and "a long fat carpet snake called goonia rolled into lengths and roasted". Finally, after twelve days and no rain, they arrived at Yalata station.

Here, "under the most kindly and hospitable pressure from the owners, Mr. and Mrs. Murray", Daisy took time to adjust from one world to the other. She needed the few days she allowed herself. She could still bridge the gap between bush and town life but the former had now taken precedence over the latter. Privacy had become an essential. She told Miss King that she did not think she could ever again share a bedroom. She preferred to wash in a bowl or a bucket brought to her room, rather than to use the family bathroom. Fortunately her clothes, expensive and well preserved, remained the height of fashion. By the time she moved into the South Australian, the most expensive hotel in Adelaide, she had assumed the appearance, as well as the assurance, of a lady about town.

She arrived to find herself the talking point of Adelaide. Her articles had been having their effect. Published now in most of the leading newspapers of the country, her highly personalized treatment of her subject was already the cause of controversy.

To the ordinary reader, she had introduced the Aborigines as human beings. From objects of contempt they had been transformed into personalities with identifiable emotions. The specialist minority acknowledged her as a journalist but dismissed her as an anthropologist. The more publicity she received—and she continued to be a source of fascination to the press—the greater the resentment among academics who considered that they had something more positive to say and were not given the same chance to say it.

Especially unpopular was her insistence that the black Australians were a doomed race.

On this premise, her ethnological studies, her personal attitude and her application for the Protectorship were based. For, "if only for a moment we put ourselves in their position, if through some sudden cataclysm we were thrown back to the Stone Age of these aborigines, would not our passing be even more tragically quick than theirs?" she asked.

It sounded reasonable. But anthropologists were already questioning the adjective "stone age"—questioning, in fact, the superiority of white culture, so implicitly accepted by this pre-war epoch. But Daisy's experience had been too long and too immediate. She was no longer capable of objective theory. She saw only the problems, never the promise of assimilation. Although she appreciated her black friends as did no other white woman; although she openly stated her affection for them, her horizons were limited. Neither a reformer nor a revolutionary, her one concrete suggestion was segregation, though for the sake of the blacks and not the whites, "since any aspect of the white man's relationship system the native absorbed has reacted disastrously through the years on his own domestic relations."

To Daisy there was nothing more pathetic than the "civilized" native, lost in his no-man's land between cultures. Like a moth he was at once dazzled and destroyed by the bright flame of the white man's vices.

"It is so extraordinary to me," she wrote to Miss King, "the sudden and hopeless longing of the natives for the white man's drink. After the first taste of it they appear to be irrevocably inoculated with it and of course the end comes soon to them."

Alcohol was the main currency in the thriving trade that had sprung up between the Aborigines and the doggers and linesmen

Pyap, on the Murray

Daisy Bates with the late Lady Hayward of Adelaide

of the Plain. Lubras were bartered for the price of a can of beer. They lived with their "temporary husbands" until the latter were recalled to the town. Then they were returned to their lords and masters. It was an amicable enough arrangement. They were accepted back into their niches in the relationship system. They might, of course, contract the white man's venereal disease, but otherwise the adjustment was made without difficulty. But, Daisy pointed out, it was the offspring of these unions who were the sufferers.

"The heritage of suffering and woe that a white man leaves his half caste child!" she exclaimed to her diary. "Set apart as children of a Ghetto, with every avenue of advancement except that of servitude and prostitution closed to them, they see themselves —those of them who read and think—left out of account or absolutely ignored by those leaders who shout for a white Australia. Not a single influence except the doubtful ones of mission or institution—neither of which fulfil the human purpose intended —is exerted to uplift them and when, naturally, they go wrong, the whole race of them is accused. They cannot defend themselves against wrong—for who will believe a half caste man or woman against a white man?"

Sometimes the child was loved, in which case the mother did her best to blacken the pale skin with oil and charcoal, but it was seldom if ever given an inherited place in the group. When it was not wanted, it was very often suffocated by filling its mouth with sand. It was then disposed of down a rabbit burrow.

Daisy's application was based on her belief that she could put an end to cohabitation between black and white and so to the problem of unwanted children. For it she blamed the white man and never the black women, who, she said, were "the absolute slaves of their men".

Public opinion was behind her. In 1914 the word "half-caste" carried its own stigma. A white woman who shared the popular point of view and had the courage to try to do something about it brought the journalists flocking.

Their first reaction was one of surprise. Here was no grim-faced do-gooder. The fashionable lady with the upper-class English accent, the expensive clothes and the delicate hands that showed no sign of the sun, was something of a revelation.

"She is as far removed from stereotyped notions of the 'new' woman as chalk from cheese," enthused one lady journalist. "Her personality is magnetic but . . . it is her gentle womanliness that one finds most charming," said another.

"The published interviews have swamped me with callers," she told Miss King. "Sir Henry Galway, at a Government House reception, singled me out and told the others what a celebrity I was. Most of the guests intend to call."

Daisy made the most of her fame to ensure her appointment. "Working here there and everywhere", she saw Glynn, the Federal representative; South, the Chief Protector, who was "kindly disposed". The Galways, "friends of my brother-in-law", expressed themselves "anxious to help".

She agreed to lecture for the women's non-political unions, and for the Royal Society. Her former host, George Murray, offered to contribute a pair of camels if the Government would supply her with the buggy needed for her work.

She arrived on 11th July 1914. Less than three weeks later she was called for an interview by a Commission representing the Minister for the Department of the Interior.

Daisy's wants were modest enough. At first she asked merely that her honorary protectorship be extended over the South Australian border; later for this to become a Commonwealth paid appointment, carrying a J.P.-ship. To be mobile she would need a camel buggy and £200 a year.

As the following extract shows, her questioners were much concerned with the current scandal of cohabitation:

QUESTION. Is it your opinion that natives would be better left alone in the interior than by being taken and treated at mission stations, or allowed to go to townships and other camps?

DAISY. Is is much better for the natives to be left by themselves.

QUESTION. You suggested that if you had a pair of camels and could travel about from camp to camp it might be the means of preventing immoral habits among the women?

DAISY. Yes. I am quite sure that it would prevent the immorality of the native women with the white men.

QUESTION. Were there any births [in the Eucla district]?

DAISY. No, but at Fowler's Bay a native woman procured abortion and killed her half-caste child before it was born.

QUESTION. Do you find any business being transacted between the black man and the black woman by the former handing the woman over to the whites?

DAISY. The blackfellow's woman is his chattel. He deals with her just as he deals with his boomerang. If you offer a price for the one he will take it and if you offer a price for the other he will take it. The boomerang is not such an asset to him as the woman because if he parts with a boomerang he parts with it for good. But he has his woman still.

QUESTION. I suppose you resent the mingling of the black with the whites on moral grounds, irrespective of whether the white men feed the lubras?

DAISY. I think I do. I detest the immorality between the blacks and the whites, because it is taking advantage of the weaker creature.

QUESTION. I understand that you have disposed of your private property and devoted your capital to this work?

DAISY. I have sold my property and I am spending my capital. I have nearly spent it all.

QUESTION. If the Government are prepared to make this appointment how would you employ your money?

DAISY. I propose traversing the districts from Streaky Bay in the east to Balladonia in the west. Then I would go north and travel along the line to get among the natives. Wherever I found a native camp there I would make a stay in order to keep in touch with the blacks and help them. My position would be one of intermediary between them to help settle their quarrels and help protect them from their own people and the whites. I could do this without raising any fuss or causing worry in any way. The chief objection in the West to my appointment as protector was that the Government considered the risks too great for a woman but I have proved there is no danger for any decent woman who wishes to travel from one end of Australia to another, either from blacks or whites.

"Wanted a Protector," trumpeted the press. Determined to make a heroine out of her, women journalists printed long interviews under such headings as "Woman's Heroic Work", "Love that is Service". Her presence at the Congress compelled the journalists to mention her book, still being "subjected to exhaustive revision", but her ethnological status took second place to "the noble work she had undertaken". Daisy saw herself referred to as a missionary "in deeds if not in words", her success attributed to "the love that she brought her work".

With her nobility thus insisted upon, her ethnological stature secure, her social influence at its height, Daisy left Adelaide for the second section of the Science Congress in Melbourne, with the Protectorship insured against all possible circumstances.

The impossible happened and war was declared. Probably stunned by the magnitude of the catastrophe, the Congress continued regardless. Daisy was interviewed with the same deference that had been accorded her in Adelaide. She had a chance to exchange views with "that charming man" John Mathew; to meet for the first time "God's good woman", Miss King; and, perhaps rashly, to cross swords once again with Radcliffe-Brown, newly created Professor of Anthropology at the University of Cape Town.

"At one of the meetings his paper was all an extract from my MS.," she wrote. "At the close of Brown's paper, Sir Everard im Thurn asked me if I would like to add to Mr. Brown's paper.

"I said that Mr. Brown had given my notes so nicely there was no occasion to add to them. The meeting 'grimaced audibly' and I don't think Brown will ever forget the incident. The paper was on the Myths of the Western Australian Aborigines."

She returned to Adelaide in September of the year, to find her cause already lost.

She did not know it at the time. She remarked with some irritation to Miss King, that "nothing but war is fashionable", but she gave her lectures and continued to hammer at the gates of Government. The presidents of the women's clubs followed the example of their sisters in the West and sent a deputation to plead for her. The chairman of the Aboriginal Board, Sir Richard Butler, was reported as expressing surprise that she was not already at work.

But the fate of the Aborigines had suffered a sad eclipse. Anxiety on their behalf could not compete with the new and terrible fear for the safety of the young men who were leaving in their thousands for slaughter overseas.

Daisy, the nine days' wonder, had to return to Yalata station "with no satisfactory news from the Government".

And so things remained. During the four years of war she was given neither yes nor no. There were moments of hope. A paragraph appeared in the papers announcing that she was to be given the appointment, which induced Daisy to bring over her gear from Eucla and establish herself in her tent in Fowler's Bay. Nothing happened.

Then came a surprise visit on the part of South, the Chief Protector.

This was on 27th June 1915. His arrival, "which could not have been more opportune, though not arranged for", coincided with that of a contingent of women and children who had travelled twelve miles to be fed, "almost naked and very hungry".

"It is my last hope," she wrote to Miss King, "and I beg you to pray that it may be fulfilled."

But Miss King's prayers, though doubtless offered, were not enough. Daisy reported that "Mr. South has consented to let me have some flour, tea, sugar and rice for the old and feeble. So that in itself is a great relief to me." He had also "advised sending a personal letter to the Premier as the appointment would have his approval".

It was never made.

As always, Daisy turned for solace to the bush. She took one of the native roads to Wirilya, twenty-six miles from Yalata, and settled down at a camping ground of the groups that passed through on their way to the lovely Yuria waters.

Surrounded by a ring of soft green valleys, bounded by hills of mallee-trees, she lived on a Government subsidy of £7. 10s. a quarter. On this she looked after three blind patients and a woman suffering from venereal disease.

This was in the spring of 1915. A press interview gave no hint of disappointment. When she was asked the reason for her "voluntary exile" her answer was that she was "really happy in the bush".

"I love the space and the peace and the freedom . . . the light of early dawn in the scrub and the twittering of birds . . . the wonder of sunsets and the peace of lengthening shadows."

If she needed stimulus, there was the never-ending fascination of primitive life: geological marvels such as the fossilized footsteps near the coast left by far-off ancestors who walked over the soft mud of long ago in search of oysters and mussels; the native hunters who came to Wirilya to drink the blood of the emu.

"In nature," she declared, "there can be no real loneliness—and there can be no bores!"

It was a gallant attempt at cheerfulness, denied by the jottings in her notebook.

"Alone, all alone I have roamed through the trees and over the gentle wooded slopes and my soul is at rest in Nature's bosom, where her sweet voices—for she is myriad voiced—lull me to forgetfulness of sorrow and suffering."

The different groups added to her store of vocabularies, customs and legends. For her patients she "hunted and cooked, tend-ing them in every detail of their poor lives." Her Eucla training proved its value and she managed to bring them back "iguana, lizards and rabbits".

She was no longer "Queen Government". Her status now was "family". She was Kabbarli, the grandmother. She was the friend who fed them, gave them clothes and trinkets and sometimes doctored them.

"My young native girl whose breasts were so bad and whom I attended is now all right again, but she had a very narrow escape," she reported to Miss King. "The matter in her breast had become hard and the skin was looking dreadful. The remedies I applied were strong but necessarily so and the matter forced a hole in the breast and passed outward. If it had gone inward nothing could have saved her as it was almost green and mortified."

Dowie, one of her blind patients, had attacks of dementia and developed the habit of rushing out of the camp and hiding himself in the bush. The first time it happened, Daisy found him naked and exhausted in a clump of bushes about a mile and a half from the camp. "With great difficulty I hoisted the poor old fellow on my back and, leaning for support upon my digging stick, slowly carried him back."

Fortunately her sense of the ridiculous came to her aid and she wrote that "the recollection came to me that I was still a present member of Perth's most exclusive women's club. My very chuckle at the thought made the load lighter."

Her most harrowing experience at Wirilya was the illness of the young lubra who was a victim of venereal disease caught from her "temporary" white husband.

"Jeera lived six weeks with me, rotting visibly away, and screaming through all her conscious hours," Daisy told Hurst. "I had to think of some remedy for her. I got brandy and stopped the pain by giving her doses in cupfuls. Such a relief to her, poor creature."

As Jeera approached the end of her sufferings, Daisy was faced with a problem that had occupied her during her years amongst the black people.

Her faith, though she admitted to no creed, was the sustaining force of her life. Since she believed in "deeds and not words", most religions were found wanting because "they lack that humanity which should be the very pith and centre of spiritual activity."

How could she pass on so very personal and private a belief to a people so recently deprived of their own?

In her letter to William Hurst, she told the story of Jeera's dying moments. On this occasion at least she could provide consolation because of the girl's faith in her:

> "Where's my firestick, Kabbarli? Where am I going?" she asked.
>
> I ventured a word. "Did you ever hear of the white man's God?"
>
> "Oh yes, Brophy (the wretch who had brought her to this state) often told me about his God Jesus."
>
> Well do you know, I simply could not claim the same God as Brophy. I said to Jeera, "You know Kabbarli loves you and tried to make you better?"
>
> "I've only you, Kabbarli. No one else would be good to me."
>
> "Well," I said, "you're going on a little journey only and to a place where my Father is. I've asked him to look out for you and he'll take your hand as I'm taking it now."
>
> "Your father, Kabbarli. Then Jeera will be all right."
>
> And she died so quietly that I did not know she was dead until her poor small hand was cold in mine.

By September 1918 Daisy had need of her faith. Her health had given out and there was no more money in the bank.

"My last payment at Yalata store was in September 1917," she wrote to South, "and since then I have had to book my few needs . . . how few you will judge when you know that my account up to July 19th 1918 totalled £13.

"I am indebted to Yalata store for the cup of tea I drink. I have brought my needs to the point when further curtailment would mean starvation . . . if there were an appointment that I could fill immediately in Adelaide then I would most gratefully accept my fare."

She asked him to bring her case to the notice of the Government and had "put the matter barely and plainly to you so that you should be fully aware of the desperate circumstances in which I have placed myself through my devotion to these unfortunate aborigines."

It was the closest she ever came to an admission of defeat. Pride had yielded to circumstance; but she could still reprove South because he had asked the constable to issue her with a train ticket.

"I'm sure you did not think of the excessive humiliation to me of having to apply to the local police for a fare to Adelaide," she admonished him.

The Government's response was the sum of fifty pounds and the offer of the matronship of a returned soldiers' home.

Daisy accepted both. She appeared to settle down, and told Hurst that "the committee—busy and bustling—seems to like me and I have been able to choose my own cap and uniform, so you will see the extent of my victory!"

Three months later she had resigned. The work was too difficult. She did not know the ABC of her job. These and other reasons she gave, although "infinitely regretful" at leaving her "beloved boys".

The real reason was the final blow dealt her on the subject of her appointment as Protector.

To Hurst she confided that a German Australian called Dr Basedow had "taken up the cause of the native women and children"; his ambition was to become their medical superintendent and his appeal was based on his claim that he could "ensure their survival". She told him that she would "wait with interest, the outcome of his appeal".

The result of it was a commission to Basedow to "investigate", with a grant of £500. It was the death blow to her hopes, too galling for her to tolerate without bitterness.

She had prepared the ground, awakened the citizens of Adelaide to the problem, and had been passed over in favour of another.

Her letters at the time reveal the venom of outrage.

She had reason for bitterness. Her experience was unique, her knowledge of the field unmatched, her devotion proved. Against her was her femininity, her extravagance, and—the word "survival".

Basedow, with the benefit of medical training, was offering hope to a situation that Daisy persisted in presenting as hopeless. Against her negative he presented a positive. This alone would have ensured him his £500 from a Government anxious by now to appease its conscience.

Daisy, unable to compromise, found instead a new "enemy". So violent was her animosity that it lost her the friends who had rallied to her support.

Most powerful amongst them was Sir Henry Galway, the Governor.

"Sir Henry said I was biassed against Dr. Basedow. I replied I am not biassed against a man I've never seen but I strongly object to the sick, diseased native women of this State being exploited in the interests of German bacteriological research.

"Sir Henry got cross (the first time a Governor has ever been cross with me and over a German too!). I maliciously quoted the *Bulletin* and said there must be something in the statement that Germany had lost all its colonies except South Australia. I then bowed myself off, laughing."

It was not the most tactful way to gain an objective.

Dr Basedow left on his expedition and Daisy boarded the train for Ooldea. As security she had the remains of her fifty pounds and the promise of freelance journalism to come. But news had reached her of a mob of Aborigines wandering from stop to stop along the railway line. Amongst them were her blind friends who had sent a message asking her to return.

She left the cool haven of the Adelaide foothills and set out for the burning sands of Ooldea soak, to pitch the tent that was to be her home for the next sixteen years of her life.

CHAPTER TWENTY-ONE

La Rochefoucauld rightly says that philosophy triumphs easily over past and future evils but present evils triumph over philosophy.—Daisy Bates: Notebooks.

Ooldea

"We generally return to our muttons don't we," Daisy wrote to Hurst on 5th October 1919. "I've come back to my natives again, since it's the only work I've proved that I'm fitted for. I could not prevail upon the Adelaide Government to recognise a Woman Protector [but] I could not resist the 'call' (a different call to that which takes a popular clergyman to a more lucrative district!)."

Daisy's call took her to a pinprick on the white man's map four hundred and twenty-seven miles north of Port Augusta on the eastern tip of the Nullarbor Plain.

A siding on John Forrest's dream-come-true, the Trans-Australian Railway Line, Ooldea consisted of a squat little row of four iron-roofed bungalows that housed the employees on the line. In Aboriginal language it was Yooldil Gabbi, the name of a miraculous subterranean water under a hollow in the eternal sandhills that undulated for a thousand miles parallel with the Bight.

The proud possession of the Emu totem men, it had been a perpetual fountain available at less than the depth of a spear in the sand, no matter how severe the drought. When Daisy arrived there the Soak, as it was called, was already orphan ground and forbidden to the people whose discovery it was. Pumping plants conveyed water at the rate of 10,000 gallons a day along the three-mile pipeline to the siding. Aborigines had to ask permission to turn on the taps along the line.

In spite of the heat, the flies and the sand that bit through the face veil to scourge her delicate skin, Daisy returned to tent life more than ever convinced that it was "the answer to everything".

Her brief contact with white civilization had decided her that she was "now a stranger to the ways and thoughts of my own people". The welcome she received from her black friends confirmed this sense of homecoming. News had spread over the bush telegraph that "Kabbarli" was back. They crowded round to greet her, advising on her camp-site, and helping her to build the breakwind, more than ever necessary in this land of the north wind. As they did so they passed on the "family" gossip.

Daisy learnt that her predictions of 1914 had come true. Little groups of derelicts had established their camps at the different stops along the line. They were begging from the passengers on the train, presenting a humiliating spectacle of filth and tatters. Prostitution was rife. Women being in demand, the men brought more down from the north. The breakdown in their laws had penetrated as far as the great central reserve. Bands of desert Aborigines drifted down towards Ooldea, bringing with them recent histories of tribal feuds and intermarriage. In the safety of white civilization, the white man's fire drink and the white man's vices were already taking their toll. There were several reported cases of venereal disease; more than one case of the death of half-caste offspring.

Kabbarli had a job to do.

Her first camp was beside an extension of the railway known as the wood line; an ever-growing finger of destruction, flanked by the broken stumps of precious trees cut down to feed the fires of the new *ganba* monster of the Nullarbor. It was not an ideal place for a seeker after solitude and it was not long before she moved to a tree-encircled site on a rise in the sandhills between the Soak and the siding. Below her were the Aboriginal mias dotted at discreet intervals in the scrub. Far in the distance was the saltbush sea of the great Plain.

Close to available water, equipped with two tents now instead of one, her new quarters were as comfortable as could be expected in a climate where rain could hold off for years at a time and the barometer could push to its limits and stay there.

Her "furniture" was much the same. To the stretcher bed, packing-case table, and mirror encircled by pockets, she had now added a deck-chair, and a tank sunk into the sand and lined with shelves to house her books. Newspapers arrived in bulk on the weekly "tea and sugar" provision train. These she devoured, line by line.

In her bough shed was the tin trunk in which were her precious manuscripts, "to the compilation of which," she told the press, "I have devoted my whole life." To study the star-pierced desert skies, she erected a Heath Robinson type observatory, consisting of a deal platform to support her telescope. An important asset was the cool safe made for her by one of the fettlers. It was a primitive enough affair, the old-time "Coolgardie safe" consisting of a wooden frame moistened by wet hessian, but it obviated the need to bury her perishables in the sand. She could now keep a tin of butter, sometimes for a month. She could even keep meat, if she could bring herself to touch it.

In Ooldea, her revolver was kept in the pocket close to her bed. Not that she was afraid, then or ever, of her companions. It was a protection against snakes and to frighten away the dingoes which, she said, could still howl in the sandhills at night.

Her portmanteau under the bed remained the only wardrobe she possessed. In it, neatly folded, were her collection of long-sleeved white blouses, blue ribbon ties, and serviceable ankle-length skirts. In these desert conditions she chose wide-brimmed hats, ballooned with fly veiling. Her straitened circumstances did not prevent her from wearing silk next to her skin. Her underskirts dated back to her schooldays, and were as long as her skirts, shaped to the figure, with knee-high flounces.

"All my native gear is made to be able to swing my tomahawk and move every part of my body," she explained.

As she could not afford to buy new clothes, she made a virtue out of necessity. Her outfit became her "uniform of Empire" and part of her "Kabbarli image"; she even wore her size-three boots buttoned to the calf and high heeled, so that the sandhills were dotted with tiny pointed indentations. But an observation in her notebooks shows that she was not always as happy with her uniform of Empire as she pretended.

"The women who wore these dresses in the old days never had to move in a hurry," she complained. "They never went for long country walks nor . . . ran hither and thither as we do in our strenuous modern—but not ungraceful life."

More than ever did she need to wear gloves, not only to protect her skin but to prevent infection. The Adelaide store of John Martins supplied her, as a gift, with endless pairs, mostly of white cotton. She was never without them. On the one occasion when she did forget, she pricked her finger while attending a diseased patient. Faced with the alternative of a trip to hospital or of immersing the infected finger in boiling water, Daisy chose the latter. The infection was burnt away and the lesson was painful enough never to be forgotten.

Part reason for her "call" was the initiation ceremony for which the groups were already gathering at the Soak. Daisy hoped to garner more invaluable data and armed herself with pencil and pad, walking the three miles there and back each day to "sit down" with them. No sooner had she settled down to the familiar rhythm of her bush life than it was rudely shattered by the discovery that she was in disgrace with the Department for Aboriginal Affairs.

The reason was her "Kabbarli camp", as she called it.

Proud of her "family" status—she boasted to Hurst that she knew the names of each member of the groups along the line—Daisy had resumed her role of matriarch together with her researches. But at Ooldea, unlike when she was at Eucla, she was now in the public eye. In fact she had become something of a curiosity, pointed out to the passengers of the train as she tended her patients in her picture hat and long skirts, pannikins of food swinging from her wrists.

As Kabbarli it was incumbent on her to distribute largesse, especially as she had been given the young initiates to feed.

Daisy, who had decided on sweetened porridge as the best and cheapest fill-up for hungry young men, took pride in their rounded bellies which they patted with the words *jooni bulga*, meaning "bowels full", by way of thanks.

By now, too, she understood the lesson first taught her by Ngilgee so many years before, that to accept the gift of information in the way of vocabularies and legends, she must reward the donor, perhaps with a tin of fruit, perhaps with a new shirt. But now she had no money of her own on which to draw. To supplement the Government rations she applied to the Department of Aboriginal Affairs in Adelaide.

It was not long before she was reprimanded. She was encouraging the Aborigines to depend on the Government. Official policy was to help them to fend for themselves. Only this way could the begging along the line be discouraged.

Daisy's chagrin can be imagined. Even if the Protectorship had been denied her, her work had never before been openly criticized.

She had grown used to her press image as a heroine. It was not easy to accept the fact that, officially speaking, she was now regarded as a public nuisance.

The irony of the situation was that, in principle, she was totally in agreement with Government policy—a fact that the Department would have seen for itself, if it had bothered to read the report of the 1914 Commission of Inquiry. More immediate proof was her application to establish a camp at Windunya Water, north of the railway line. With Government backing, she could entice the groups away from white settlement and prevent new arrivals from joining them. This she considered to be a positive answer. The departmental policy of forcing the Aborigines to "move on" meant that they were banished from their only available water, with the result that they drifted back farther down the line.

Her suggestion had been refused, probably because, by the time she made it, she had thoroughly antagonized South, the Chief Protector.

The root of the trouble was the equivocal position in which she had placed herself.

At Eucla she had the authority of her honorary Protectorship, and had private funds to supplement Government handouts.

South claimed, with some justice, that her presence at Ooldea was a personal and not an official matter, and therefore not under the jurisdiction of his Department.

Her requests for increased rations became an irritant which, because of her prestige, could not be ignored. He authorized the local police officers to investigate and their reports contradicted hers. Her requests were refused.

As usual Daisy countered official opposition with an appeal to a higher authority—a move that did not help her case. Amongst the civil servants of Adelaide, the impression grew that she was an irresponsible eccentric, requesting Government help to further her own ends.

In the battle of wills that followed, Daisy strained every nerve to gain her point. Unfortunately for her cause, her habit of exaggerating the situation weakened rather than strengthened her case. Finally all cooperation was lost.

The first brush with the Department was precipitated by the announcement of a train strike.

In the late spring of 1919 the little community of Ooldea was presented with the disturbing news that the line was to be closed down until further notice. Isolated by eighty miles from their nearest white neighbours, they would be cut off from all sources of supply.

Volunteers brought a train to take the fettlers' wives and families to Port Augusta. Daisy, faced with the responsibility of eight sick or elderly dependents, elected to stay.

Her immediate step was to send off a wire to the Department, asking for rations to be put on the last train to pass through the siding before the strike came into operation. She was answered, she said, with a request to send a report in writing. She then hired a buggy and drove into Cook, loading it with necessities to last for some weeks.

November came and went. By mid-December the strike was still dragging on.

Life became a question of survival. Two of the pumpers who had remained behind to ensure the water supplies, set out on foot for Fowler's Bay. The younger Aborigines went north. The women foraged daily for lizards and goannas. Daisy used her revolver as a hunting weapon and went rabbit shooting with the temperatures mounting from 100 to 107°.

She broke the news to Hurst with the flippant comment that "we are all doing a starving stunt." Her letters written, though unposted, during the strike, were filled with comments designed to console.

"At least my body is free from the ailments of too much food," was one. And another: "I can live off a biscuit and a sunset and so am closer to the Gods."

But a biscuit must be swallowed with at least a glass of water and after a time even the water supplies were threatened. In the last painful days of the last painful week, Daisy's letters were no longer cheerful.

On one day of great heat she was forced to remain prostrate on her stretcher, deaf to the appeals of her black friends who crowded round her tent calling for her. Only when night had come to disperse them did she dare get up and make herself a longed-for cup of tea.

The first supply train drew into the siding on 21st December; but Christmas 1919 was not a festive occasion. Daisy's Christmas dinner was "a damper failure, made without baking powder, tea and jam". But she had "learned the secret of true contentment"—she could "live without a good cook!"

After such a prolonged ordeal, depression was inevitable. Daisy yearned for "her own kind". A letter from Harry Gregory, Minister of Mines for the West, had brought news of Arnold; now "a fine man" of whom she could be proud, married and with a family of his own. Daisy kept his letter and busied herself with her black *boggali* in order not to think of the two white grandchildren she had never seen.

Her friends had not altogether forgotten her. Letters appeared in the Adelaide papers urging that her "noble work" be remembered. Her honorary Protectorship was renewed for the State of Western Australia. She was made a J.P. for the Line and was, therefore, the only woman to be a Justice of the Peace in two States.

In 1920 the *Melbourne Herald* took up her cause, stating indignantly that: "There should be a limit to the voluntary work which Mrs Bates has performed uncomplainingly for so many years at her own expense. She has blazed a trail which seems to show the necessity for the appointment of woman administrator of native affairs."

But South, who had originally favoured her appointment, was now against it.

"You know, my friend, I must have some enemies," Daisy wrote to Hurst. For, "no man or woman, who tries to pursue an ideal in his or her own way, is without enemies."

She had even lost the support of the Adelaide Women's Guilds who had worked so hard on her behalf. Now, she told him, they were saying that "Mrs. Bates does not adhere to the facts." Predictably, she attributed the "little meannesses, pinpricks and vulgarities" to which, she said, she was subjected, to the pro-German element in South Australia.

Much closer to the truth was the comment that appeared later in Government files.

"It is clear that Mrs Bates has no idea of the value of money."

There was precious little left. Without the help of the Aboriginal Affairs Department, she was having a struggle to continue her camp life. Her newspaper articles brought in scarcely enough to support herself, and certainly not enough for the gifts necessary to matriarchal prestige.

If she had not made public her rejection of their aims, she might have been able to draw on mission funds. Here again she paid the penalty of her refusal to compromise, openly discounting the possibility that the Aborigines could be converted to Christianity, if only because "they had no sense of original sin".

Their mission prayers, she said, were repeated "pitter patter parrot fashion"; after which they went back to their ancestral tribal beliefs.

She repeated her statement, shocking to those comfortable citizens with an unchallenged belief in the superiority of their culture, that, by Aboriginal standards, the whites were condemned. "Our consanguinous marriages," she wrote, "would be punished by instant death . . . our lenient divorce system . . . reduces us below their own level . . . our drunkenness, misery and vice—though so often tragically adopted—receive their contempt."

If we did succeed in Christianizing them, what do we offer? she asked. Who will treat them as brothers and sisters, though they are fellow Christians?

For that matter what virtue was there in European religions, since "we dare to limit God's universality and lessen that mercy to which all hearts are open to this or that puny creed, all others being anathema."

"Aborigines," she declared, "could not accept this or that dogma, nor hell fire . . . nor any of the abstract ideas confusing even to ourselves which we call, collectively, religions."

These were not the kind of arguments designed to win the support of the missions.

She was too proud to ask for charity and incapable of playing the part of a civil servant. She thought "black" not "white". Her constant demand was that "the native question should be looked at from the native point of view."

Convinced that she, more than any other white person, understood the Aboriginal mentality, she was ready to give but seldom to take advice.

In her own eyes she might be Kabbarli, woman of Empire and matriarch of a black family, in the eyes of the Aboriginal Department she was Daisy Bates, a self-willed eccentric who refused to acknowledge their authority while demanding to represent them as though she did.

In March 1920 South paid her a visit. He repeated his instructions that her group must disperse. More humiliating still, he had chosen a local pumper as his representative in the district. This man would, therefore, be the distributor of rations in Ooldea.

Daisy's reaction was to order him off her camp-site. From then on her relations with the Department were severed.

As though this were not bad enough, by the end of the year she was in even more serious trouble with the anthropologists.

Receipt of the final payment from her leaseholds had decided her on a trip to Perth. Her official reason was to see an eye specialist. Unofficially it was to persuade Neville to give her the appointment refused by South. To this purpose she had enlisted Frank Hann, now an explorer of note. Again the answer was no.

Hann wrote, bluntly enough, that neither Neville nor his assistant wanted her to have a say about the blacks. She had no chance because "neither of them understand the blacks outback but they think they do and that goes down with the Government."

The reason for their refusal is not hard to find. On her way to Perth Daisy had released the first of her "cannibal" sensations.

In spite of opposition from the anthropologists, she had persisted in her belief that, among the circumcised groups of the North-west and North Central areas, cannibalism was practised. It was limited, she said, to certain regions, and was due in part to a shortage of available meat, in part to the custom of blood-drinking at initiation ceremonies. Amongst the uncircumcised Bibbulmuns it was unknown. In fact it was the sight of a human thigh being prepared for cooking in the Kimberleys that had sent her old friend Fanny Balbuk hurrying back to the South.

To the gruesome phenomenon of infant cannibalism she had been introduced in the very early days at Beagle Bay.

In the past, she had been reticent on the subject. When she did make a brief mention of it to the *Western Mail*, she had been careful to add that it was a custom that died out after contact with the whites.

In saying so, she had shown more compunction than Surveyor Brown whose report on the Eucla district had included a statement from a resident that "the natives of the area ate their children and quite frequently their old men and their enemies." He mentioned by name "Old Dick Dorie, Swan and Smith's dog poisoner, [who] said that he had seen a black child killed and eaten. He could do nothing as he was being felt at the same time to ascertain his condition for killing."

Daisy had taken it for granted that her presence in camp was enough to prevent any form of cannibalism as it was enough to prevent prostitution. She was, then, extremely upset to find that she was wrong.

Shortly before she left for Perth a contingent of twenty-six Aborigines had come down from the Musgrave Ranges, one among them a "heavily pregnant woman".

According to Daisy's account, the lubra had vanished from the camp and, suspecting the worst, Daisy had tracked her over a distance of twelve miles. The woman had doubled on her tracks, returned to within a mile of the camp, and given birth to a baby girl. She then "killed and ate it, sharing her dreadful meal with her youngest child aged about three or four."

"Later with the help of her sons and grandsons, the spot was found but nothing was to be seen, only the ashes of the fire. The boys said 'the bones are under the fire' and, digging with the *wanna* (digging stick) we came upon the broken skull and one or two bones which were forwarded later to the Adelaide Museum."

This benefited Daisy's reputation not at all. The bones were analysed by her old friend Professor Cleland, now Professor of Pathology at the University of Adelaide, and discovered to be the bones of a feral cat.

That the incident occurred, however, is corroborated by A. G. Bolam, the Ooldea station-master, in his little book *Trans Australian Wonderland*, in which he says there was "unchallengeable proof" of cannibalism, including a case that "occurred so recently as October 1920 at Ooldea". On top of a difficult and disappointing year that had ended with a frightening attack of blindness resulting from sandy blight, Daisy had been confronted by failure in the one area in which she had known only success.

It was too much to be borne. Discouraged and depressed, she determined that the world should understand something of what she had to face, and released the story to the *Kalgoorlie Miner*.

It appeared on 12th May 1921, and was introduced with the damaging admission that "few more gruesome pictures have ever been drawn of the Australian native than that recently given by Mrs. Daisy Bates." To the story of the lubra Daisy had attached the comment that "there is not one child [at Ooldea] who has not eaten portion of his brother or sister . . . [for] all the natives in the area . . . are cannibals."

Sweeping statements, as the interviewer commented, but borne out years later by an unexpected source.

In *Ooldea*, her book on the Ooldea Mission, Violet Turner, writing with the earnestness of the zealot, makes the astonishing claim that the Aboriginal mission children did not find it difficult to accept the Christian significance of the eating of bread and the drinking of wine, since many of them had been given the flesh of a baby brother or sister in order to partake of their strength.

Miss Turner's book was not in time to appease the indignation of the Chief Protector. Nor do many anthropologists, let it be said, share her opinion.

Daisy found herself the centre of a controversy that was by no means confined to the West.

A letter she sent to the Commonwealth Government is proof that she regretted what she knew to have been a betrayal of trust on her part. But to defend herself against the accusations levelled against her, she was forced to back up her statements. She did so in the form of an article published in the *Australasian.*

Proof that cannibalism existed, she contended, lay in the Aboriginal children's games; in the legends that represented black history, and above all, because there was a dialectic keyword meaning "human meat" from Kimberley to the Great Bight. Only by inserting this word "quietly and ordinarily" into the conversation could she obtain her information on the subject. For, "it is no use asking a native, are you a cannibal?" she wrote. "He will reply, no, but those other fellows eat blackfellows. When the other fellows are questioned they also deny the accusation and say their accusers are man eaters."

While mending his trousers Daisy had prevailed on Tharndurri, an old man of the Andingirini group, to talk about the last man-eating ceremony in which he had partaken.

On this occasion a young adult had been killed. "Tharndurri extracted the raw liver and placed it on some bark. Certain young men of his group . . . held their *miros* (spear throwers) across their backs with the ends in the crook of the elbow, thus rendering them unable to use their hands. Tharndurri sliced the liver with a large chipped flint and threw a piece at the mouth of each young man, by whom it must be caught and swallowed without mastication. Should a stomach reject the portion, or should the young man be unable to swallow it without mastication, or should it drop before he could catch it in his mouth, the young man's death followed soon afterwards."

This and other incidents she repeated. Then, considering that the article was sufficient vindication of her opinions, Daisy withdrew from the controversy.

One more article appeared in the *West Australian* in 1924 but the controversy did not flare up again until 1927, this time because of a private letter written to geologist Lyell Brown.

A group had arrived in her camp in possession of a blood-stained bag on which was written the name Robbins. Daisy felt it incumbent upon her to inquire if a man of this name was missing.

News of the bag leaked to the press and the argument began again.

"As far as I know there have been no cases of cannibalism at Ooldea," said Neville.

"Though many authorities in Australia assert that cannibalism among the Australian blacks is unknown, enquiry among the residents in the Kimberleys and lower Western Northern Territory disproves such statements," wrote the *Adelaide Advertiser*.

"There is no such tribe in Australia as a cannibal tribe. In times of unusual distress such as starvation through drought, they might kill and eat one of their own people, but I'm sure it would be done in all grief and regret," said Daisy's old "enemy", Dr Basedow, in the *Adelaide Register*.

Daisy returned to the attack with an article for the *Adelaide Register* under the heading "Aboriginal Cannibals: Mothers Who Eat Their Babies". This was provocation indeed. The storm that followed compelled her final article on the subject in the *Australasian*, published in May of the following year. Once again she bowed out of the controversy that followed but not before delivering one parting shot, published in the *West Australian*:

"I should like your readers to know that the circumcised tribes of the interior from Kimberley to the South Coast were all active cannibals."

Proof that she believed what she said is to be found in her notebooks. Here are recorded comments made to Kabbarli that would not be made to strangers, not even to visiting anthropologists.

> The distribution of human meat must be made according to traditional law. If a man has ribs given to him when he is entitled to a shoulder or some other portion, a quarrel arises.
>
> When a boy is given his baby sister to eat, if he has been very fond of the baby he will not eat it. His mother and father therefore pretend it is emu flesh and show him *wibia* (emu feathers) which they wrap round his portion.
>
> Old natives, Jingabulla and others said when the long dry times came and root and plant foods went, cannibalism became an epidemic and everyone was afraid both in his own little group and of his neighbours.

To Hurst she mentioned the subject as casually as any other aspect of Aboriginal life:

"They are all cannibals here. One poor old creature, unbelievably thin, was feeling my body yesterday. Of course I am not in the least afraid but I could not help reading the poor soul's thoughts—I never get scraggy even when I've had short commons for weeks."

In a letter to Professor Fitzherbert in which she gives her sources for her Eucla vocabularies, Daisy commented that "Gauera's mother procured abortion of all her other babies and cooked and ate the foetus. Gauera ate infant flesh many times and liked it!"

But to publicize a practice condemned by the black community itself was not to "play the game" with her friends. Daisy knew it and regretted, as she so often regretted, the impulse to shock that had started the whole controversy.

One more article did appear from her in the *Western Mail* in September of the year, but it was not until she wrote *The Passing of the Aborigines*, when she had established proof of her affection for the black people, that she discussed the subject in depth.

To Daisy, Aboriginal cannibalism was a fact, but only one among the many not understood by the white man. Its reappearance among the refugees from the North she saw as another manifestation of disintegration.

Typically, she overstated her case and so weakened it.

CHAPTER TWENTY-TWO

"Kabbarli", an old woman who undertakes the office of grandmother to the tribe. She settles quarrels, and separates men who fight.—Living Races of Mankind.

"The Great White Queen of the Never Never"

The "cannibal" controversy was only one battle in a campaign that lasted for the sixteen years in which Daisy was at Ooldea.

A lonely David in her near-desert, she tackled the Goliath of officialdom. Unlike David she was vanquished. The coveted goal of a paid Protectorship was never achieved. But her defeat was not without honour. When the news came, in the autumn of 1920, that the Prince of Wales was to cross the Nullarbor by train, it was Daisy who was asked to arrange the Aboriginal display for his benefit. It was to be held at Cook, next stop on the line from Ooldea.

His visit was scheduled for July. Though cooler conditions had now come, a drought of months, with its accompanying thirst and hunger, had stirred some aggression among the groups along the line. A contingent arrived at Daisy's breakwind, led by three mutinous "civilized" men.

At the sight of their spears and the sound of their voices, the women fled to hide under neighbouring clumps of saltbush.

"The general temper," Daisy noted, "was not peaceable."

Nabbari, Dhanggool and Winnima, the three leaders, began to shout.

"Blackfellow king belong to this country."

"Whitefellows have frightened all our game away and taken our waters."

"You send paper to Gubmint and tell them we don't want white fellow King. We want our own King."

They had a case; and Daisy, their Justice of the Peace, considered it.

"Who would you choose for King?"

"Nabbari."

"And will the men of the grey kangaroo sit down under a dingo at this water?"

To this they could not reply but their silence gave an opening to the eldest who was, she said, usually the gentlest among them.

"This country belong black fellow. *Wijela* [white fellow] Gubmint take dousand dousand pound, close on five pound. . . ."

Their grievances were real enough but heresy against the British monarchy could not be tolerated by a servant of Empire.

Daisy became uncomfortably aware of isolation. The fifteen whites of the little community were out of sight. The nearest police station was a hundred and seventy miles away. She decided to create a diversion.

"Put the biggest billy on the fire," she instructed.

The prospect of tea brought one of the women out of hiding and preparations went ahead. The sight of such mollifying delicacies as sugar and flour relaxed the general tension.

"Now, *Boggali*, sit down."

They sat.

"Suppose you make Nabbari King. All right. Maadu Queen. Our King's wife we call Queen. Maadu your Queen now."

This was not so popular. At the best of times an Aboriginal is reluctant to recognize the authority of a mere woman. Maadu was more than usually unacceptable because of her ill-nature and fine command of what Daisy called "Billingsgate".

Daisy pursued her advantage.

"When Maadu Queen, Thanyarrie must build her breakwind. Dhanggool will bring her firewood . . . everything Maadu say you do."

This was too much.

"No Maadu," they decided.

"Very well," Daisy said agreeably, "King must have wife. You give Nabbari one of your own women. Whichever one he wants."

She had won the day.

Daisy busied herself in making damper while they argued among themselves. The revolution ended in an impromptu feast that emptied her larder but reconciled her guests to the coming of the English Prince. They began to look forward to "King Gubmint". The display was reported as "a triumph of tactful organization". The Prince stayed well beyond his scheduled time; watched the crushing of seeds, the making of string from human hair and the *I-Wal-Eenma* or spirit dance, chosen by Daisy as it could incorporate all the groups. As a special tribute to King Gubmint the young initiated men swung their bullroarers, the women banished to their wurlies meanwhile.

The future King Edward VIII sat beside Daisy on his dais, "a nice English boy, interested and pleased throughout". The Royal party reported news of a triumph, impressive enough to convert her critics in the women's clubs at least.

"I used to think you were a crank. Now I know you are a saint," said old Mrs Burt of the Karrakatta Club.

"So what could I do but give her a hug and waltz her down the corridor?" remarked the saint to her friend Hurst.

One result was a visitor from Government House, Perth. In August 1921 Miss Ruxton, friend of Lady Newdegate, wife of the Governor of Western Australia, made the 999-mile trip from Perth to Ooldea. Sir Francis sent a new tent, a hamper of food, a parcel of pipes and "'bacca". Daisy prevailed on the Murray family to lend her the buggy and the "two mangy camels" of former days and filled her cool safe with stores of bacon and eggs. Miss Ruxton stayed for five days and returned to write a eulogy that covered one entire page of the *Sunday Times*.

Her first impression of "a miserably inferior race", dirty and dejected in their cast-off clothing was, she said, superseded by the "starlit corroboree" by which she was greeted. She watched the lithe bodies decorated with ochre and feathers dancing to the thud of clubs beaten on the ground. She tasted "bardee" grubs and described them as resembling "oysters flavoured with almonds." She noted the constant little crowd of *boggali* calling for the services of their Kabbarli. She marvelled at the fastidious Daisy kneeling in the ashes of their wurlies, rubbing liniment into their suffering bodies with her neatly gloved hands, impressing on them as she did so, the evils of cannibalism.

Miss Ruxton returned to civilization determined that the world should be told of Daisy's "noble work".

It was a sentiment to be echoed many times over. Eighteen months later *Woman's World* promoted her to royal status as "The Great White Queen of the Never Never", and the article concluded with a rap over Government knuckles that they were so dilatory in giving official power "to the only person competent to handle the situation".

Unfortunately for Daisy, such support was too partisan to be effective. The nobility of her work was presented in direct relation to the unworthiness of its recipients. *Woman's World* described in loving detail the "ragged, unkempt, grimy aborigine on the platform, clothed in tattered khaki which flapped about his skinny limbs". He was "a study in drab browns" relieved only by "a bandage of snowy whiteness which hid one of his revolting sores". When Daisy made her appearance she was "surrounded by the most ragged and most disreputable escort white woman ever had." Her breakwind abounded with "unwanted piccaninnies" left in her care. Adults and children could utter only two words of the English language: "Daisy Bates".

"Rubbish," wrote Daisy firmly in the margin. And, Rubbish, echoed her critics.

If they did not help her cause, her visitors were necessary to her morale. To be forced to remain for so many years in one place was to deny her strong nomadic instinct. Since she could no longer afford to visit, her visitors must come to her. She looked forward to them as "joyous little interruptions from my own kind", contacts that bridged her two worlds.

There were not so many over the sixteen years. She reported the arrival of "a jolly little artist called Miss Pink, who stayed for five days and cooked and did for me and painted the children"; a circus party who had been performing along the West Coast and lost some of their animals in the great heat—"so like Dickens's characters that . . . I had to have the whole lot down at my camp. I made them a big damper, gave them a few curios and enjoyed it no end."

There were two young explorers who wrote their own account of the kindly samaritan who appeared out of the bush at a moment when thirst had reached danger point. Daisy invited them back to her camp, gave them the inevitable damper and tea and talked as they had "seldom heard a white woman talk".

Then in 1923 came a party of scientists that included the future Professor of Anthropology to follow Radcliffe-Brown at the University of Sydney, A. P. Elkin.

Daisy, whose ambition was still to be regarded first and foremost as a scientist, enjoyed their visit until the moment of departure.

She had made the state of her finances abundantly clear, her motive, as always, to provoke the Government into offering her a salaried post. The scientists had a kindly but disconcerting reaction. They clubbed together and offered her £20 out of their own pockets. Daisy, mortified that her complaints should have been interpreted as a request for charity, threw the money into their distinctly aggrieved faces. It was not a gesture that the scientists were likely to forget.

In the main her visitors were travellers who summoned her, by wire or letter, to meet them at the train.

She never failed to be there, a tiny figure on a desolate platform, lost in the perspective of nothingness, impeccably and resolutely old-fashioned. The express stopped for an hour. The travellers scooped her up into their carriages, offered her iced champagne and the gossip of the town, and roared away into the blue haze of distance.

They might be politicians, bishops, presswomen or reporters. They might be Governors, sometimes Governor-Generals. Lord and Lady Forster, or the Stradbrokes, or Sir William and Lady Campion.

There were friends innumerable. Even Sam McKay, now minus a leg and so accorded a privilege that not even his donation had won him, of using her Christian name. Once or perhaps twice, there was her son Arnold. Of Jack there was no mention at all.

As her fame increased so did the curiosity of the train travellers, their comments often embarrassingly audible:

"There's Daisy Bates. The one in the funny clothes."

"How can she touch those filthy blacks!"

"Fancy, gloves in this heat!"

"I feel like a two-headed elephant," she complained to Hurst.

Campion, Governor of Western Australia, was a special friend. When he and his wife travelled to the East they never failed to do their best to persuade her to return to Perth—if only, they said, to liven up the conversation in their drawing-room.

To which Daisy replied that "if the Premier asked me very nicely to accept a thousand a year", she would agree. But she must come back "royally or not at all". "Not as Flora Casby but as Daisy Bates, who says the most startling things in the most startling way."

Her visitors returned her to the siding, to the dust and the north wind that tore at her clothes. Daisy took off her best coat and hat, put on for the occasion, turned up her skirt and "plodded through sand and limestone pebbles to fret for a wee while for the old days and the bright lights."

Her answer to depression was work. The struggle for survival never eased and articles poured out in a never-ending stream to meet her increasing markets. Arthur Mee had written asking for contributions for his *Children's Newspaper*. Daisy sent him no fewer than forty-seven, under such titles as "The Chase of the Thirty Wild Men", "Life in Lonely Australia", "A Cannibal's Conscience".

Like Hurst, Mee became an admiring friend as well as editor, for whom Daisy's life and the dangers she faced represented an ideal as romantic as it was heroic. Daisy did nothing to diminish the picture. Her articles were coloured to suit the imagination of the young.

Learned societies from overseas still asked for scientific papers. In 1923 one of her essays was translated into French by the Abbé Breuil as "*Observations sur les Pierres Taillées de la Région d'Ooldea*" for the *Revue d'Ethnographie*, Paris. An article on the "Sexual Mores of the Australian Native" was sent to America.

Nearer to home was the *Adelaide Register*, which published a series under the provocative title of "Our Aborigines, Can They Be Preserved?" On more general topics of Aboriginal interest were her articles for the *Australasian*, sometimes one a month. Hurst considered their publication to be of value as a record of black Australian history. He seldom refused her suggested titles and, in 1923, answered a critic in the correspondence column with a statement of faith in Daisy's authenticity.

In her letter of thanks she wrote: "The *Australasian*'s faith in my accuracy is a greater incentive than anything could be to keep me to statements of facts. Though for my own sake I am too keen for decency in little and big things to go against truth and try to broider my facts." And yet this is precisely what she did do, as was demonstrated by her articles on Stead written in 1926.

In search of new material, she had approached Hurst with the idea of a series based on her years in London, provided he did not think it "a breach of good taste".

The result was four long articles entitled "W. T. Stead and His

Friends". They were well written, amusing and inaccurate and provoked a letter of protest from Stead's daughter Estelle.

An ardent spiritualist, Miss Stead had already written a memoir of her father in which she expatiated at loving length on the subject of Stead's psychic experiences. These Daisy had dared to dismiss. What is more she presented herself as a not inconsiderable factor in the demise of *Borderland*, the psychic weekly.

In answer to Miss Stead's implied or stated accusation that she was nothing of the sort, Daisy gathered together documentary evidence in the form of two notes from Stead, one from Madame Novikoff, another from James Grun. These she sent in to Hurst.

The letter that accompanied them came unusually close to an apology. Though not prepared to budge an inch on the subject of spiritualism, she hoped that Miss Stead would accept any inaccuracy as a lapse of memory, for, "I much prefer people to dislike me if I dislike them, but I would not like any member of the Stead family to think unkindly towards me."

To Hurst she was capable of admitting that she was wrong. She even appeared to welcome correction. "Tell me my fault that I can mend and not again offend," she wrote. And again: "The *Australasian* always seems to show me where I am not playing the game and I like it all the better for the lessons it teaches me."

But Hurst had, intellectually speaking, replaced the "wise father" of memory. Towards the rest of the world she was not so tractable.

Proportionate to her gratitude for encouragement was her hostility towards discouragement. She admitted to hypersensitivity and provided her own reason for it.

"Before I lost my means . . . I did some good work because I had no thought other than the work itself. Now sordid thoughts, anxious thoughts, will hover."

Anxiety was a constant companion. For the exaggeration of the written word quite as much as for the exaggeration of her public image, fear of want was directly responsible. She could endure starvation, blindness, heat and solitude well beyond the capacity of the ordinary woman, with no concrete prospect of financial relief to offer a way out, and with too much obstinacy to give in. Instead she fought back, using any weapon that came to hand.

Inevitably the struggle took its toll. Signs of a persecution complex began to manifest themselves.

"So overwhelmed was I with the insults, obscene remarks, the raging hostility with which I was surrounded, that I went absolutely blind for some three weeks with the horror of it all," she wrote and perhaps believed. Everything, including sandy blight, had become grist to her mill.

Whether real or imagined the persecution had its effect. Her pride, always a dominant factor in her personality, became inflamed to the point of mania. She would accept no service without payment. When the fettlers offered her a cup of tea she would accept it only if she could give them a penny for it.

Contrary to an often repeated accusation, she developed a hatred of publicity. She began to avoid the siding, only meeting the train on special occasions. When curious passengers came in search of her she retreated farther into the bush. If they spoke to her she turned her back on them.

A few years after her arrival, the exploitation of the Soak came to an end. Over-zealous drilling had produced brackish water in all but one of the pipes. The works closed down and Daisy's tap was no longer operative. She took it as a personal affront, writing in protest to the Commissioner. His admittedly logical advice that she move her tent closer to the siding she interpreted as indifference. Instead, she chose to walk there and back for her water. This meant as many as three trips a day, her buckets carried in a yoke across her shoulders. She confessed to Hurst that in great heat the distance felt closer to ten than to two miles. Even so she refused all offers of help, either from fettlers or Aborigines, while making sure that her friends knew of her plight. Her reaction to a suggestion from Lady Forster that she keep goats to ensure a supply of fresh milk, shows that her sense of humour was not quite lost.

"Can anyone who knows me see me chasing or hunting my goats, carrying water from the siding for them and paying for the clothes lines they eat!" she demanded.

Once again she sought and found a convenient bracket within which to enclose her persecutors.

"Labour" employees lost her post, delayed telegrams announcing the arrival of friends on the Express. The "labour" stationmaster refused to take delivery of her goods. When she got the Commissioner to intervene on her behalf, the "labour" owner of the one vehicle for hire at the siding refused cooperation, forcing her to carry the heavy bags herself.

"Labour" was corrupting employees, white-anting governments and substituting materialism for the pioneer spirit.

Her letters to Hurst were often long tirades on the subject, by which means she wrote her resentment out of her system. Less forgivable was the change in her attitude towards the problem of mixed bloods. A deeply felt and reasonably argued approach to the subject became a personal vendetta against the sufferers. Not only the act but the product of the act became evil. Deprived of authority to prevent, she regarded its manifestation as a personal affront.

Not surprisingly her hostility was resented. In 1928 a deputation consisting mainly of mixed bloods called on the Premier of Western Australia to petition for the rights of white citizenship.

Daisy saw herself described as enemy number one, who lived among the black people for the sake of the publicity she received for doing so and whose matriarchal largesse encouraged begging and so argued against self-respect.

This was the last straw. She protested to Hurst that "I never give or take money from the natives. From the moment of their arrival at my camp I keep them out of the doldrums by [using] their own exchange and barter laws. The men and women make some exchange even if it is only bringing me a mouse or an armful of small chicks . . . anything as long as it isn't begging."

The camel's back remained unbroken but Daisy in her battle position retreated deeper into isolation, from which she sent appeals to such organizations as she hoped might still listen.

"Over and over again I sent a veritable *cri de coeur* to the women of Adelaide, and, as far as my distracted mind and worn body enabled me, begged them to get the native women and children away from the low whites and back in my charge."

One at least of her *cris de coeur* was listened to. Although she had broken off relations with the Aboriginal Affairs Department, she could not allow the birth of a half-caste child in her area to go unreported and she informed the Inspector of Police at Port Augusta.

The result was a visit from one Police Constable Claxton, whose report shows that, on this occasion at least, she had converted a champion to her cause.

"Mrs. Bates has more influence over the natives than she is usually given credit for," he wrote to the Department. "She has spoken to the men of the tribe and told them that the child must not be killed . . . but the mother will probably cause the child to die. In a futile attempt to correct the mistake of colour, I might mention that it has already been thoroughly cleansed with 'nugget polish'."

His last words could have been Daisy's own:

"Since . . . large camps of men, none of them saints—are scattered over 300 miles of railway, why not keep the aborigines away from temptation?"

The Department elected to continue its policy of keeping the Aborigines away from Mrs Bates. "I haven't a native near me and I am most frightfully lonely without them," she wrote to Hurst. Then, later in the year 1928, she told him that "because of the bias of the Department against me I am now in no inconsiderable danger."

Her own little group had been "moved on" and a new one was collecting ready to come into Ooldea. They had migrated from the north, leaving behind them a trail of tribal murders. Their avengers were in pursuit and the pervading mood was ugly.

"I just trust in God, simply, as I have always trusted Him; and I hope I shall be able to help these new people and avert tragedy."

Tragedy was averted, but not by Daisy.

The avengers duly arrived and their *mul'dharri*, or murderer's slippers, deposited in a nearby tree. These were the foot-coverings of emu feathers which enabled a man on murderous intent to approach his sleeping victim without sound or track. Justice was about to be done when, out of the dust of the dreaded Nullarbor Plain thundered the great *ganba* Express. The two avengers, convinced that it was the snake monster of legend, turned and fled for their lives.

Malnutrition took its toll and Daisy went down with a bout of pneumonia, followed, the next year, with a return of sandy blight. The pneumonia might have proved fatal but for the persistence of the fettlers' wives, who, after she had been absent from the siding for a week, went in search, invaded her privacy and nursed her back to health. Daisy repaid their kindness with the Edwardian gesture of two bottles of vintage champagne, one for each.

Pneumonia she could endure, but the recurring attacks of sandy blight were a nightmare that she acknowledged with dread.

In *The Passing of the Aborigines* she described how she dealt with them.

"By covering all the things I used most with white tops I could manage to attend to most of my needs and to feed the natives, who daily brought me firewood. They were amazed at my affliction and looked upon me with 'Physician heal thyself' written very legibly upon their faces, for was I not Ngangarli, doctor of all magic healing?"

Alone in her tent she felt her way among the familiar objects,

Daisy Bates with Lady Gowrie in Adelaide, 1939 (*Photo*: *Adelaide Advertiser*)

Old age in Adelaide, 1948 (*Photo*: Douglas Glass)

Her eyesight was affected by her long years in the desert (*Photo*: Douglas Glass)

venturing into the breakwind with bandages to protect her granulated eyelids from sun and wind. By now she had warning of an attack and took the precaution of propping open her eyelids for long enough to read her beloved newspapers before being "plunged into outer darkness".

She survived the attacks as she survived the heat that she said "melted the marrow of my bones". But to Hurst she admitted that "each summer of isolation and privation makes a more distinct mark."

Then, as hopes of the paid protectorship diminished, whispers reached her of a reward of a different kind. Her Perth friends wrote to tell her that "if Sir William Campion had his way, she would be made a Dame of the British Empire."

Overjoyed, Daisy wrote to enlist the help of the *Australasian*. She explained that she was hoping to find a successor, "some such woman as myself [who] may take up the firestick when I drop it". If she were to be made a Dame, her successor would recognize the value of her work, not only to Australia but to the Empire.

She needed the help of his newspaper, because "I am not a public woman at all and I have nothing but graves to show what my work has been."

So she rationalized ambition, the driving force of a lifetime. Honorary distinctions were hers. Her work was recognized and applauded. But, in the end, officialdom had beaten her. After ten years of battle she was still deprived of the recognition as well as the security that went with a salaried position.

An honour from the King would represent a victory snatched from the jaws of defeat. Those jaws were closing and she knew it.

"I am beginning to realise all I have cut myself away from," she admitted. She missed "her own kind". Her health was failing. The natives were increasingly difficult. There were more and more days of prostration from the heat.

Now, at long last, it looked as if she was to be rewarded. But between hope and fulfilment were six long and gruelling years.

CHAPTER TWENTY-THREE

One must love solitude for its own sake to taste in its fullnes the perfect happiness that these beautiful open spaces give.—Daisy Bates: Notebooks.

The Years of Drought

These were the years of drought; slow years of torture in which rain clouds rolled pitilessly overhead, to disgorge a few drops like a spit of contempt before passing; in which the earth became dun brown and the atmosphere colourless with dust.

Until now Daisy had been asked the question, "Why?". From this time on it became "How?".

How could she, a woman of late middle age, endure the discomforts of camp life a mile from this dusty siding in the middle of nowhere? How could she wear her long skirts and her high collars in such heat? How could she survive the isolation from her own people with only a few diseased relics of a primitive society for company?

Daisy did more than survive. Forgetful of anxiety, of failure, even of drought, she could look back on her years at Ooldea with a nostalgia so keen that her old age was spent in a constant attempt to recreate them.

The reason stemmed from her inner resources, always at their most effective in the bush.

Perched on this ancient and eroded land surface her tent flapped its lone but never lonely defiance to the north wind. In a "world of silence and moving shadows" the clumps of saltbush could shimmer into "lakes of water studded with palms and islands, trees upside down".

Mirage consoled for reality. In solitude she could recapture the "bright aura" that excluded all that was ugly in herself and in others.

Away from the intransigence of her own kind, she could graft happy endings onto her life's histories and there was none to argue.

Make-believe perhaps—and yet her response to nature, as Alan Moorehead said, bordered on the mystical.

"It is curious," she wrote to Hurst, "but there is another 'me' that seems even closer to stars and moon and trees and wind than the ego of the long trying days. I have retired at night worn out with anxiety over my poor hungry natives—hungering with them for I shared all I had (there were so many and the Government would send no relief), and just as soon as I lie down this other 'me' comes out from the shell of the day 'me' and whispers lovely things—master poems—to the stars and the winds."

Living close to the black people she developed their "spiritual power of seeing which exists apart from the limited bodily organs".

"It takes some time for the beauty of the open places to reach one's soul," she wrote, "but once there, hills, sea, river, wood, all are as nothing beside the beauty of the flat land that goes on and on in infinite open space from sunrise to the glorious sunset."

From her breakwind she watched the change of colour on the distant ranges—yellow to royal blue, purple to red. At twilight, the moment of dreaming, ". . . a hundred mixtures seem to blend just before final darkness brings the fleeting dimness of moonlight like breath melted upon a mirror.

"With one's own shadow mingling with the long shadows of evening, the violet after-glow which is only seen to perfection in desert areas, spreads its glorious mantle over the plain. The million windows of the heavens open and in their clear light the trees are silhouetted against the gorgeous transparent background."

Like an echo from her Celtic past, the "thud of clubs beating on the ground, the stomachic cadences of aboriginal song comes softly in the silence.

"All the music of the wild folk is in these sounds . . . the earliest instruments of man, the roughly fashioned stone that beats time on the hard earth and the open palms of the women slapping the inner parts of their thighs or groin.

"Believe me the natives have compensation in their closeness to mother earth and their wide untrammelled sense of sky and stars, moon and clouds and silent places."

There was much that she had learnt from them that she did not, because she knew that she could not, try to interpret for the benefit of the whites. What they taught was woven into the fabric of living. When she woke in the morning she would look as they did to the sky. She could tell the direction of the wind from its cadence in the trees. She drew strength even from their improvidence, because it allowed her to absorb the peace that knows only the present.

It was, in fact, a never-ending diversion to compare her quiet life with the hectic futility of the cities.

"These tired society women!" she exclaimed, "worn out from a constant rushing from bridge to cocktail parties. How glad I am not to be them!" Sometimes she pitied Hurst, condemned to live in Melbourne with its "noise and chatter and artificiality", bombarded by "electric light dazzling the eyes, the cling clang of trambells mixed with the purrings of paper engines".

At other times she envied him, "wallowing in intellectual abundance" while she made porridge and mended trousers for "folk who've never had a wash except when they got caught in the wet!"

"Just let me picture my little home to you and see the contrast in our lives," she wrote to him. "My canvas tent is an 8 by 10 lined and open at both ends and at each end is a Thallyury (Acacia) tree. The one beside my front door is my particular friend for its leaves often stroke my tent when the wind is making fierce love to it, as though it would say—the wind is my lover but you and I are friends.

"Away on the plain there is the tinkle of a camel bell. Crickets are nearby and curious little night creatures. Each wind brings its own weird sound from the blowholes that are but the opening of those spaces between the cliff shelves."

Sometimes they were "loud moaning voices that blend together and in an odd way take me back to a cell in a Trappist Monastery where I lay on a coarse bed listening to the poor wretches moaning to their God at 3 a.m."

Sometimes they were "the voices of the old native dwellers in these parts—long since dead—their voices raised in anger or in song or in the fanatical initiation incantations."

She was never bored because her curiosity extended to all forms, no matter how minute, of natural life. Even a visiting insect was examined. It was "an animated aeroplane, doing stunts", "the embodiment of energy". When it came to rest it "throbbed as if refilling its engine".

She noted the procreative capacity of her six *ming-aris*, or mountain devils. Tiny reptiles, as gentle as they were fierce looking, they filled the important role of ant-eaters and Daisy attached red wool to their legs as a mark of ownership. If one should wander from her tent, her friends removed the piece of wool and "sold" the *ming-ari* back to her, knowing how she valued the creatures.

Daisy had already bought her *ming-ari* six times over before she woke up to the ruse.

Her small reptiles were second only to her birds as companions. Jaggal, her bicycle lizard, who "trailed a banded tail like the trains of our grandmothers", was so tame that he sat on her lap and caught flies while she dozed in the sun. Both her *ming-ari* and Jaggal had a job to do as scavengers; and, if a poisonous spider appeared on her canvas, Daisy captured it for Jaggal who "tossed it about until he had subdued its fighting spirit."

She liked to watch the combat of her tiny reptiles and anticipated Walt Disney in her reflection that, "if the combatants could be enlarged to saurian size the battle would make the most interesting prehistoric reptile film in the world." She described how they "manoeuvred and circled for the final rush, aiming at the head and mouth, resplendent in the colours of war, red, yellow and blue, black expanded throat, erected spikes along head and neck. . . ."

Birds were her love—so much so that she was known as the "birdwoman" by some of the townspeople. No matter what the temperature, she walked to the siding and back for water for them. As a result her water vessels were alive with finches and with *melga*, or ground thrushes, for whom she kept a special crumb patch. When her *melga* were devoured by the murderous butcherbirds she grieved over their loss as for a friend.

With *Burn Burn Boolala*, the bell-bird, she "chattered all day". She did in fact establish communication with him and understood his warning at the approach of an enemy, perhaps an goanna or a snake inside her breakwind. For this she was grateful, especially after an incident that happened not long after her arrival.

"I was busy typing an article and I looked down for a moment to see *Joonoo*, a poisonous black snake," she wrote. "He was just under my feet so what do you think I did? My movement sent the snake wriggling between my hold all and portmanteau. As I had no other weapon near, I cut it in half with a dinner knife. The front half was further away or I should not have dared to do such a stupid thing. His mate must be watched for now. I hope I get it before it gets me!"

She was often solitary but never without creatures of one kind or another. When it was not a crippled dingo needing refuge it was a *jaggal*, with a mouth split open from a fight, to be immersed in warm and antiseptic water and fed with flies and apple crumbs until his wound healed. Cats were all too abundant, because of a stray female kitten she was bequeathed. She christened her Lady Kitty and put up with her regular litters until some Aboriginal children presented her with five more kittens to look after. She could scarcely move for pets who ran about under her feet "knowing that I would not tread on them, the wretches!" Then Daisy decided that the time had come to clear the decks.

Her abiding joy was the piccaninnies. She nursed and massaged them against croup, writing to Hurst that she was "rubbing one of my black babies with olive oil . . . one that I prevented from being eaten so I am anxious to save it."

To her breakwind came the unwanted orphans, commented on by *Woman's World*. Left with no adults to provide for them, they led, she wrote, "a life of semi-starvation up and down the line". This continued until they were able to catch reptiles and rabbits which they could bring back as "propitiatory offerings" and so take their place in the group.

Daisy fed them as she had fed the young initiates, with sweetened porridge and damper, and taught them to play the game so popular at Beagle Bay, ring-a-ring-a-rosy.

Only one white child did she find to take the place of Ainslie Fairbairn. This was the lonely only daughter of the fettler's wife who nursed Daisy through her attack of pneumonia. She had been sent with custards cooked each day during Daisy's convalescence. From this a friendship developed that the fettler's daughter was to remember all her life with wonder and delight. To the eleven-year-old child Daisy was a fantasy figure who conversed with birds and revealed the mysteries of the bush, and in whose presence even the lizards were tame.

The ebb and flow of nomadic drifters brought with them interest that had the added virtue of variety. The ones who became Daisy's friends were the constants, in other words the old and the ill who needed her care. The men she respected and sometimes admired but because of her adoption of women and children the rules of her camp reversed the Aboriginal law in one important respect. The matriarchal largesse went first to children then to women and last of all to the hunters to whom tribal priority normally gave first preference.

Consequently it was among women that the name of Kabbarli carried greatest significance. She was the white protector, a pied piper of black legend whose name drew at least one migrant across a thousand miles of desert to look for sustenance for herself and her crippled son.

Four seasons had been lived through while this lone woman, clutching the firestick that must not be allowed to go out, cooked snakes and rabbits and bandicoots and "every living thing that provided a mouthful". Even her dingo puppies were killed except for one to which her son clung lovingly to the end. When game was not available, the woman chewed grass seeds to moisten them before cooking, and looked for water in the mallee roots. The puppy was taught to hunt for game and to share his kill. They came to wallaby country, passed dried-up swamps, and finally she found the tracks of her relatives and made a "woman smoke signal" to announce her arrival. Mindari, a hunter, being the first to greet her, she was claimed as his woman and presented at Daisy's tent, naked except for the bright red seeds that threaded her long hair. Mindari remained in the background.

"With due regard for dramatic effect," she wrote, "he had sent mother and son to make their own acquaintance with Kabbarli the Grandmother . . . food, clothing, and welcome were given. The big happy sigh that came from the woman was eloquent of the joy and relief at her long journey's ending."

The groups moved on but Daisy stayed, at once a refuge and an interpreter who spoke as they spoke and answered their bewilderment with the comfort of her gifts.

In interim periods between arrivals her companions were books and newspapers.

The *Australasian* especially was her "rock", "every issue like a friend coming to tell me all about things in just the way I like to hear them."

Dickens she read and re-read. As faithful to her enthusiasm as she was to her prejudices, she claimed that for the bush dweller he provided every need.

"I grumble and think the Adelaide Government have not played the game with me and I remember Mrs. Gummidge. Flora Casby restrains me and so does Mrs. Nickleby . . . the Cricket and the Hearth helped me to get through the awful heat."

Her strength was her self-discipline. In spite of her impulsive, spontaneous temperament this never failed her. Because of it she maintained the distance necessary to keep order in her Kabbarli camp. Towards the black people her manner was calm, her voice quiet. Above all she remained conscious of her appearance. Every day of her life she did her "figure exercises". And, "In order to prevent the untidiness that goes to mind and soul if neglected, I have my travelling glass straight forninst me on my table. I've never yet sat down untidy to any meal tho' I have not even a native visitor. Tired, exhausted with heat and failing health though I may be, I look at myself about to sit down untidily and I am up and repairing the damage."

She admitted to another "rather quaint practice". When the urge was strong to establish contact with her "kind", "I dine with H.R.H., Lord and Lady Forster, or Sir Francis and Lady Newdegate and a few others whose photographs I have the honour and pleasure to possess and I talk or am silent with full thoughts and it does me good and it helps to keep my poise and my self respect."

Alone in the lamplight of her little tent, a mere glow-worm in the limitless desert, Daisy used her Kallower magic and Cinderella was transported from the little box table in the emptiness of the tent to the subdued glitter of the Governor-General's dining-room.

Her correspondence was voluminous—with Georgina King, with Arthur Mee, with Sir William Campion, with treasurer Tom Gill, with philologist Thomas and above all with her "dear unknown friend", William Hurst, editor of the *Australasian.*

"I just feel I want to talk to you and so I write," she told him. "I ought to apologise for flooding you with letters . . . I know how very busy you must always be."

Although she assured him that "I do not think of a reply to my effusions", his answers were a much needed reassurance. Here was a relationship that could be sustained because it was at one remove. There was no fear, by letter, of the abrasions of personal contact; nor of the conflict of wills that had so often terminated her more intimate relationships. Confident that she had discovered an "understanding and lenient spirit", she poured out her "scatter-brainy thoughts".

As early as 1919 they exchanged photographs and Daisy, though nervous of "committing a sin against good form in thus discussing [him]", wrote down her reactions to his "counterfeit presentment".

"It is as if we had met and you were quietly and yet livelily waiting for my words. They would be of pleasure now that I see you in the—spirit. You have humour and melancholy but, praise the Gods, the former predominates. If we ever meet it will be as jolly friends who know just a little of each other's minds."

He was more than that. He was at once an outlet and a lifeline to the world she had left behind.

Inevitably there were moments when she felt as trapped as the birds of Ostend; when her work appeared to be "slavery", or "manual labour unpaid". At such times she thrashed around for an escape. Her letters were filled with suggestions, practical and impractical. She offered herself as an immigration officer to be sent to England; as a lecturer to talk about the Aborigines in the capital cities of Australia. Something, anything in order to be on the move again.

Her one hope of escape remained her book, her "King Charles's Head" as she called it. If she could find another Syme to finance her . . . another £1,000 perhaps from a publisher, perhaps from a collection of her articles. But when an offer came from Radcliffe-Brown, installed as Professor of Anthropology at Sydney University in 1925, she refused it out of hand. The very word "collaboration" had become anathema to her. Ironically, it was by reason of her refusal that her researches were never published.

As early as 1924 hope was beginning to wane. It was then that she offered Hurst her chapter on the Broome initiation ceremonies, and began to use other sections of her material in her articles for the *Australasian.*

This did not mean that "the virus of research" was any less of an obsession. To her anthropological gold-dust, left to tarnish in her tin trunk, she continued to add new material. By now she was a collector for collecting's sake. Disappointment had made no difference to her faith in the value of her data, whether or not it was scribbled on the back of an envelope or a torn piece of wrapping paper; nor to her conviction that one day its value would be recognized.

She followed the will-o'-the-wisp of new information as a detective follows a new lead, for the sake of the chase as much as for the solution of the problem.

Even those Empire Day feasts that she so rigorously celebrated, provided her with material for study.

For these occasions she saved her stock of good things, "lashings and lavings of flour, tea, sugar, tobacco, lollies, jam and clothing", distributed according to "Kabbarli law" but eaten according to native etiquette. Her guests sat with their backs to each other as was polite, and the conversation was limited to impersonal topics, as was traditional.

As the matriarch distributed largesse, the ethnologist looked round her, "helped yet again in my study by observing the personnel of each little mob, its distance from the others, its relationship to the group nearest it, and even its manner of placing itself by the fire."

More notes were jotted onto more pieces of paper. When Christmas 1930 brought the threat of a bushfire, Daisy's first and only thought was to save her manuscripts.

Fire was the only catastrophe she had dreaded. In 1913 she had written to Miss King that "after a death, the natives must move away from the vicinity. As they cannot walk over or near the tracks of the dead, they set fire to all their shelters and the trees round where the dead person's hut has been. . . .

"Just think of the risk!"

Now, almost two decades later, her fears were realized—not for reasons of death but because of the greed of young Dhalberdiggin, who had set fire to a bush to smoke out a goanna. The shrivelled fruits and berries, the withered mulga and mallee, dried to the substance of tinder by years of drought, flamed to the dusty skies.

Dhalberdiggin's goanna was well cooked when he ate it, and by Christmas Eve the Soak was a flaming inferno.

Daisy conscripted some of her native friends and, with their help, managed to dig a pit seven feet deep.

"With perspiration streaming from our faces, the roaring and crackling of the fire fiend coming steadily closer, in a fury of choking smoke and flying cinders, the natives and I worked grimly against hope and against time."

The manuscripts were buried and covered with sand. Then, after the fire, the flood. Ushered in by a grey mountain of cloud, moving threateningly across the plain . . .

"Suddenly it was upon us," she wrote. "The mountain became a whirling mass of sand and wind and rain. I clung to the ridge pole and shut my eyes in a tornado of blowing canvas and lashing branches and corrugated iron, while the thousand and one water vessels beat about me in pandemonium."

And the desert became a rose and Daisy's birds sang again in her breakwind. And she wrote to Hurst that "today is cool and already I've forgotten my limpositiness. Thank heaven for Irish resiliency!"

CHAPTER TWENTY-FOUR

A life with no shadows, a place of no corners and delusive piquancies . . . how flat! I like the world of mood and change.—Daisy Bates.

The Kabbarli Legend

The bushfire brought to an apocalyptic end a decade that had been, in many ways, the most taxing of Daisy's life.

After eleven years in the wilderness, she had reason to hope for better things, but the year 1931 was ushered in with yet another attack of pneumonia, caused this time by damp bedding—an ironical anticlimax after so many years of drought, and one which forced her to face the problem of malnutrition.

Her claim was that she could live on ten shillings a week, enough to pay for her weekly train-load of supplies: two loaves of bread, toasted to the last stale fragments, one tin of powdered milk, a pound of rice or sago, butter when she could get it, a quarter of tea, an occasional lettuce or cabbage, dried potatoes bought in bulk.

Luxuries sent by her friends were exchanged for flour or tea and sugar for camp use.

Supplemented by quandongs, or the occasional goanna cooked for her by the Aboriginal women, this was enough for survival. But now drought had put an end to native foods and even the ten shillings had become a doubtful quantity.

Help came in the diminutive form of Professor FitzHerbert, philologist and head of the department of Classics at Adelaide University. At the suggestion of John Cleland, Daisy sent him samples of her dialects. FitzHerbert asked to see the rest and she began the difficult job of transcription, slowed down because of her eyesight, now permanently damaged by sandy blight.

She wrote to warn him of her limitations as a philologist, since she "hadn't the haverings of knowledge of the science". For this reason, she had kept to the two thousand word structures recommended by the Royal Geographical Society. FitzHerbert's answer was to recommend to the University of Adelaide the purchase of her collection.

In due course the sum of £50 was paid into her sadly depleted account in the National Bank of Australasia.

Daisy was overjoyed. "I knew that once I contacted a real enthusiast of Australian philology he would be as keen as I am on the subject. I am delighted to have my wish come true," she wrote. It was a much needed boost to her morale, since "official recognition of my work is more satisfactory to me than anything else could be."

It also enabled her to eat. The Express provided an available mobile restaurant. Daisy crawled out of her sick-bed, walked to the train and carried home her food. As her strength returned she remained in the dining-car, partaking at leisure of her first regular meals for many years.

At long last her dream of publication seemed closer to realization. In 1932 the Lothian Press wrote offering to publish a selection of her articles written for the *Australasian*. Daisy, who had made up her mind to donate her original MSS. to Perth University, changed it temporarily and sent to Lothian a batch of typescript that included her early work. Lothian Press was more than ever enthusiastic but with their final offer of publication came the suggestion that she collaborate with a trained anthropologist. Daisy's refusal was polite but firm.

Not long afterwards came the momentous visit of Ernestine Hill.

The success of Daisy's relationship with the already famous Australian writer was as predictable as her failure with Radcliffe-Brown.

Here was a journalist with an instinct for all things Australian; for whom the map of Australia was the face of a friend. The story of the white woman who chose to live as a tribal matriarch among the first Australians was bound to appeal to her imagination. She took the train to Ooldea with the intention of finding out more about her.

Such criticisms as she had listened to were dispelled by the first words of the fettler's wife who introduced them.

"We don't see much of her. She won't listen to gossip and she hates publicity."

At the sound of Ernestine's name the "blue eyes burnt colourless by the sun" brightened to animated life, the "restless hands" gestured an apology.

"I thought you were someone's niece. Come and stay."

Ernestine stayed. She occupied the "guest bedroom", watched Daisy at work by day and sat beside her fire under the velvet night skies absorbed in the kaleidoscope of her memories as they unfolded out of the misty Dublin streets into the bright sunshine of Australia of the eighties and plunged back again into the gloom of Dickens's London.

A wave of her *nowinning* and Kabbarli was back in the bush, pouring olive oil over suffering black bodies, pencilling notes on the backs of envelopes.

After five days Ernestine Hill left to enhance her fame.

Inch headlines introduced the "White Grandmother of Ooldea", the drama of symbiosis cleverly captured by her description of the "charming little lady of the old school, daughter of the sporting gentry of Ireland", who "told the time by the passing of the sun and was accepted as a tribes-woman and guardian spirit of the most occult race in the world."

Even more newsworthy was a second feature, headed "Black Baby Saved from Being Eaten" and subheaded "Cannibalism on the East West".

Ernestine's articles were widely syndicated. Anyone who had not previously heard of Daisy Bates now had a chance to remedy the omission. Again the price of fame was paid in anthropological circles. The fact that her name was not mentioned in the second article did not protect Daisy's anonymity. The reaction of her accusers varied from scepticism to the outrage of a schoolmaster who finds his school notorious because of its delinquent minority.

What they did not, because they could not, know, was the extent to which Daisy shared their point of view. But Ernestine's headlines were balm to a wound left unhealed for too long. By such unqualified support from so respected a source, Daisy's pride was assuaged.

The Kabbarli legend had arrived. The prophet was no longer without honour even in her adopted home State of South Australia. The newspapers found excuses for interviews, if not with, then about her. As her most recent guest, Railway Missioner William Cowan was given a half page, devoted largely to his enthusiasm for "this amazing woman" who might well have snubbed him since she had "welcomed Vice-Royalty and turned her back on important officials", but who had, instead, entranced him with "the most brilliant conversation I have ever heard from a woman".

Her eccentricities were now regarded as lovable. She was "a quaint hour-glass figure in the chin veils and shirt waists of other days", who laughed that she was "historic perhaps, prehistoric certainly", and whose opinion of modern life was summed up in two sentences:

"I have never heard a talkie or a jazz orchestra. Tell me, have I missed something?"

In August of 1933 the Commonwealth Government set its seal of approval on the new image by inviting her to Canberra to ask her advice on the thorny question of the Aboriginal minority.

The press applauded their invitation. To the *Adelaide Advertiser* her summons was further evidence that "at long last the Commonwealth Government is awakening to its responsibilities in respect of the Aborigines."

Yet the dispute that had been part cause of the summons, between Perkins, official investigator, and Rosenthal, accuser of pastoralists, was much the same, in content if not in length, as the Gibney controversy that had resounded throughout Western Australia some forty years before. Rosenthal laid similar charges of exploitation against the white settlers, this time of North and Central Australia. They were refuted by Perkins with arguments similar to those used by Daisy in her answer to Malcolmson. The question that followed was the same:

"What is the Government doing to save from annihilation the race we have dispossessed of their continent?"

This, as Daisy had predicted, was becoming a problem of increasing urgency as the Aboriginal Protection League had been doing its best to point out.

In 1929 Bleakley, Protector for Queensland, had produced a report for the Minister for Home Affairs, pessimistic enough to have come from Daisy herself. In answer, Genders, secretary of the League, had circulated his comments and followed them with a concrete proposal.

Using the extremely modern arguments, endorsed by anthropologists such as Lévi Strauss, that the Aboriginal was endowed with mental powers the equal of any other race; that his social life had been cleaner and better than that of his conquerors; that his concept of brotherhood was superior to the so-called democracy prized by the whites, he advocated the establishment of an Aboriginal State, on a level with the white States.

He warned that it might be already too late. The white settlers had disregarded the instructions given to Cook that the land should not be taken without the consent of the native inhabitants, whose interests were supposed to have come first and not second to those of the white immigrants. They were now landless proletarians. A native State was a last-minute attempt to repair wrongs to a people who had numbered at least 300,000, now reduced to a maximum of 60,000 in all.

Typically, Daisy had refused to sign his petition. The signatories, she said, "hadn't the haverings of knowledge of the native mind." Official bodies were "all philanthropy and Honeythunderositiness". As a member of the black family she knew that "they could not rise to being an ordered self governing people."

It was not as contrary as it sounded. Her own proposal, presented to the Commonwealth Government, was along very similar lines, but with one important difference, the appointment of a High Commissioner for Native Affairs.

Her recommendations were that the Aborigines should be gathered into "a large central contiguous reserve", forbidden to white people until they had worked out a community along their own lines of government. In this they should be allowed to live in their own shelters, to be treated with their own medicines, but be trained to manage domestic herds, to plant seeds and to build roads.

It was not a separate State she advocated, but her insistence that her High Commissioner be appointed from England was based on the idea of the State Governors who, free from local pressures, could represent their King and Empire with impartiality. He could choose a small committee to work under him and with their help "blend mission institutions and settlements into one harmonious whole."

Her plan was dismissed as impractical. She had been too long away from the problems of administration. Her idea of a High Commissioner was laughed at, though gently, because of her proviso that he should be "an anglican and a gentleman".

Here was the rub. In learning to "think black" she had forgotten how to "think white", at least in the changing phraseology of the twentieth century. It was the manner and not the matter of her scheme that was old-fashioned. Later appointments were not, after all, so far removed from her original concept.

She enjoyed her visit. The Government provided her with a car, a driver, a courier for the journey, a room in the best hotel. In Melbourne she had been able to meet her "dear editor friend" Hurst, bursting into his office in such an excess of high spirits that she wrote later to hope that she had not been "rather too boisterous".

On the train she travelled with Lady Casey, wife of the future Governor-General—a meeting of significance since it was to lead to one of the few works to be written in her memory, an opera with the libretto by Lady Casey, the score by Margaret Sutherland.

Not long after her arrival in Canberra, the *Sydney Morning Herald* hailed a triumph of a different kind with the tale of the Tasman map.

This was a story that had begun on 2nd September 1926, seven years to the day before the article appeared, and its origin lay in a book that Daisy happened to be reading at the time. In it the author, Dr J. P. Thomson, stated that Prince Bonaparte had given a verbal guarantee that he would leave to the Australian people the 1644 map of Tasman's voyages that was in his possession. She wrote off to Hurst, asking for confirmation. This he was able to give and she lost no time in contacting W. H. Ifould, the Principal Librarian of the Public Library of N.S.W., to notify him of Australia's right to the map.

Her letter was the start of a serial story that was to last for the remaining seven years.

At Ifould's instigation, the Agent-General in London, Lord Chelmsford, took up the matter with Lord Crewe, British Ambassador in Paris. Lord Crewe approached Princess Marie, daughter of Roland Bonaparte and wife of Prince George of Greece. At this stage the map was in the possession of the Geographical Society in Paris, who were, not unnaturally, reluctant to part with it. Ifould persisted until finally Princess Marie was persuaded to intervene personally. On her instructions the map was sent to the Mitchell Library in Sydney. Drawn from Tasman's original sketches, it was pronounced "one of the most important original documents bearing on the history of our continent".

This represented another very considerable feather in Daisy's cap. Her six weeks holiday became something of a triumphal progress that came to a reluctant end with her return to Ooldea.

The funeral of Daisy Bates
(*Photo*: Hal Missingham)

The plaque erected in her honour at Ooldea

Hughie (*left*) and Jackie, two of Daisy's friends, on the Reserve at Yalata. Hughie's proud claim is that he is the grandson of King Billy, depicted opposite Daisy on the plaque at Ooldea.

Detail of the plaque at Pyap

For the first time she resumed her tent life without the joy of homecoming. Only the memory of Hurst's "kindly face" that, she told him, she "carried constantly before me", compensated for the cold aftertaste of failure.

Her advice had been rejected. No appointment had been offered to transport her to the corridors of power in the Federal capital.

As though this were not bad enough, she was greeted with the news that her "claim" had been "jumped".

Two valiant ladies, missioner Annie Lock and her friend Miss Marshall, had set out in a pony trap to drive to Ooldea. There, beside the one remaining pump at "Yooldil Gabbi", they were constructing a two-roomed headquarters, a bush church and a dispensary. The police were already at work, rounding up the itinerant native inhabitants to be settled under their protection.

Daisy arrived to find her black empire in the process of disintegrating. There was no future for a "Kabbarli camp" when official pressure commanded and mission tucker lured her black friends away from her.

"Of course I play the game and tell the natives they must sit down at the Mission," she wrote miserably to Hurst, "but they come to me and say . . . they want Kabbarli.

"I really am crying as I write, but only to you. I do not let myself go and I make no comment whatever, even to Canberra."

Clashes between the three women were inevitable. Financially supported, approved of by the Chief Protector, Miss Lock's Mission flourished. In a remarkably short space of time she could declare that there were two hundred and fifty Aborigines in her care. When the Duke of Gloucester followed in his brother's footsteps and visited the Nullarbor, it was Miss Lock and not Daisy who was put in charge of the Aboriginal display.

Kabbarli, the beloved grandmother, had become an anachronism. To endure her humiliation, Daisy was forced back onto Dickens, and after one acrimonious encounter wrote to Hurst that she was "patting Mr. Crisparkle on the back for his little bout with Honeythunder".

Neither she nor the missionaries were aware that nature was already in the process of affecting a slow and remorseless revenge.

With each north wind the sands of the Soak blew deeper. They invaded the cracks in Miss Lock's buildings, piling deep beneath windows and behind doors until the inhabitants, courageous though they were, had to admit defeat and abandon the Mission. In time there was nothing left except a circle of fruit-trees and

Q

an occasional pump-head like a question mark above the rising sand.

The year 1933 dragged to its depressing conclusion and then, with the New Year Honours of 1934, came the longed-for "pat on the back" from the King.

Daisy had been awarded the Order of Commander of the British Empire.

In one stroke her labours were rewarded and her enemies confounded. In May of the year she was on the train bound for Adelaide and so to Government House to receive her honour.

Hers was a popular choice. She was congratulated on being "the only woman in the world who can claim the distinction of the C.B.E. and blood brotherhood with an aboriginal tribe." There were the usual criticisms against "those who have the recommending of the Honours" but it was generally admitted that "none can take exception to the honouring of people like Mrs Daisy Bates."

Praise and more praise but no £1,000 a year to enable her to make her royal come-back. She did, however, jog the elbow of the Commonwealth Government, to whom she had offered her material for the price of the time it would take to put it in order. The amount she asked for was £500 and her suggestion was backed by the Australian National Research Council, by Charles Hawker, M.H.R., and by her staunch ally, Professor John Cleland. Even the National Council of Women rallied to her cause.

The Department of the Interior made a cautious assessment of what they had been offered and were told by their National Librarian that "it was a representative collection of outstanding value" and that "any risk of losing it should be avoided."

Recommendation of purchase was offered with the proviso that Daisy work "under the direction of, or in consultation with the best research ethnologist available."

Daisy withdrew her offer. She might be "as poor as wood" but collaboration, whether suggested by Lothian Press, by Idriess the writer, or by the Government of the country, was out of the question. She would choose her own colleague or not collaborate at all. Never again would she allow a Radcliffe-Brown to pass judgement on the accumulated knowledge of Kabbarli the grandmother.

The battle began. She wrote to Prime Minister after Prime Minister. Her letters were referred to the Department of the Interior who reacted first with politeness and finally irritation. When they yielded it was from despair.

In the meantime Daisy had accepted a "commercial proposition" from Lloyd Dumas for the *Adelaide Advertiser.* The go-between was Ernestine Hill, who alone knew how to make palatable the bitter pill of collaboration by banishing the word before it could be uttered.

"I did not want you to collaborate with anyone and it must not be," she wrote. "Cannot you realise that it must be your book? 'My Natives and I' by Daisy M. Bates—no other person must intrude." And again: "A commercial association would be intolerable, an acknowledged collaboration would be wrong."

She, Ernestine, would "help with the presentation because it will be such a joy to me." "It would be unfair to Australia not to get the book published."

So, with her dream of years at last in sight, was Kabbarli persuaded to leave her 8 x 10 tent on the sandhills of Ooldea for the "pains and penalties" of civilization.

Out of her Irish gift for telling a tale and with the literary guidance of a gifted writer, came the serial "My Natives and I", syndicated through the leading newspapers of Australia.

Three years later John Murray red-pencilled the first chapters, edited the remainder, and produced a European best-seller, *The Passing of the Aborigines.*

CHAPTER TWENTY-FIVE

I cannot live in town under £400 a year and there is no via media between that and tent life.—Daisy Bates.

Re-entry into Civilization

Her re-entry into civilization was royal enough even for Daisy. A sad procession of her black friends walked with her to the siding. The men carried her cases, the women were crying. One or two of the young ones went ahead to kick aside the stones that might injure her *bookati*, the buttoned boots worn for special occasions. As a farewell present she gave each one a shilling.

Black hands waved the *ganba* monster out of sight. From the sandhills came the wailing of the old women left in their wurlies.

Waiting for her in Adelaide was the "motor" sent by the *Advertiser* to take her to her club; an invitation to dine at Government House; the solid reassurance of £100 in her bank account and the promise of another £100 to come.

Success suited her. Her cheeks, protected at last from the abrasive north winds, glowed pink. Each morning she swung out of her club with her forward-thrusting, skirt-lifting stride to walk to her office in the *Advertiser* building. She walked in all weathers. If it rained, so much the better. She would arrive at the office soaked and rejoicing.

"Just to feel the rain on my face! It is such a pleasure!" she exclaimed to the concerned young secretary.

The much-needed moisture brought the colour back to eyes as well as skin. As she was now over seventy, her complexion was of the kind described as Dresden china, giving a look of frailty, wholly deceptive. Her Adelaide friends remember the packing cases that she could move. She demonstrated the fireman's lift as the means whereby she had been able to carry demented old Dowie back to her camp.

Her personality radiated energy. Scorning the *Advertiser* lift, she ran up and down the stairs. Her talk bubbled with a child's inconsequence, but her range of subjects extended from politics to the theatre, from books to the latest court case, punctuated by an earthy store of Aboriginal anecdotes.

By now she was proud of her old-fashioned clothing. Having "hitched [her] sartorial waggon to Queen Alexandra", she admitted that she could see no reason to unhitch it. Her clothing distinguished her from the crowd. She clung to it as a symbol of Victorian dignity, now debased, to her unaccustomed eyes, by the "monied oafs and oafesses, running and shouting and smoking" through the streets.

White technology had never impressed her. Now she recoiled from it as she recoiled from the slang of the day.

"I don't remember a word approaching the vulgarity of 'jitters', which quite blends with 'titters' and 'bitters' and other such mean words," she complained to Hurst.

She was far from oblivious of the curiosity aroused by her appearance or of the "titters" that sometimes accompanied it. Her compensation lay in recognition. This she was egotist enough to enjoy.

Having given its allegiance, Adelaide was, on the whole, content to pay her homage. The stories that circulated about her were now told with the indulgence shown to the famous, whose idiosyncracies are forgiven because they are proven exceptions to the prosaic rule.

She walked through traffic lights and motorists applied their brakes, no doubt muttering under their breath, but prepared to humour this "child of many prayers" as Bishop Gibney had called her. Her economic values were as old-fashioned as her wardrobe, but tram conductors accepted the penny she offered them as good-naturedly as Edward Hayward, owner of John Martins—and the benefactor from whose bounty she had clothed her black children—accepted the pound she sent him as a deposit on a debt of four figures.

Even her bankers, who had reason for protest, allowed her overdraft to remain as a fixture on her account. Far from reproving her, the manager congratulated her on being able to keep up the impression she created as a "£1,000 a year lady".

"How do you do it?" he asked.

"Genius, my lad," Daisy answered modestly.

It was a kind of genius—will-power so strong that it could sustain her against anxiety as her clothing was sustained in the careful folds of her boxes. It was born from pride, aggravated now to the point where she would write a cheque for the smallest service done for her, whether or not there was anything in her bank to cover it.

But anxiety remained, to sabotage what should have been the Indian summer of her life. The struggle to protect her independence continued until the moment of her death. Because of it she would accept no charity, even for her cause. As an Empire woman her salary must come from the Government of the land. This she claimed as her right, to the discomfiture of those officials who did not share her point of view.

In January of 1936 "My Natives and I" made its debut in the Australian newspapers. Daisy judged the time to be ripe for a letter to the Prime Minister, asking that he "most urgently finalize the matter of securing my valuable MSS for the Commonwealth."

By now she was able to give him a precedent to follow.

She had been provided with an office and a typist by "my esteemed friend Lloyd Dumas, to whom I am indebted for many kindly courtesies". If the Government agreed to do the same, she would undertake the job of putting together her untidy mass of notes. Her price had gone up. She asked now for £400 a year for two years.

The Prime Minister, J. A. Lyons, passed on her letter to the Department of the Interior who suggested that she might reconsider her refusal to allow an expert to inspect her manuscripts and pronounce on their value.

Daisy, who was not in the habit of reconsidering her decisions, sent back her regrets that "your department has decided against acceptance"; she would now "regard your decision as final."

A department of mere males was no match for such feminine obstinacy. They capitulated.

A short twelve days later, she was writing in honeyed terms that she was "willing and delighted to submit my MSS" to Sir William Mitchell, Chancellor of the University and Sir George Murray (Lieutenant Governor), whose judgement she would accept.

Sir William Mitchell called in those same experts recommended by the Government, Professors Cleland and FitzHerbert, whose verdict was even more enthusiastic than the Commonwealth Librarian's:

"Irreplaceable, authentic, close to the mental as well as the social lives of the people."

Encouraged by their verdict, urged on by Charles Hawker, the Government offered Daisy an office in the Exchange Buildings, Pirie Street, Adelaide, with a secretary to help classify her material.

What they did not offer was the £400 a year she had asked for.

In an attempt to fix an adequate subsidy for the period of time that it would take her to finish the marathon job ahead, Sir William Mitchell had consulted Professor Elkin.

Elkin, with memories of the £20 that had been thrown in his face at Ooldea, wrote back that she had been known to "treat rather scornfully" any suggestion of financial help. He added that this did not mean that she did not need any. It might be a graceful gesture to offer her a small sum such as £2 per week "to ensure that she could not need for room and food."

Daisy had, then, won the battle and lost the campaign. Since she had agreed to accept Sir William as final arbiter she could hardly refuse the stipend though, even in 1936, it is difficult to understand how such an income could have been thought sufficient to cover board and lodging. Seeking about for a means to add to it, she again offered her services as a lecturer. The Government decided that the work in hand was more important. There was no alternative but to return to tent life.

This was never a prospect to daunt her though now it offered inconvenience. She moved a hundred miles north to an idyllic little camping ground at Pyap. Here she could wake each morning to the sound of birds and the sight of the gum-embroidered reaches of the River Murray. She put up her tent and surrounded it with a breakwind. Within this were her work table and typewriter.

At Pyap there were no Aboriginal friends to help. The native inhabitants had moved away long since, crowded out by white settlement. But it was within easy postal access to her office. Daisy continued to direct, collate and supervise. Progress was slowed down but not discontinued.

On 10th February 1938 the Director of Works sent in a request for an extension of time, but took the precaution of obtaining yet another value judgement of Daisy's material. This time it was from the Reverend Love, of the Kunmunya mission. The "great scientific value of her notes" re-established, the extension was granted. The £400, however, was not forthcoming.

A few months later, John Murray launched *The Passing of the Aborigines*. On the strength of her publisher's advance, Daisy moved back to the Queen Adelaide Club to savour in comfort the admiration that poured in with every press cutting.

Even by those case-hardened sceptics, the English literary critics, Daisy found herself referred to as "Goddess" or "Saint" or "The Greatest Woman in the Empire".

"One of the most remarkable women of our time," said one. "Of our generation," amended another.

"I doubt whether in human history the single virtue of kindness has even been so perfectly practised," said Richard Hughes in the *Sunday Times*.

James Agate declared her to be "an entirely heroic woman", a mixture of "Father Damien, Florence Nightingale, Miss Edna May Oliver, Miss Cicely Courtneidge and Dickens' Mrs Jellyby", an all-embracing list of which Daisy may well have approved.

The element that was missing was the recognition of her work as an anthropologist. Few amongst her admirers bothered to mention "the virus of research" that had motivated her life. The world insisted that she be a heroine.

In the annals of history there could be few heroines who received such acclaim with so little to show for it.

By the end of the year 1938 Daisy was in the Loxton hospital "semi blind and looking very frail". She had contracted an eye disease and needed medical attention but she had no money to pay for it.

The Government of South Australia did its best to make amends for past neglect by offering her treatment in a private hospital. Daisy refused it. She had neither forgotten nor forgiven what she continued to regard as their treachery over the appointment of Protector. She insisted that she be regarded as the responsibility of the Commonwealth. Her future was to be in the hands of Federal and not State Government.

Her preference was not, alas, reciprocated. The official sigh of exasperation is almost audible in the comment on the files of the Department of the Interior.

"From previous correspondence with the lady it can be accepted that, having made up her mind, no amount of persuasion would make her accept the offer of the State Government."

Hospitalization was authorized and Daisy's eyes operated on. Once convalescent she took charge. Her routines were by now ingrained. One of her nurses remembers her daily menu: tea and toast for breakfast, an egg and fruit for lunch, tea and a bar of chocolate for the evening meal, a glass of milk with brandy for supper.

To another she demonstrated her "figure exercises" that kept her body in its youthful shape to the end of her life. A bath was still a luxury. As soon as she was strong enough she insisted on washing herself. The surprised nurse found her standing in her footbath. "You see, my dear, there is a great shortage of water all over Australia, and it must be regarded as precious," Daisy explained.

She was invariably grateful for the care she received and tended to stroll out from the hospital as she had from her camp, distributing hand-outs archaic enough to be regarded as touching by some and ridiculous by others, depending on the disposition of the recipient.

She returned to Pyap to find its peace disturbed. Tourists made the journey expressly to photograph her, with or without her permission. Daisy called on her friend Mickan, the schoolmaster, and with his help had her camp officially closed to visitors.

In spite of such brash intrusions, Pyap was a peaceful enough interlude, warmed by the friendliness of the "fine German settlers" as she described them—thereby renouncing one of her most dearly held prejudices. Life was a combination of tent life and city stimulus. For her black children she substituted the children of the town, to whom she gave sweets and recited A. A. Milne, already committed to memory. As the local celebrity, she was besieged with requests to open fêtes, to give the school prizes, to lecture on the Aborigines; invitations that she seldom failed to accept.

To the more intelligent among Adelaide's "first families" her oddity was a breath of desert air, scattering the dust that tended to settle over the staunchly conservative little city. Since she loved nothing better than to shock, her conversation could be relied on to be stimulating and sometimes devastating. The faces of the elderly at the Queen Adelaide Club blanched before her stories of the lubra who ate four of her babies. Dressed in a cream suit and straw boater that had been the height of fashion when she bought them, her complexion matched in delicacy by her manicured hands, she scandalized a luncheon party with her story of the "billy of all purpose". This was a tale from her expeditions in the Nor'-west when her bushmen guides offered her the only available shelter with a blanket and a billy for her "night convenience". A tap on the door in the early morning hours was followed by a request for the billy. "We want to go ahead and make the tea," the voice explained.

To celebrate success she asked Hester Cayley to come and stay, an invitation that was in itself a witness to her audacity, as the acceptance witnessed to the courage of her guest.

Miss Cayley, daughter of baronets, accustomed to five-course meals served on the polished mahogany tables of London's genteel suburb of Bayswater, was to occupy "the guest bedroom", and partake of Daisy's spartan menu. In spite of it she enjoyed her visit, largely because of the generosity of Daisy's friends.

By the time her ship pulled in at the outer harbour, Sir William Mitchell's luxurious motor was there to meet her. The Haywards had provided the champagne and caviare commanded by Daisy as the feast of welcome. Clad in their Edwardian coats and skirts, the two women posed for the photograph of reunion, Daisy's ankle-length, Miss Cayley's the more fashionable calf-length, but crowned with that symbol of Empire, a pith helmet.

At Pyap the Mickans offered the luxury of a bath and added rations to supplement camp fare. Miss Cayley boarded her ship for the return voyage with her khaki suit fitting perhaps a shade more loosely, but with the friendship of forty years unimpaired.

In the meantime, work at the office pressed on.

Twilight had always been Daisy's favourite moment of the day. In this, the twilight of her life's span, events conspired in her favour as they had done in Perth during the early years of the century.

The secretary appointed by the Government could not have been better chosen. A university graduate, she tackled the sorting of Daisy's "scatterbrainy MSS" with a conviction of privilege. Slowly but surely order was created out of chaos. The young Miss Watt applied herself while Daisy breezed in and out of her office, announcing her arrival with the click of rapid footsteps up the stairs, always ready to talk, always impatient of officialdom, courteous of manner, unfailingly alive. Her escape valve was the office of the bush nurses on the floor below. When the effort of concentration was too great, Daisy "burst in" on Miss Howie, the nurses' secretary, as she had "burst in" on Hurst, to "talk black" over a cup of tea.

"To sit with you, to take up your time with my chattering, eased my mind and I went back to my office spiritually tidied up," she wrote to her.

But disaster was on its way. The year 1939 ushered in the second major global war in the white world. It was also the year chosen by Daisy for her 80th birthday. Her memory, never to be relied on for detail, was now capricious enough to obey her command, at least on the subject of dates. Whether she had put her age back for her wedding, or forward in old age, can be left as a matter of opinion. The press, no doubt welcoming the diversion, reported Government House luncheons, bouquets of sweets donated by the Governor's wife. In many ways it was reminiscent of a similar moment in white history, twenty-one years before.

But the Department of the Interior was becoming restive. The work had now extended to four years. Miss Watt was engaged to be married. Daisy was requested, firmly, to complete the compilation. Her one real need, a salary to go with the job, appeared never to have been considered. Honours she continued to receive. A Silver Jubilee medal, a Medal of Commemoration of the Coronation of Their Majesties. But in October of the year 1939 her overdraft amounted to three figures. Since she had no time to write articles and no properties left to sell, she cast around for the means of return to the city. There was only one possession left that was worth money.

She instructed her solicitors to charge the Government the sum of £1,000 for her manuscripts.

Departmental reaction was one of outrage. The Government could not be held responsible for the overdraft of Mrs Daisy Bates. The fact that she had no idea of the value of money was no justification for breaking an agreement, extended already through Government generosity by two years.

Her request was refused. But a compromise of a kind was reached. She would be given an allowance of £5. 5s. per week for a period of three months. This should be sufficient to enable her to live in comfort for the amount of time which, by her own reckoning, was all that was needed to finish the work.

Daisy had no alternative but to accept what she was offered. If she looked into the future, tent life was all that was promised. But, at the approximate age of eighty, the future is an uncertain prospect. At least her life with the Aborigines had trained her to live in the present.

By the end of the year 1940 the scraps of paper, torn envelopes, Pitman notebooks, newspaper cuttings, manuscripts and correspondence were typed and bracketed, filed and enclosed in ninety-four folios destined for the archives of Australia's national library.

Her treachery forgiven in the matter of the £1,000, she was invited to Canberra for the donation ceremony to take place in the new year.

Glory again was hers. She was received with the deference due to the Queen Government of her black kingdom.

Neither son nor grandchildren were with her. No native Australian had been asked to witness the donation of this record of his history. Daisy stood alone, her O'Dwyer chin held high; back erect and buttoned boots squarely planted. The cardboard boxes were placed one after the other on the library shelves.

If she heard an inaudible fanfare of clubs beaten on hard earth, the slap of palms on thighs, the ascending scale of a ceremonial incantation, she showed no sign. Her eyes were not wet with remembered tears shed for a black people who suffered and "to their death made no moan nor hurled no fury at the dreadful white."

At this moment she was the scientist she had always aspired to be, standing to regal attention while her work was ensured for posterity.

Eight graves round her Ooldea camp were monuments to a friendship. The ninety-four folios on the shelves of Australia's national library were her legacy to the future.

The "virus of research" was exorcized.

CHAPTER TWENTY-SIX

I'll keep my personal dignity and pride to the very end—it's all I have left and it's a possession that only myself can part with.—Daisy Bates to William Hurst.

"The Commonwealth Government Is No Gentleman"

It was the end of the chapter and she knew it. By March 1941 her camp gear was on its way to Wynbring Siding, a stop east of Ooldea on the Trans-Australian Railway line.

To show the finality of her decision she "fired her past" Aboriginal fashion, by making a bonfire out of diaries and personal correspondence not included in the Canberra collection. Since she now despaired of realizing her dream of a cottage in the Adelaide Hills, to which she had once hoped to invite her grandchildren, she took, so she said, "a garden plot" with her. "Here you and I will walk and talk," she wrote to Hurst.

To finance her she had her stipend of £2 a week, attached to the title of "Consultant For Native Affairs". The choice could scarcely be regarded as hers to make, but she went with relief.

"I really have no place and no desire to have a place in the bewildering and I must say vulgarizing atmosphere of today," she wrote. "I don't smoke and I don't drink or raise my voice.

These fashionable attributes remind me of tales of London's East End."

To friends such as Ursula Hayward and Winifred Howie she called it her "war work", her ambition being to establish a new native camp to take care of the nomads still drifting along the native route from the Murchison district in the west, through Tarcoola and so north. It would be another "Kabbarli camp" run along the lines of Ooldea. She would tend to the old and sick, massage the babies and distribute tucker and clothing. Her old age would be protected and at the same time made useful by her role of tribal matriarch.

With this in mind she pitched her tent a half mile from the siding, beside an extension of the railway on which she could wheel her water cart. At a suitable distance were the native wurlies.

In the first cool months of winter her letters recorded only relief. She wrote that her mental poise had been restored by the quiet of bush life.

Then came the first shock of disappointment.

Those same boys who had been initiates when she was at Ooldea, had banded together to form what she called a "police mob". They were stealing from the herds of the pastoralists, their dogs were destroying the vermin fences. Their weeks were spent in hitching rides on the train between Wynbring and Ooldea to obtain food, first from Daisy, then from the soldiers on the train, and finally by collecting their Government rations at Ooldea. There was a report from the Tarcoola mailman that his tent had been broken into and his food stolen.

The gentle laughing people whose honesty had so surprised her at Beagle Bay had degenerated into camp thieves.

This was not the end of it. It was not long before she was writing to Hurst that "the worst vice known to civilized man has become theirs."

Like an avenging angel, Daisy invaded their camp and "razed it to the ground". Its occupants were "sent to Coventry", her punishment for the most dire offences. They were told that they must stay away until they were "clean inside", a phrase they understood, since kidney, liver and intestines represented spirit, soul and mind in their terminology.

But a decade had brought changes to her *boggali*. Her Kallower magic no longer had its effect on these young men who had been a witness to the breakdown of tribal rules and so learnt to live outside the law.

Only the old and the sick people returned to her camp. The bands of young men continued on their disreputable way, enjoying the pursuit of the police much as they had enjoyed the chase when hunting.

"You can gauge my sorrow and regret," their Kabbarli wrote sadly to Winifred Howie.

Her war work was, then, limited to the making of sweetened porridge for her old people. Occasionally she was able to tend to her black babies when their mothers reappeared in camp. Her nursing was more restricted than before but she could report at least one cure, of an old man "near dead from disgrace" as he was suffering from venereal disease.

"I bought cod liver oil and massaged him with it," she wrote, "pouring it over the infected organ and giving it to him as medicine as well, two or three times daily."

"Oh my dear, the poor old fellow saw the dreadful sores falling off and, well, you never saw such a happy good old face as he turned to me."

But the failure of her hopes depressed her. She had now the added burden of old age to contend with and the physical activity that she had once welcomed as an outlet for her energy drained her failing resources of strength.

The effort of chopping and carrying wood had become too much. Even the ritual of dressing was a chore. She could scarcely see clearly enough to knot her tie or to lace her corsets. Drought returned, bringing with it inevitable losses among her birds. An infection of the toe refused to heal.

Locally she was denigrated. The pastoralists blamed her, unfairly, for the loss of their stock due to the "police mob". The Aboriginal Affairs Department blamed her, almost equally unfairly, for the traffic between Ooldea and Wynbring. With no *boggali* to take their place, she missed her "child friends" who, she mourned, "were always my delight."

Coupons, in the wartime ration-books, presented an insoluble problem. She wrote irritably that the books took up too much room on her table, but the trouble again was her eyesight, no longer good enough for the labour involved. After so many years of training it was easier to go without food. Meat presented no problem, butter was more of a loss, tea was a disaster. Once again she was forced to live off her "biscuit and a sunset", boiling and reboiling her tea-leaves, Irish fashion.

The result was malnutrition to which, this time, her ageing body was unable to adjust. A cancerous ulcer developed on the skin of her face. By 1943 her sight was so bad that she found it difficult to read even with the help of a magnifying glass. Letters came but remained unanswered, unless she wrote "blind". Many of her letters to Hurst and to Winifred Howie are pointed scrawls that waver across the page, accompanied by the comment "I hope you can read this. I cannot." When the north winds tore at her tent she could no longer see to mend it.

Her guardian angel during this endurance test was Winifred Howie. To her, Daisy sent lists of her requirements in such matters as knitting wool and materials, usually accompanied by cheques for ten shillings or perhaps a pound, torn up without comment by the tactful Miss Howie. As often as they could, the bush nurses sent up parcels of cakes, sweets, tea and butter. Daisy distributed the sweets, divided up the cakes and kept the tea and butter.

"You cannot imagine how much your dear love means to me," she wrote thankfully.

Loneliness was harder to endure than it had been at Ooldea. Trapped in the sad confines of her deserted "Kabbarli camp" with no money even for her fare to Adelaide, there were moments when, she said, she felt like "an internee in a concentration camp".

Signs of her persecution complex began to reappear. When the local storekeeper refused to give her rations without coupons, she took it as a personal affront. A new argument blew up with the railway authorities, more acrimonious even than at Ooldea.

She told Miss Howie that she was in "new and frightening straits". The extension to the line, necessary for the transport of her water, had been removed. Daisy reacted much as she had done after the closing down of the Soak. Instead of accepting offers of help from the fettlers, she chose to carry her own water and continue the battle with the authorities. Fortunately for her, there was at least one among the fettlers who ignored her refusal and daily deposited water inside her breakwind. Daisy used the water but refrained from acknowledging the fact. To have done so would have been, in itself, an admission of defeat.

It was too much to expect a community of practical men and women to understand the pride of an old woman living in the paling shadow of her own legend. By 1944 the consensus of local opinion was that she was "slightly mental".

That nothing could have been further from the truth, is proved by her letters to Winifred Howie. They are the letters of an old woman, egocentric and vulnerable, generous and perverse, exaggerated and brave. Imperious she remained, but her gratitude for favours done was correspondingly heart-felt:

"It is truly lovely of you to think of this ancient, unwanted, plus-average woman and tell her in that darling cake [that] I was not forgotten by my little stair sanctuary," she wrote to Miss Howie after one of her lonely bush birthdays.

What emerges is her courage.

In these anguishing years at Wynbring she could have been forgiven for playing on the sympathies of her friends. Instead she made light of her vicissitudes, reporting them with her own brand of humour that hovered between the schoolgirl's and the sophisticate's.

"My toe is listening to reason and behaving in a most gentlemanly way," she wrote after weeks of battle with her poisoned foot. A few months of near-starvation diet and, "I am getting thinner and more genteel daily."

Her pride continued to insist on cheerfulness, and she warned Miss Howie "never [to] judge my health by my gaiety, because I shall be gay as long as life is in me."

The reason, she told her, was the strength of her personal faith. About this she spoke little, but to Miss Howie she admitted that "the secret of my lightness of heart is that every night I lie down and commit my soul to God." This she had done during forty years of tent life.

But He was more to her than a mystical concept. He was a presence with whom she joked as she had joked with her earthly father. She could endure the isolation of blindness, which prevented her from reading or even writing, because she "never lost the feeling that God is on call."

Then, in June of 1943, to her "everlasting sorrow and regret", came the news of the death of Arthur Mee.

It was the closing of another door. Mee had been more than a "loved correspondent of twenty years". He had been a financial and moral support. His newspapers had been ranged behind her work, providing a never-failing market, a prompt pay cheque. Faced with a new insecurity, Daisy sent a fresh proposal to the Department of the Interior.

She would prepare a book of Aboriginal legends from her collection. It would be for the use of schools and in payment she would accept £400 a year for as long as it took her to compile.

The Government answer was to increase her allowance to £3. 3s. per week.

Once again Daisy had asked for a commission and been offered charity. The "rise" was refused with the comment that "the Commonwealth Government is no gentleman."

She did not leave it at that. She strained her eyesight with yet more letters written to acquaintances powerful enough to intercede on her behalf. Her situation was suitably exaggerated to match the urgency of her need and at least one plea that her case be re-examined appeared on the files of the Department of the Interior to show that her efforts were not wasted.

But the wheel had turned full circle. Australia's heroine was once again eclipsed by Australia's heroes, spending their young blood in defence of white democracy. Concern was officially expressed but no official action was taken.

Then, in 1944, came breaking point.

It manifested itself in the form of a long and alarming telegram sent to the Prime Minister, John Curtin. In it Daisy presented a grim picture of herself, standing at the door of her tent, revolver in hand, though too blind to see, in order to ward off a mob of hostile Aborigines who had got off the Friday night train. She reported herself in "great danger" as they had been banished from her camp and were now seeking revenge. She urged the Prime Minister to see to it personally that the Ministry "play the decent British game" and finance her move to Adelaide so that she could prepare her books of legends.

From one whose proudest boast had always been that she could travel anywhere over the length and breadth of Australia in perfect safety, the telegram told its own story. It was effective enough. The Department wired the roadmaster of the line to make immediate inquiries. Daisy was interviewed. But the report sent back was entirely negative.

No Aborigines had got off the train on Friday night. There were only six in all at Wynbring. Daisy's alarm was put down to her failing sight that had led her to imagine things. Less charitably, it was suggested that she had sent the telegram to draw attention to her work.

The Government wrote that it could not see its way clear to increasing her income to £400 a year.

It did, however, offer a compromise solution. She could apply for a Commonwealth Literary Fellowship to supplement her income. It would amount to £250. Together with her approved salary of £3. 3s. this would provide her with the sum of £400.

In September 1944 the Fellowship was approved, representing one year of grace.

It also coincided with the arrival of a new group of Aborigines, come to "sit down" with Kabbarli at Wynbring.

With their coming the picture changed. Surrounded by her black family, Daisy was no longer in a hurry to leave the siding. Her "Kabbarli camp" re-established, she wrote that she was looking forward to the happiest Christmas she had spent since she left Ooldea. She began to put off her departure with excuses. She was waiting for her health to improve before embarking on the journey. Since she would not travel on the train, she asked for a car to take her to the coast. In January 1945 she wrote that she was worried about her eyes, about her debts, that she felt unable to travel.

If this letter was sent as a delaying tactic it failed in its object. The Department commented sourly that it could not be held responsible for her debts but that it was obvious she needed treatment. Arrangements were made for an ambulance to be driven to Wynbring to take her to the Port Augusta hospital. The driver and the policewoman who accompanied him were instructed to see that she got there.

The result was an ambulance journey that must surely have been the most publicized in Australian history.

The press, having got wind of the "rescue" of its heroine, reported events in stages rather as it might a Monte Carlo rally.

Such was the resistance that Daisy put up against her "capture" that the ambulance managed only twenty-three miles in two hours. The driver sent on a wire to prepare the Tarcoola hospital to receive her. The policewoman was quoted as saying that Daisy's health was "deteriorating fast". She could travel no farther than Tarcoola.

According to Daisy's own account it was battle all the way. So fierce was her struggle against the two "gangsters" who manhandled her that she had actually fallen out of the car. Even less forgivable, her native friends had seen the tracks of her fall and so been a witness to her humiliation.

Perhaps like the menacing mob of non-existent Aborigines, her ill-treatment was a figment of her imagination. But to the day of her death she complained of strained tendons of the back. Nightmares in which she "battled" with her captors recurred to disturb her sleep.

That she was admitted to the Port Augusta hospital suffering from malnutrition is on record.

The plight of its heroine brought a flood of response from a sympathetic public. Offers of accommodation poured in.

A new champion took up her cause. Alan Moorehead suggested in the *Sydney Morning Herald* that more generosity might well be accorded her.

This provoked an answer from Professor Elkin, who pointed out, with some truth, that Daisy resented either assistance or reward that might be interpreted as charity. He declared her well compensated since she had been decorated by the King and her work published. He would personally see to it that her material in the Canberra library would be edited by an anthropologist. Credit would be given her for her contributions.

She was then to be satisfied by glory, since she would accept no charity.

What she had aimed at was neither charity nor glory but a salaried position with which to ensure her independence.

Had this been granted, pride might not have been aggravated into obsession and the author of *The Passing of the Aborigines* dismissed by local gossip as "slightly mental".

CHAPTER TWENTY-SEVEN

My dear I don't think even you—so kindly and dear a pal, can fathom this intense feeling of love and sorrow and desire to be with my natives.—Daisy Bates to William Hurst, 1946.

"To Be with My Natives"

She did her best to adjust back to white ways, agreeing sensibly enough to move into a room in the Trent hospital in Adelaide's South Terrace, so that the deep-ray treatment on her cheek could be continued. But there were indications that Kabbarli was no longer prepared to abdicate in favour of Daisy Bates. Her farewell presents to the nurses at the Port Augusta hospital, though admittedly governed by her empty purse, were matriarchal hand-outs; an old sun hat, a digging stick. When she walked the streets of Adelaide with her new secretary, she insisted on being the royal step ahead.

She still managed a daily stint of work that began at ten and ended at four, but now reminiscences tended to spill over into work time. She finished a children's story, based on the legend of the *ngargalulla* spirit babies, for which she had hopes of a separate publication, dashed because of wartime paper shortages.

In appearance she was as vigorous as ever, still scorning lifts and escalators, preferring to walk rather than ride by car or tram.

The world marvelled at the straight back, the neat figure that had not altered in forty-five years.

To prove her changelessness the *Daily Telegraph* printed two photographs in both of which she wore the same suit, bought in Perth in 1900. They were a feature of a double page profile appearing in June 1945. In itself it was a recognition of her fame, but its objectivity brought a new element to her public image.

Publicity for Daisy had been sharply divided between the kind that increased and the kind that decreased her prestige. The former she valued, as she proved by the number of her press cuttings, kept sometimes in triplicate, from 1901 on. The latter she did her best to avoid. The *Daily Telegraph* profile was neither one thing nor the other. It neither debunked nor eulogized. But a new note of scepticism had been introduced. The emphasis was on her curiosity value. She was a museum piece, to be hailed with respect but without hosannas.

"An interview with Mrs Bates is like stepping into fairyland," her interviewer observed. "Many of her quaint gestures and phrases are like passages from a novel by Jane Austen. She sits bolt upright on a hard chair. You feel that armchairs and rocking chairs . . . usually the choice of women over eighty, are not proper chairs for a Victorian gentlewoman."

She was a "picturesque and familiar figure" in a "family album dress". "Her relations with civilization" were "full of gigglywinks, the name given by Mrs Bates to anything of which she disapproves." Daisy, who had been so careful to keep her private emotions out of the press, now saw herself labelled as "lonely", "hurt because the Government had not availed themselves of her services as consultant". Her work was dismissed by a "prominent" —though anonymous—"scientist and friend" as "of little value".

It was not encouraging reading for one engaged in whipping her failing concentration and straining her failing eyesight in an attempt to publish further examples of researches described, a short ten years earlier, as scientifically invaluable.

Since her rapport with the fashionable world was also a thing of the past, her club was no longer a haven. When the hospital broke the news that it was closing down, Daisy reported that the club secretary had "failed to put down my request for a fortnight's stay." Sensitive to her change in status, she took it as a slight and resigned her membership.

Her need to escape back to the bush was now as great as her need had been, twelve months before, to escape from it. An announcement in the press that drought had brought an influx of Aborigines into Ooldea prompted yet another letter to the Department of the Interior, asking that she be sent back there.

"My very presence will quiet them," she promised.

The Government consulted South Australia's Department for Aboriginal Affairs and received back an alarmed request that no such action be taken. Like a malign echo from a battle long past was the comment that, as far as they knew, "no especial services had been rendered by Mrs Bates to the aborigines."

The Department of the Interior took their advice and no doubt regretted that they had. Their files began to be peppered with letters from friends and organizations referring to them the problem of Daisy's accommodation.

Adelaide was filled with her admirers, but, it was pointed out, there was no single person to take responsibility for her. An attempt was made to contact Arnold but he was now living in New Zealand and suffering, Daisy said, from loss of memory caused by a war wound.

After months of fruitless search for a room that matched the limitations of pocket with the demands of independence, Daisy decided that the time had come to take responsibility for herself.

She walked out of the hospital, took a taxi and boarded a Birdseye Bus to Streaky Bay.

It was a long journey of over four hundred miles, tiring for one of half her age. The tedium was relieved by her child's glee at the thought of the matron's face when her absence was discovered. She looked forward to the joyful prospect of rejoining her black friends.

Before doing so she had to finish her compilation of legends.

With this in mind she took a room in a hotel owned by a landlady with the Dickensian name of Mudge and with a balcony that overlooked the navy-blue bay, named Streaky by Flinders because of the grain-like weed that darkened it.

Here were peace and a sea breeze; the leisure to remember and, she hoped, the energy to write.

Flinders had captured her imagination and she wrote to Hurst that she was working on the legend of the Konnarup Corroboree, inspired by Flinders and his two companions when they put in at King George's Sound in the early years of the nineteenth century. It was Flinders, she said, who had first been hailed as a *jangg'a* or spirit man. If all who had followed them had been like these three men, the story of settlement would have had a different ending. The legend of the Konnarup Corroboree had been told her by old Nebinyan, whose grandfather had been one of the first to paint the pattern of the naval uniform on the chests of the dancers.

But she was "tired, tired, tired". There were thirty letters left unanswered. Her pen-strokes were a grey haze in front of her eyes. The year of her grant came and went with nothing to show for it. An SOS sent to Ernestine Hill had found her in the West. It would be months before she would be returning East.

Daisy walked, climbed up and down stairs, did her "gymnastics", and wrote to Miss Howie, with some pride, that she had managed to lose the "fatositiness" that had resulted from her long spell in hospital.

"I am getting fit again in order to be with my natives," she explained. "There is now no place that is home to me except their company. My happiness is bound up in them only."

In 1946 the Australian edition of *The Passing of the Aborigines* made its much delayed appearance. This meant money in the bank at last. Daisy hired a "motor" and began her search for her black friends. The roads were bad, she had to put up at the one desolate little hotel at Penong, but she found them in Bookabie, a disreputable little band, as old and tired as she was, renowned as beggars in the district.

They were part of her old mob and she reported "tears of joy" at the sight of her. They sat down together to plan their future. They would move to Yuria Waters. Her friends would go ahead, Daisy would join them as soon as she could to establish a new Kabbarli camp in which she would look after them and they would look after her.

Before she left, she gave money to the local storekeeper with instructions that "Kabbarli tucker" was to be available to them on demand. She drove back to Streaky Bay, to be followed by a letter from the storekeeper reporting that more black people had arrived in search of her. One of them, "old Charlie Queenma", had walked a hundred miles in the hope of seeing her.

The question was how to manage. She had no camping equipment. If she had, she knew that tent life was no longer possible.

The visit of Ernestine Hill brought with it a solution of a kind. She came in a caravan. It was too modern for Daisy's liking—"multum in uno, full of gadgets and knobs that I ran into or rode over and under"—but it gave her an idea.

If the Government would give her an old-fashioned horse-drawn caravan, she could be happily independent for the rest of her life.

Daisy sat down to write off her request.

There was no answer. She wrote again. Chafing against uncertainty, she moved from one hotel to the other, writing to Miss Howie that "my heart is heavy and won't lighten, but please God it will later when my natives and I are together."

The white world had not quite forgotten her. In July of 1946 she received a visit from the Governor, Sir Willoughby Norrie, and his wife. Daisy made her curtsey in the dress she had worn for her presentation in 1901. Each night she appeared in her hotel dining-room, regally alone, barricaded by her "pride and dignity" from the curiosity of fellow diners.

Her sense of isolation deepened. In a community in which she found no "quiet cultivated voice"; in which she "started a monologue" if she attempted conversation; among people whose idea of entertainment was to "mimic the quaint ditties they heard on the wireless", she felt a stranger even to herself.

She sought consolation, as she had always done, in the company of her child friends. It became one of the sights of the town to see the dignified little old lady in faded black, hand in hand with a circle of children, playing "Here we go round the mulberry bush".

Time passed. Her dream of a caravan became a mirage, dissolved in the silence of Governments. The waiting group of Aborigines broke up and drifted on their nomadic way, forlorn ghosts of a lost world.

A second visit from Ernestine Hill brought hope of another kind. "She is going to collect and collate all my remaining Aboriginal matter," Daisy wrote happily. But the shadow of an old fear returned, and she added that she hoped the typescripts would be back soon so that she could "send them all home where they would be of use."

Ernestine Hill did what she could. Her letters to the Department of the Interior brought Daisy's pension up to the respectable sum of £5. 5s. a week. Bolstered by a new security, Daisy accepted the offer of Beatrice Raine, now living in Adelaide, to share her bungalow in the Adelaide foothills. It was an uninspiring little haven with its Victorian fretsawing, but there was a patch of garden and a clam shell of water for her birds.

She seemed happy enough when Douglas Glass, the photographer, found her there in 1948. His search had not been an easy one. The legend was well in eclipse and few people knew the whereabouts of Daisy Bates. She welcomed him as she had welcomed the writer Roderick Cameron, with humour and without self-pity, making a joke out of her life's disappointments, even skipping on the square of lawn to prove to him that she still could.

But it was all too late. Memory, that Aladdin's lamp of her desert nights, had become too deeply rooted in the past to be a reliable register of the present. Her imperious will could no longer command solitude. Outside the confines of her bungalow, she could forget where she was and with whom she lived. She was a prisoner to the devotion of her friend who humoured her with the indulgence shown to children.

She escaped from patronage as she had escaped from the hospital. The Department of the Interior received a last and distressed letter from Ernestine Hill, informing them that Daisy had taken a taxi and left the house. Through the offices of John Preece, an Adelaide bookseller, Ernestine Hill had received a request for the return of the manuscripts. The legends, she wrote, were "among the few authentic left of tribes now gone"; they would make an outstanding book for general reading; but imaginative handling was necessary, and for this she needed time.

Time was the one gift that Daisy did not have to give. The legends were returned to her. Preece arranged with John Murray for an advance on royalties sufficient to cover the bulk of Daisy's overdraft. Her "beloved bank" agreed to forget the rest.

She was moved into a convalescent home at the beach suburb of Semaphore, from which she emerged only for the occasional garden party at Government House. During the last year of her life she drifted between past and present, as lost a relic of another age as her black friends of Bookabie. She came to rest at last in a private hospital in the suburb of Prospect.

Kabbarli, who had yearned for the red roads of Yuria, which gleamed from the white rock like the points of a star, died alone under the prosaic roof of a suburban rest-home.

The date was 18th April 1951. Her age was given by some as ninety, by others as ninety-two. The white grandmother who had chosen the site for her grave beside the eight she had dug out of the lift of sandhills above the eternal Plain, was buried in one of a regiment of graves in Adelaide's North Road Cemetery.

There were a few to weep, a grandson to represent her white family, but no *boggali* to represent her black. A photographer with a sense of history got off his ship to record the occasion.

She had made a will, though she had no money to leave. Future profits from her work were to go to the Australian Aborigines, so that they could call at any outback store and ask for their "Kabbarli tucker".

Obituaries appeared in two hemispheres, paying homage to a heroine. But her legends remained unpublished, lying in the archives of the Adelaide University, sent there by John Preece. The ninety-four folios in the National Library have been accorded no more than a passing mention in the annals of anthropology. The doom of the Aboriginal race, in which she so stubbornly believed, has been contradicted by statistics: their numbers are increasing.

If we are to judge by results, her life must be written off as a failure. But the woman who had followed her own star throughout the span of her years needed no commendation from others to give value to her work. She had seen to it that her records were available. She was confident that sooner or later would come a new generation who would find them of use.

Her "perfect reward" was her honour from the King. Her obituary she wrote in one sentence:

"God knows I have done my best for my poor natives."

Nor was she greatly fretted by her hospital bed. Death was of no more than passing moment to this nomad who had been impatient for four long years to put down her firestick and to reach out her child's hand to be led into territory unknown.

And the death within her eyes was a peaceful one. . . . They looked steadily and quietly into the Dreamland of her forbears whither her soul went.

SELECT BIBLIOGRAPHY

SELECT BIBLIOGRAPHY

National Library of Australia (Canberra)
The major collection of Daisy Bates papers is divided according to her own plan into the following categories: (1) origin, (2) geographical distribution, (3) social organization, (4) initiation ceremonies, (5) totems, (6) religious beliefs and superstitions, (7) myths and legends, (8) food, (9) weapons, arts, crafts, (10) diseases, remedies, death, burial, (11) dances, songs, (12) language, grammar and vocabularies, (13) general notes, (14) notebook, (15) annotated books, (16) published articles, (17) correspondence, (18) notes, newspaper articles, (19) photographs, (20) maps.
Barr Smith Library (Adelaide)
Correspondence with Mrs I. E. Sior, Mary Lange, Winifred Howie, Mr and Mrs Mickan, Sir Charles M. Barclay-Harvey. Also photographs. This library holds a transcript of the main collection in the National Library of Australia.
J. S. Battye Library of West Australian History (Perth)
Typescripts and manuscripts of articles, also correspondence with Dr Thompson, L. Glauert, Mrs Macdonald, the Department of Native Affairs, the *Advertiser*, Ernestine Hill, Miss M. St Clair Layman and the Minister for the North-west. Also (when Daisy Bates was working in the office of the Registrar-General), correspondence with John Mathew, R. H. Mathews, Andrew Lang and A. R. Radcliffe-Brown. This library holds a transcript of the main collection.
Mitchell Library (Sydney)
Correspondence with Georgina King, W. H. Gill, J. F. Thomas, W. H. Ifould, N. Campbell.
University of Queensland Library (Brisbane)
Correspondence with A. J. Vogan.
State Library of Victoria, La Trobe Collection (Melbourne)
Letters to the editor of the *Australasian*, also to W. P. Hurst (who became its editor). Also articles and photographs.
Private Collection of the Fairbairn Family
Letters to Ainslie Fairbairn.

Adams, David (Ed.). *The Letters of Rachel Henning*. First publ. *Bulletin* 1951-2. Hard-covered ed., with foreword and pen drawing by Norman Lindsay: Sydney, Angus & Robertson, 1963.
Bates, Daisy. Aboriginal Names of Places. *Science of Man*, n.s. 14, 1913, pp. 74-6.
———. Aborigines of the West Coast of South Australia: Vocabularies and Ethnographical Notes. *Trans. and Proc.*, Royal Soc. S.A., vol. 42, 1918, pp. 152-67.
———. Australian Aborigines, Western Australia, 1921-7. Aborigines —Press Cuttings 1902-27, vol. 2, pp. 19-30. (Mitchell Library.)
———. Brands Act of Western Australia. Dept. of Agriculture, W.A., *Journal*, vol. 7, Jan.-June 1903, pp. 184-90.
———. Fanny Balbuk-Yooreel, the last Swan River (female) Native. *Science of Man*, n.s. 13, 1911, pp. 100-1, 119-21.
———. From Port Hedland to Carnarvon by Buggy. Dept. of Agriculture, W.A., *Journal*, vol. 4, July-Dec. 1901, pp. 183-202.
———. The Marriage Laws and Some Customs of the Western Australian Aborigines. Royal Geographical Soc. of Australasia, Vict. branch, *Journal*, vol. 23, 1905, pp. 36-60.
———. Measles in Camp. *Science of Man*, n.s. 14, 1913, pp. 31-2, 51-2, 67-8.
———. *My Natives and I*: Press cuttings 1932 (n.p.).
———. Ngilgi, an Aboriginal Woman's Life Story. *West Australian*, 1935.
———. Notes on the Topography of the Northern Portions of W.A. Royal Geographical Soc. of Australasia, Vict. branch, *Journal*, vol. 23, 1905, pp. 18-36.
———. Ooldea Water. Royal Geographical Soc. of Australasia, S.A. branch, *Proceedings*, vol. 21, 1919-20, pp. 73-8.
———. *The Passing of the Aborigines: A Lifetime Spent Among the Natives of Australia*. London, Murray, 1938. 2nd ed., Melbourne, Heinemann, 1966.
———. Possibilities of Tropical Agriculture in the Nor'West: the Beagle Bay Mission Experiments. Dept. of Agriculture, W.A., *Journal*, vol. 4, July-Dec. 1901, pp. 6-13.
———. Rabbit Drive in Riverina, N.S.W. Dept. of Agriculture, W.A., *Journal*, vol. 7, Jan.-June 1903, pp. 111-15.
———. Social Organization of Some Western Australian Tribes. Aust. Assoc. for Advancement of Science, Melbourne Meeting 1913, *Report*, pp. 387-400.
Berndt, R. M., and Berndt, C. H. *The World of the First Australians*. Sydney, Ure Smith, 1964.
Bolam, A. G. *Trans-Australian Wonderland*. Melbourne, 1923.
Borderland. Copies from 1894 to 1896. (In British Museum, London.)
Cameron, Roderick. *My Travel's History*. London, Hamilton, 1950.
Crowley, Francis K. *Sir John Forrest*. Qld University Press, 1968. (John Murtagh Macrossan Lecture 1967.)

Durack, Mary. *Kings in Grass Castles.* Constable, London, 1959.
———. *The Rock and the Sand.* Constable, London, 1969.
Efforts Made by Western Australia Towards the Betterment of Her Aborigines. Perth, Government Printer, 1907.
Elkin, A. P. *The Australian Aborigines: How to Understand Them.* Sydney, Angus & Robertson, 1938. 4th ed. 1964 (extensive revisions).
Friend of a Dying Race. *Desiderata,* Nov. 1938. (Abridged from article by Arthur Mee.)
Kabbarli. *Salt,* 23rd Nov. 1942, pp. 18-23.
Kirwan, Sir John, *Empty Land.* London, Eyre, 1934, pp. 99-101.
———. *My Life's Adventure.* London, Eyre, 1936, pp. 269-74.
Mead, Margaret (Ed.). *An Anthropologist at Work.* Boston, Houghton, 1959.
Moorehead, Alan. *The Fatal Impact.* London, Hamilton, 1966.
Reay, Marie (Ed.). *Aborigines Now.* Sydney, Angus & Robertson, 1964.
Review of Reviews. Copies from 1894 to 1896. (In British Museum, London.)
Stanner, W. E. H. *After the Dreaming: Black and White Australians.* Sydney, Australian Broadcasting Commission, 1969. (Boyer Lectures 1968.)
Stead, Estelle W. *My Father: Personal and Spiritual Reminiscences.* London, 1913.
Tennant, Kylie. *Australia, Her Story.* London, Macmillan, 1953. Reprinted 1962.
Turner, Violet E. *Ooldea.* Melbourne, Bacon, 1950.
Watson, E. L. Grant. *But to What Purpose.* London, Cresset Press, 1946.
———. *Where Bonds are Loosed.* London, Duckworth, 1914.

INDEX

INDEX

BIBL. UNIV. LAUR. UNIV. LIB.
3 0007 00255775 8